Thüsing
European Labour Law

European Labour Law

by

Dr. Gregor Thüsing, LL.M. (Harvard)
Professor at the University of Bonn

C. H. Beck · Hart · Nomos

Published by
Verlag C. H. Beck oHG, Wilhelmstraße 9, 80801 München, Germany,
eMail: bestellung@beck.de

Co-published by
Hart Publishing, 16C Worcester Place, Oxford, OXI 2JW, United Kingdom,
eMail: www.hartpub.co.uk

and

Nomos Verlagsgesellschaft mbH & Co. KG, Waldseestraße 3–5,
76530 Baden-Baden, Germany
eMail: nomos@nomos.de

Published in North America (US and Canada) by Hart Publishing,
c/o International Specialized Book Services, 930 NE 58th Avenue, Suite 300,
Portland, OR 97213-3786, USA, eMail: orders@isbs.com

This book is mainly based on *Gregor Thüsing*, Europäisches Arbeitsrecht, 2nd ed. 2012. It was shortened, translated and adopted in its references.

ISBN 978-3-406-65047-5 (Beck)
ISBN 978-1-84946-488-8 (Hart Publishing)
ISBN 978-3-8487-0297-8 (Nomos)

Printed in Germany by
Nomos Verlagsgesellschaft
In den Lissen 12, 76547 Sinzheim

Typeset by
Reemers Publishing Services GmbH, Krefeld

Preface

In the beginning Labour Law and Social Security Law were of little significance in the development of European Law. They only played a very minor role in the founding Treaties of the European Communities as their aim was primarily to harmonise economic, not social conditions. More than 50 years after the Rome Treaties the situation is completely different: There is more and more awareness that the only way to further develop European Law and the European Union as a whole is by not only getting rid of competitive constraints but also by making the citizens of Europe aware of its social dimension. The Saint Pope *John Paul II* once made the quite beautiful remark that Europe must breathe with both lungs, East and West. This image can be applied here: Both lungs, i. e. the economic as well as the social breath of air must feature in the future development of the law.

Therefore today is a good time for an outline of European Labour Law. This book was written mainly with students in mind that are specialising in Labour Law but it also gives practising labour lawyers an overview of the most important regulations and judgments on this subject. References were deliberately kept to a minimum, instead numerous examples and a summary of the most significant judgments of the ECJ illustrate vividly the contentious issues. This publication focuses on the key issues of the debate. Therefore, some points have been left out to make room for a more profound discussion of others.

This book is dedicated to the memory of my dear father, *Dr. Rolf Thüsing*, who first introduced me to European Labour Law.

Bonn, August 2013 *Gregor Thüsing*

Table of Contents

Selected Abbreviations

ADA	Americans with Disabilities Act
ADEA	Age Discrimination in Employment Act
AGG	Allgemeines Gleichbehandlungsgesetz (German Anti-Discrimination Act)
Art.	article
AuR	Arbeit und Recht (German law journal)
BAG	Bundesarbeitsgericht (Federal Labour Court)
BetrVG	Betriebsverfassungsgesetz (Works Constitution Act)
BGB	Bürgerliches Gesetzbuch (German Civil Code)
BGBl.	Bundesgesetzblatt (Federal Law Gazette in Germany and Austria)
BGE	Entscheidungen des schweizerischen Bundesgerichts (Leading cases of the Swiss Federal Courts)
BGH	Bundesgerichtshof (Federal Court of Justice)
BUrlG	Bundesurlaubsgesetz (German Federal Leave Act)
BVerwG	Bundesverwaltungsgericht (Federal Administrative Court)
BVerwGE	Entscheidungssammlung des Bundesverwaltungsgerichts (decisions of the Federal Administrative Court)
C.M.L.R.	Common Market Law Review (journal)
Calliess/Ruffert/ *author*	*Calliess/Ruffert*, commentary EUV/AEUV, 3rd ed., 2007
CEEP	European Centre of Enterprises with Public Participation and of Enterprises of General economic Interest
cf.	confer
CFREU	Charter of fundamental rights of the European Union
CMLR	Common Market Law Review (journal)
COM	Proposal by the Commission of the European Union
DB	Der Betrieb (German law journal)
E/A/S	*Oetker/Preis/Balze*, Europäisches Arbeits- und Sozialrecht – EAS, 174. Ergänzungslieferung
e. g.	exempli gratia
ECJ	European Court of Justice
ECR	European Court Reports
ECSC Treaty	European Coal and Steel Community Treaty
EEC Treaty	European Economic Community Treaty
ERA	Employment Rights Act
ESC	European Social Charter
ETUC	European Trade Union Confederation
EUROATOM Treaty	European Atomic Energy Community Treaty
EWiR	Entscheidungen zum Wirtschaftsrecht (journal)
EWS	Europäisches Wirschafts- und Steuerrecht (journal)
H/S/W/*author*	*Hanau/Steinmeyer/Wank*, Handbuch des europäischen Arbeits- und Sozialrechts, 2002

v. Hoyningen-Huene/ Linck	*von Hoyningen-Huene/Linck*, Kündigungsschutzgesetz, 14th ed., 2007
i. e.	id est
Ibid	Ibidem
ILJ	Industrial Law Journal
ILO	International Labour Organization
InsO	Insolvenzordnung (German Insolvency Act)
IRLR	Industrial Relations Law Reports
ITF	International Transport Workers Federation
KR/*author*	*Etzel*, Gemeinschaftskommentar zum Kündigungsschutzgesetz und zu sonstigen kündigungsschutzrechtlichen Vorschriften, 8th ed. 2007
KSchG	Kündigungsschutzgesetz (German Protection Against Dismissal Act)
LEBEP	Ley del estatuto básico del empleado público
MLR	Modern Law Review
NJW	Neue Juristische Wochenschrift (German law journal)
NZA	Neue Zeitschrift für Arbeitsrecht (German law journal)
OJ	Official Journal of the European Union
para.	paragraph
PWD	Posted Workers Directive (96/71/EC)
RdA	Recht der Arbeit (German law journal)
RRA	Race Relations Act
SAE	Sammlung arbeitsrechtlicher Entscheidungen (German law journal)
SDA	Sex Discrimination Act
SE	Societas Europaea
sec.	section
SNCF	Société nationale des chemins de fer français
Streinz/*author*	*Streinz* (ed.), commentary EUV/AEUV, 2nd ed., 2012
STSJ	Spanish Supreme Court of Justice
TFEU	Treaty on the Functioning of the European Union
TUPE	Transfer of Undertakings (Protection of Employment) Regulations 2006
TzBfG	Teilzeit- und Befristungsgesetz (German Part-Time and Temporary Employment Act)
UNICE	Union of Industrial and Employers' Confederation of Europe
WLR	Weekly Law Review
ZESAR	Zeitschrift für Europäisches Arbeits- und Sozialrecht (German law journal)
ZEuP	Zeitschrift für Europäisches Privatrecht (German law journal)
ZfA	Zeitschrift für Arbeitsrecht (German law journal)
ZZP	Zeitschrift für Zivilprozessrecht (German law journal)

§ 1. Basics

Literature: *Bercusson*, European Labour Law, 2nd ed., 2009; *Blanpain*, Comparative Labour Law and Industrial Relations in industrialized Market Economies, 10th ed., 2010; *Blanpain*, European Labour Law, 12th ed., 2010; *Chalmers/Hadjiemmanuil/Monti/Tomkins*, European Union Law, 2006; *Craig/ de Búrca*, EU Law: Text, Cases and Materials, 5th ed., 2011; *A.C.L. Davies*, Perspectives on Labour Law, 2nd ed., 2009; *K. Davies*, Understanding European Union Law, 4th ed., 2010; *Fairhurst*, Law of the European Union, 9th ed., 2012; *Fuchs/Marhold*, Europäisches Arbeitsrecht, 3rd ed., 2010; *García et al.*, Lecciones de contrato de trabajo: Materiales adaptados al Espacio Europeo de Educación Superior, 2nd ed., 2012; *Hanau/Steinmeyer/Wank*, Handbuch des europäischen Arbeits- und Sozialrechts, 2002; *Haverkate/Weiss/Huster*, Casebook zum Arbeits- und Sozialrecht der EU, 1999; *Henssler/Braun*, Arbeitsrecht in Europa, 3rd ed., 2011; *Kenner*, EU Employment Law: From Rome to Amsterdam and beyond, 2003; *Oetker/Preis*, Europäisches Arbeits- und Sozialrecht (loose-leaf collection, Service 169 July 2012); *Ottavi/Roset/Tholy*, Code annoté européen du travail, 5th ed., 2010; *Schiek*, Europäisches Arbeitsrecht, 3rd ed., 2007; *Teyssiévon*, Droit européen du travail, 2010.

I. What is European Labour Law?

1. Concept

The term "European Labour Law" can mean different things. On the one hand, it can refer to the **labour law of the individual European states**. The development of the law in this area has been very different in the various countries, but over time similarities have emerged in the different legal systems with respect to some areas. Subsequently, these elements of labour law are no longer only relevant on a national level but constitute the beginnings of a ***ius commune*** in labour law. 1

The individual **European states** have very **different rules** regarding e. g. the protection against **unlawful dismissal and the right to co-determination**. In Germany there is a two-tier system: There is co-determination at supervisory level which is achieved by posting employee representatives on the supervisory boards of corporations (Mitbestimmungsgesetz, Montan-Mitbestimmungsgesetz, Drittelbeteiligungsgesetz) and there is extensive co-determination at operational level (Betriebsverfassungsgesetz, Sprecherausschussgesetz, Bundespersonalvertretungsgesetz). In contrast, France acknowledges the right of the *comités d'entreprise* to send an advisory representative to supervisory board meetings and even on an operational level a representative is restricted mainly to consulting (see in detail § 10 para. 32 *et seq.*). Great Britain has no general statutory co-determination. Only where Europe has prescribed mandatory co-determination by law worker participation rights can occasionally be found (especially as regards consultation: *Davies*, Perspectives on Labour Law, 2004, pp. 187 *et seqq.*). The Netherlands employs a different model altogether. Its co-option model gives the supervisory board the power to select its own members. However, the employee representatives are given a right to object if the objection is founded on objective reasons. The power to make a decision on such an objection lies with a state arbitration agency (*Hopt/Kanda/ Roe/Wymeersch/Prigge*, Comparative Corporate Governance: The State of the Art and Emerging Research, 1998, pp. 352 *et seqq.*). The same can be said for the protection against unlawful dismissal. German law concedes reinstatement when an employee is unlawfully dismissed and provides extensive dismissal protection after the first six months (§§ 1, 23 Kündigungsschutzgesetz). In contrast to this, the English *Employment Rights Act* only takes effect after two years of employment and there is no right to reinstatement in French dismissal protection law; in case of unlawful dismissal the only remedy is to make a claim for compensation (Art. L. 1231-1 *et seqq.* Code du travail; see also § 6 paras. 14 *et seqq.*). In Great Britain the Employment Tribunal can grant an order of reinstatement as well as award compensation (sec. 113 *et seqq.* Employment Rights Act 1996). 2

3 On more fundamental issues there is a somewhat larger consistency amongst the different legal systems, for instance with respect to the question of **who is considered an employee**. The prevailing view in Austria and Switzerland – most likely influenced by the German legal system – is to apply a test of 'personal dependency' when distinguishing between employees and self-employed persons (compare *Rehbinder*, Schweizerisches Arbeitsrecht, 15th ed., 2002, p. 27; *Marhold*, Österreichisches Arbeitsrecht, 2nd ed., 2012, p. 46). In Italian law the employee is defined in Art. 2094 Codice Civile as a person who works dependently and under direction of his employer ("*alla dipendenze e sotto la direzzione dell' imprenditore*"). The significant factor, according to general opinion, is the employee's dependency (*subordinazione*) on the employer. The two relevant criteria for this – with emphasis on the latter – are the binding force and frequency of the employer's orders and the performance and incorporation in a product organization (Corte di Cassazione 86, 4152; 83, 2728; 81, 5807; see also *Cian/Trabucchi*, Codice Civile, 8th ed., 2005, § 2223, section 2 para. 1). This is largely in accordance with the 'personal dependency' test applied by the Federal Labour Court of Germany. The German legal scholar *Wank*, applying a slightly different definition, considers the relevant factor to be a lack of entrepreneurial risk (*Wank*, Arbeitnehmer und Selbstständiger, 1987). This concept has found support in English law. Judgments emphasize that the greater the skill and expertise of the employee, the less significant is a definition of employee that pertains to the employer's control over the work (Beloff vs. Pressdram Ltd. [1973], 1 All ER 241 at 250). From the late sixties onwards the courts settled on a so-called *mixed* or *multiple* test where a set of criteria was considered without one factor or another being decisive in itself. Under this test, the courts pose the question whether the working person is effectively controlled by the employer in order to classify him as an employee. In a second step, the courts assess whether the contractual agreement correlates to an employment relationship. The most conclusive indication against the existence of an employment relationship is if the contract displays an *entrepreneurial character of self-employment*. To determine this, one must ask: "*Is a person in business on his or her behalf?*". Just as suggested in German literature, *the extent to which the person takes the chance of profit or risk of loss* (Market Investigations Ltd. vs. Minister of Social Security [1968] 3 All ER 732; Hitchcock v Post Office [1980] I.C.R. 100; Ready-Mixed Concrete Ltd. vs. Minister of Pensions [1978] 2 QB 497) is applied as a criterion. Under Dutch law an employee is defined as an individual, who works on a regular basis for an employer and adheres to the instructions given by the respective employer. Therefore, it depends on the employment agreement whether an employee is in fact an employee based on a right to give instructions contained in the agreement (*Grapperhaus/Verburg*, Employment Law and works councils of the Netherlands, 2009, p. 13; *Jacobs*, Labour Law in the Netherlands, 2004, p. 45).

4 Much more often European Labour Law is conceived as the **labour provisions of the primary and secondary legislation of the European Communities**. These provisions come into effect in addition to national labour law, the labour provisions of which still predominate in the individual Member States. It pursues specific goals which are stipulated in European primary legislation. A central objective is to contribute to the improvement and harmonisation of living and working conditions (Art. 151 TFEU [Ex-Art. 136 EC]), but also to secure the freedom of movement of workers within the Union (Art. 45 TFEU [Ex-Art. 39 EC]).

2. History

5 The genesis and moulding of European Labour Law cannot be regarded independently from national labour law. Oftentimes the member states' provisions are a model for better and new European Law.

6 See for instance the draft of a **directive of the Parliament and the European Council on the working conditions of temporary agency workers** – COM (2002) 149 final of 20 March 2002, OJ No. C 203 E, 1, which later led to the directive on agency work **2008/104/EC** of 19 November 2008. The composers drafting the European regulations on temporary agency work attempted to generalize what already existed in most European countries on the basis of national legislation. E.g., the principle of non-discrimination stipulated in Art. 5 of the draft was unknown in German Law until 2003, yet it was already part of the existing law in ten other European States.

However, European Labour Law also follows American Law to some extent. 7

The **Directives 2000/43/EC and 2000/78/EC** are fashioned in many respects after the US-American discrimination laws (see in detail *Thüsing*, 19 International Journal for Comparative Labour Law and Industrial Relations 2003, p. 187 as well as § 3). Moreover, the explicitly formulated institute of indirect discrimination, which can now be found in the various discrimination directives, was adopted by the *ECJ* in the Jenkins case specifically citing the US-American leading judgment Griggs v Duke Power (see Art. 2 (1)(b) of Directive 2006/54/EC; Art. 2(2) (b) of Directive 2000/43/EC; Art. 2(2) (b) of Directive 2000/78/EC) (Case 96/80 – Jenkins [1981] ECR I-911, compare Advocate General *Warner's* opinion on p. 936). 8

3. Distinguishing International Labour Law

One must distinguish between European Labour Law and International Labour Law. For one thing, it refers to the **conflict of laws**, i. e. the national provisions that determine which state's legal system is applicable with respect to a particular employment relationship. This International Labour Law, like all international private law provisions, contains no substantive law. However, rules on the conflict of laws with regard to employment contracts can now also be found in European law, more specifically in the Rome I Regulation (Regulation (EC) No. 593/2008, p. 6). For details see § 11. 9

Another form of International Labour Law is more related with the law of the EU. *International Labour Law* can also mean the labour law which has its origins in the **regulations of the International Labour Organisation**. This organisation is situated in Geneva and was founded in 1919 making it the oldest agency of the UN. The ILO's most important undertaking is to create internationally applicable labour and social rules, the acceptance and implementation of which is recommended to the Member States. With the help of these rules the working and living conditions of employees mean to be improved and protected. The ILO operates by adopting Conventions that must be implemented after ratification and Recommendations that are non-binding for the Member States. Between 1919 and 2013 the International Labour Conference adopted 189 Conventions and 202 Recommendations. Some of them concern the protection of elementary civil rights, e. g. Freedom of Association and Protection of the Right to Organise Convention, Forced Labour Convention or Discrimination Convention. Others pertain to individual aspects of employment politics, working conditions, social security and occupational safety and health. The protection of certain worker groups was particularly important, especially the Child Labour Convention. (see in detail *Batten*, International Labour Law, 1993, passim). In recent times ILO Conventions have been included in agreements between international concerns and trade union associations, in so-called International Framework Agreements (see *Riisgaard*, 77 Industrial Relations 2005, 707 *et seqq.*; *Thüsing*, International Framework Agreements: Rechtliche Grenzen und praktischer Nutzen, RdA 2010, 78). 10

II. Development of European Labour Law

11

The origin

- ECSC Treaty and EURATOM Treaty not labour law in the proper sense
- EEC Treaty established
  - free movement of workers in Art. 49 EEC, now Art. 45 TFEU → reason was to secure freedom of competition
  - gender discrimination Art. 119 EEC, now Art. 157 TFEU → here also emphasising freedom of competition by setting comparable protection standards

The second phase

The directives of the 70s
- equal treatment: 75/117 EEC; 76/207 EEC; 79/7 EEC
- industrial safety: 77/578 EEC; 80/107 EEC
- social security of employees: 75/129 EEC; 77/187 EEC; 80/987 EEC

Beginning of the 80s

Stagnation as some drafts were left on the shelf: Directive proposal on information and consultation of employees in companies; Temporary work and fixed term employment; Working time directive → Also in company law: European Company, merely industrial safety was moved forward.

An upsurge

1986: Creation on Art. 118a, 118b EC-Treaty, now Art. 154 and 155 TFEU
1989: Community Charter of the Fundamental Social Rights of Workers: a lot of it declaratory, some of it new
1992: Social Policy Protocol. Without England; important role for social policy
1998: Social Policy Protocol incorporated in Art. 137 et seqq. EC by Treaty of Amsterdam (today: Art. 153 et seqq. TFEU). Important new competences; Art. 13 EC (today: Art. 19 TFEU)

The boom?

Numerous directives in recent times: 2000/43/EC, 2000/78/EC, 2001/23/EC, 2001/86/EC, 2002/14/EC, 2002/15/EC, 2003/72/EC, 2003/88/EC, 2005/47/EC, 2006/54/EC, 2008/94/EC, 2008/104/EC, 2009/38/EC

1. The beginnings

12 European Labour Law developed only slowly with rather tentative beginnings. In the three founding treaties of the European Communities (ECSC Treaty, EURATOM Treaty and EEC Treaty) labour law was of only low priority. The goal of the Communities was to accomplish a harmonisation of **economic conditions**. The ECSC Treaty of 1951 therefore contained no labour law provisions in the proper sense. The EURATOM Treaty did include in Arts. 30–36 some provisions on the

safety and health of workers at work, however their significance did not contribute to the further developments due to the limited area of applicability, namely the production and marketing of atomic energy and special fissile materials. The EEC Treaty of 1957 contained more important provisions which to this day constitute a central part of European Labour Law; however here too the focus was on ensuring freedom of competition: Art. 49 EEC (now **Art. 45 TFEU**) ensured the workers' freedom of movement which was ascertained as an essential requirement for freedom of competition on the part of the employers and was protected precisely because of this fact. Of greater relation to labour law was the equality principle of Art. 119 EEC (now **Art. 157 TFEU**) which established the principle of equal pay for men and women Europe-wide.

Here it is often pointed out that these provisions had less of a labour law value than one of 13 competition law and commercial law. **France** in particular sought to prevent any competitive advantages of other Member States after having already incorporated the principle of equal pay into its national labour law and consequently having feared considerable disadvantages of its economic location (*Tobler*, Indirect Discrimination: a case study into the development of the legal concept of indirect discrimination under EC law, 2005, 37). Whether this was actually the case, is difficult to say today. Such an indication would have lead to every protective regulation of labour law being Europeanised. The awareness that discriminatory working conditions for women present an injustice, probably had some influence on the matter. For instance, the preamble of the constitution of the ILO (1919) states that it recognises the principle of equal remuneration for work of equal value; on the 29 June 1951 a Convention followed concerning equal pay for male and female workers for equal work (AS 1973, pp. 1602 *et seqq.*). Equal pay responded to a demand of the times, not just of France.

2. The consolidation

In a second phase European Labour Law gained much more significance. The 14 European Community was taking shape and the economic integration was followed by the awareness that it was necessary to create uniform European social standards. **The 70s** were the foundation of many important directives, in particular ones concerning equal treatment, industrial safety, consultation and information of employees in the event of mass dismissals, preservation of claims following transfer of a firm and the protection of employees from employers' insolvency. These very productive years with respect to labour law were described as "l'âge d'or de l'harmonisation" (*Blanquet*, L'Europe vers l'harmonisation de la législation sociale, 1992; *Bercusson*, 5 ZIAS 1991, 1).

At the beginning of the 1980s the winds changed. There was a general stagnation 15 of economic development and in the fight against the minor economic growth and increasing unemployment it seemed that deregulation and flexibility in labour law were the better arguments than the improvement of social protective standards. Numerous directive proposals at this time did not receive approval from the Council and remained unimplemented over many years. These included: The draft of the so-called *Vredeling*-directive (named after its author, the Dutch socialist and later minister of defence *Henk Vredeling*) concerning the information and consultation of employees in companies (Proposal of 8 July 1983, COM (1983) 292 final, OJ C-217/3, see note, The proposed Vredeling Directive: A Modest Proposal or the Exportation of Industrial Democracy?, 70 Virginia Law Review 1984, No. 7, 1469–1503), a proposal for a directive regarding part-time work (Proposal for the directive of the Council regarding the regulation of part-time work of 7 May 1992, see Debates of the European Parliament (1997) *Debate on part-time work-employment* (No. 4–509/65–89), 18 November 1997) and various proposals concerning temporary work and the regulation of fixed-term employment contracts (Proposal of 7 May 1982, OJ C-128/2 and proposal of 6 April 1984, OJ C-133/1). Other European projects were not carried out either, in particular the European Company which failed mainly due to lack of agreement on the question of co-determination of employee representatives on supervisory boards (see early on *R. Thüsing*, Arbeitgeber, 1980, p. 45; *Hood*, The European Company Proposal, 22 International and Comparative Law Quarterly 1973, Issue 3, 434–461; see also the official website of the EU: Worker Participation – the Gateway to Information on Worker Participation Issues in Europe, History of the European Company Statute (ECS), available at: www.worker-participation.eu/European-Company/history; for further details see § 10 para. 29).

16 A significant surge in the development of labour law came along with the Agreement on Social Policy – adopted alongside the **Maastricht Treaty** (Treaty on European Union of 7 February 1992, OJ EG No. 11 293/61) – between the Member States of the European Community with the exception of the United Kingdom of Great Britain and Northern Ireland on 7 February 1992 which was annexed to the Social Protocol of the Maastricht Treaty (*Griller/Droutsas/Falkner/Forgó/Nentwich*, The Treaty of Amsterdam: facts, analysis, prospects, 2000, 548 *et seqq.*; *Best*, The United Kingdom and the Ratification of the Maastricht Treaty, in: Laursen/Vanhoonacker, The Ratification of the Maastricht Treaty: Issues, Debates and Future Implications, 1994, 245–279). Considerable competencies to create European Labour Law were determined herein. Furthermore, this agreement for the first time included the social partners in the legislative procedure on a European level. Incorporation into the Treaty failed at first at the resistance of Great Britain who feared too strong a Europeanization of its labour and social policy. The rules of this agreement were finally incorporated into the EC Treaty as Arts. 137 *et seqq.* EC by the **Treaty of Amsterdam**, and therewith the legislative competences with respect to labour law were applicable to Great Britain. With that the danger of a divergent European development in the different countries of the European Union was warded off. Since the adoption of the Lisbon Treaty these provisions can be found in Arts. 153 *et seqq.* TFEU.

3. The present

17 **In most recent times** European Labour Law has once again been given a considerable impetus. A lot of what was left on the shelf in the 1980s was implemented over the last 15 years. A directive on temporary work came along in 1997 (Directive 1997/81/EC). Directive 1999/70/EC then dealt with fixed-term employment contracts. In 2001, after a 40-year-long struggle, a breakthrough was finally achieved at the summit in Nice for the European Company, namely co-determination at a European level (Directive 2001/86/EC). The Directive establishing a general framework for informing and consulting employees in companies came along in 2002 (Directive 2002/14/EC). Directive 2008/104/EC on agency work, which had to be implemented by the Member States by the 5 December 2011, is also an important advancement. It requires agency workers to receive the same remuneration as the permanent workers (for details see § 4 paras. 59 *et seqq.*).

Aside from these new directives, many other directives have been modernized, such as the Collective Redundancies Directive 98/59/EC, the Transfer of Undertakings Directive 2001/23/EC, the Insolvency Directive 2008/94/EC and the European Works Council Directive 2009/38/EC.

Along with these older projects a range of recent legislative plans were able to be implemented. Significant steps forward were taken in particular in the area of **protection against discrimination**. Art. 13 EC (now Art. 26 TFEU) has instructed the Member States since 1997 to combat discrimination based on gender, racial or ethnic origin, religion or belief, disability, age or sexual orientation. In execution of this order Directive 2000/43/EC regarding discrimination based on racial and ethnic origin as well as Directive 2000/78/EC regarding discrimination based on religion or belief, disability, age or sexual orientation were created. In 2006 the Directive on equal treatment of men and women was amended (2006/54/EC). For details see § 3 paras. 1 *et seqq*. 18

How things will continue is difficult to predict. An extended European Union makes political compromise more difficult. Still today there are many unfinished projects in European Labour Law. The Commission sought new blue-prints. This is why it presented a new **green paper** on the 22 November 2006: **"Modernising labour law to meet the challenges of the 21st century"** (COM (2006) 708 final of 22 November 2006; see also *Sciarra*, 36 Industrial Law Journal 2007, No. 3). Under this rather ambitious title, 14 questions were spread over 17 pages that were to help launch a debate about a labour law fit for the future. The intention was to ascertain the basic principles in order to design the future. However, the paper revealed substantial weaknesses in this respect. The text and the questions swayed back and forth between completely different concepts and perspectives without pinpointing a clear direction. The Commission quite rightly did not pursue it further. There was never a white paper to follow the green paper. 19

Sure enough: a few sentences sounded brave, for some ears even provoking. The report refers nonchalantly to findings "that stringent employment protection legislation tends to reduce the dynamism of the labour market, worsening the prospects of women, youths and older workers". It is not debated or put into perspective and so dismissal protection legislation is depicted as a recruitment staller. At the same time it points out that some devices to bypass employment protection which were chosen consciously by the national legislator with the aim of increasing employment – in particular fixed-term work – were advancing the risk of a segmented labour market. So it seems reasonable to address the root of the problem. Anyone encouraged by this and seeking arguments for deregulation in the following statements will be disappointed. The more concrete the paper gets, the more it places emphasis on searching for more extensive regulations to boost employment. The question asked is which regulations on a European level could be newly-created, not: which areas should remain unregulated – or braver still: which regulations have turned out to be off target und should be stricken without replacement? Even obviously cumbersome regulations like the European working time provisions for the health sector are not judged as completely unworkable (see § 7 paras. 1 *et seqq.*) but considered a "particular challenge" that needs to be coped with. The course the questions take and the thought process of the paper is therefore set out to increase legislation at Community level – not to trim it. The fundamental idea of subsidiarity cannot be found therein. At the same time the paper asks whether labour law should go beyond the scope of its traditional boundaries and also cover self-employment on particular issues. Labour law for the self-employed. This way of thinking is not completely unusual in European Labour Law, as the green paper rightly refers to the Directive 86/653/EEC relating to the commercial agent. The anti-discrimination directives also apply to the self-employed with respect to access to employment. 20

But the green paper goes further, and herein lies the most far-reaching position. It poses the question whether it would **make sense and whether there is a need for a universal European** 21

definition of the employee. The Commission fears – and rightly so as English practice shows – that directives could be circumvented by the national legislator defining the employee so narrowly that significant employment relationships which are commonly defined as employment contracts are not included. Were this step to be taken, other areas of national law would certainly be affected.

22 The green paper then payed special attention to those employment relationships that differ from "**standard employment contracts**". It avoids using the term in French law referring to all of these as "precarious employment". It also raises the plausible question whether the social security systems should be better adapted to labour law: Those who wish to shorten the entitlement period must think about how the employee can remain employed for a longer time. All this is formulated openly as a question, not a statement of fact. This is good and facilitates a dialogue.

23 The **Lisbon Treaty** which came into force on 1 December 2009 has served as a further strengthening of the European Union. The EU-Treaty as well as the Treaty on the Functioning of the European Union (TFEU, formerly EC-Treaty) forms the basis of the European Union; both treaties have the same legal status and are therefore on equal footing. The previous column construction has been dissolved. The Lisbon Treaty has given the European Union legal personality. It can now be party to international treaties and acts as successor of the EC pursuant to Art. 1(3) EU-Treaty. Whereas the EU-Treaty contains the main provisions of the EU, the TFEU regulates the functioning of the European Union and represents the framework for exercising its competences. Its provisions set out the scope, demarcation and details of the EU's responsibilities. But in its Arts. 7 *et seqq.* the TFEU also offers provisions regarding the general principles of the European Union. The central competence rule is in **Art. 153 TFEU** (ex-Art. 137 EC-Treaty). It represents the general rule for enacting labour legislation and will enable an extensive harmonisation of national individual employment law. However, significant parts of collective labour law are still exempt from regulation by the EU pursuant to Art. 153(5) TFEU which excludes "pay, the right of association, the right to strike [and] the right to impose lock-outs" from the scope of Art. 153 TFEU. There are still other specifically labour law related provisions in the TFEU aside from the competence rule in Art. 153 TFEU. These include the rules on freedom of movement for workers (Arts. 45 *et seqq.* TFEU) and the principle of equal pay for men and women (Art. 157 TFEU).

The Lisbon Treaty has given the **Charter of Fundamental Rights** (Art. 6(1) EU-Treaty) legal force. The latter has now become a genuine part of primary law. It sets out general rights and freedoms that are binding for the bodies and institutions as well as the Member States when they implement EU law. Union citizens can rely directly on the rights and freedoms guaranteed by the Charter against the EU bodies and the Member States; this ensures a multifaceted protection of fundamental rights.

4. The future?

24 The further development of European Labour Law is difficult to predict. In the past, development was oftentimes not determined by the necessity as much as by the political **feasibility** of a regulation. The European Directives that were agreed upon in the political process include – so it seems from an unbiased point of view – not only regulations that are justifiable by the necessity of universal or improved

employee protection, but it seems at times only their feasibility has lead to the directives. Brussels must justify itself by passing new laws – and so the Commission also proposes things that are not necessary but also unlikely to meet with much political resistance.

Again, the recent **examples of discrimination laws** prove this point. Considering current political circumstances, the creation of universal European dismissal protection in the foreseeable future is probably unthinkable. The legal positions in Great Britain and Portugal, in Germany and in Poland, are too different (see § 6 para. 14 *et seq.*). Thus, no universal dismissal protection has been created. Instead, comprehensive discrimination protection has been enacted. The fact that this can be functionally comparable to dismissal protection can be seen in US-American practice which does not know a general *good cause requirement* but often achieves the same results via intricate and sophisticated anti-discrimination legislation. It may be allowed to say that the extension of discrimination protection was feasible at European level because a different, much more central regulatory area could not be dealt with. In a heterogeneous society, like the European one, the legislator must retreat to such legislation where a consensus may be reached. The more different the positions of the national legal systems are, the thinner the margin of possible action. The fact that there is such a margin in some areas does not mean that action should indeed be taken. Where there is no need for a statute, there must not be a statute. The old phrase of *Montesquieu* is true also for European Law. 25

III. To recap: The terms used in European Law

In European Labour Law – as in European law generally – it is important to differentiate between **the types of European legal instruments and their legal effect**. It therefore makes sense to give a short outline of the legal sources of European Labour Law. One must first make a rough distinction between primary law and secondary law. Primary Union law is referred to as the rules of law in their entirety created by the Member States of the European Union as subjects of international law to constitute and shape the Union. Therefore, primary legislation consists mainly of the founding treaties of the European Union (Treaty on the Functioning of the European Union and the Treaty of the European Union and, according to Art. 6(1) TEU, also the Charter of Fundamental Rights) including their annexes, accession treaties and association agreements. It is (casually speaking) the "constitutional law" of the EU, i. e. the law from which the European Union is formed, not the law created by the EU (*Fairhurst*, Law of the European Union, 2007, pp. 55 *et seqq.*). The latter, i. e. the law that is derived from primary law, is referred to as secondary law. European primary law takes precedence over secondary law. 26

There is also unwritten primary law. **Customary Union law** is conceivable if through actions of the Community institutions and/or the Member States as a result of "consistent practice" an *opinio iuris* has developed (e. g.: representation of the Member States in the Council not just by ministers – as prescribed by Art. 16(2) TEU [ex-Art. 203 EC] – but also by state secretaries). More important are the "**general principles common to the Member States**". They do not represent custom law (as a rule) because they do not necessarily depict an *opinio iuris* of all Member States, but instead were selected and formulated by the *ECJ* following assessment of comparative law as the best solution benefitting the Union out of the statutes of the legal systems of all Member States (*Fairhurst*, Law of the European Union, 2007, 67 *et seqq.*). The main focus is on developing fundamental rights on a European level. In the *ECJ* judgment of the 20 November 1969 in the Case 29/69 – Stauder [1969] ECR 419), after hearing the Advocate General *Roemer's* opinion, the Court assessed the validity of a Community measure for the first time in light of "the fundamental human rights enshrined in the general principles of Community Law and protected by the Court" (for further development see in particular the opinions of Advocate General *Colomer* in the Case 466/00 – Kaba [2003] ECR I-2219). These fundamental rights also include the rule of equal treatment in equal circumstances: "It is settled case-law that the general principle of equal treatment is a fundamental principle of 27

Community Law" (CFI Case T-298/02, OJ 2005 C 330/17). This is only binding for the European and national legislator in areas where they implement European law. Discriminatory treatment by a private employer is not covered by the principle of equal treatment – with all due caution interpreting the not very clear chain of argument. Since the adoption of the Lisbon Treaty these principles have been acknowledged expressly in Art. 6(3) TEU. In the EU Charter of Fundamental Rights the principle of equal treatment is guaranteed by Art. 21.

28 European secondary legislation is classified into regulations, directives, decisions, recommendations and opinions. The two most significant legislative acts for European Labour Law are **regulations** and the much more common **directives**:

29 1. The regulation (Art. 288(2) TFEU [ex-Art. 249(2) EC]) is the "strongest" form of European legislative acts. It is directly binding upon citizens of the individual states. Its legal effect is therefore no different than that of national legislation. As a result of this extensive effect this legislative instrument is rarely exercised; the authorization to make regulations is usually subject to stricter requirements than the authorization to issue directives (*Craig/de Búrca*, EU Law: Text, Cases and Materials, 2011, pp. 104 *et seqq.*).

30 2. The directive (Art. 288(3) TFEU [ex-Art. 249(3) EC]) does not grant citizens a legal position directly, but rather obligates the Member States to create such legal positions (For an extensive study see *Prechal*, Directives in European Community Law: A study on EC Directives and their Enforcement by National Courts, 1995). Regarding the choice of measures, the Member States can act according to their own judgment. Consequently, this form of action is more in accordance with the **principle of subsidiarity** as a larger scope of discretion remains with the Member States (see also Case 163/82 Commission vs. Italy [1983] ECR I-3273). An exception to the principle – that directives are not directly applicable to citizens of the Member States – is made for the case of a Member State exceeding the deadline for transposition. If the directive contains a mandatory provision and is sufficiently specific so as to grant the addressee a legal position accordingly, then it takes effect as of expiry of the time limit "**self-executingly**". However, it is not true that a directive is tantamount to a regulation or to the directly applicable Treaty legislation with respect to its legal effect. For even when a directive takes direct effect, it addresses only the state, not other citizens. It does not have a direct horizontal effect, **just a vertical direct effect** (as maintained in labour law by the *ECJ* against the opinion of Advocate General *Lenz* in the Case 91/92 – Faccini Dori [1994] ECR I-3325; Case 555/07 – Kücükdeveci [2010] ECR I-365). An employee cannot therefore invoke the provisions of the directive against his non-state employer.

31 The **Mangold case** (see on this: *Schieck*, The ECJ Decision in Mangold: A further Twist on Effects of Directives and Constitutional Relevance of Community Equality Legislation, 35 Industrial Law Journal 2006, 329–341) has not changed this either (Case 144/04 – Mangold [2005] ECR I-9981). In the closely observed trial about the German provision in § 14(3) Teilzeit- und Befristungsgesetz (a provision that allowed the employer to limit the duration of an employment contract to a fixed term without any objective reason for employees over the age of 52, whereas younger employees that were employed for longer than 2 years were only allowed to be given a fixed-term contract if there was an objective reason) the court did not revert to the directive but substantiated the inapplicability of the provision with the prohibition of age discrimination as an unwritten element of primary Union law. Here too there is only a direct effect with respect to unequal treatment by the national legislator incorporating European law, not by the employer. The opinions of Advocate General *Sharpston* in the trial Bartsch (Opinion of Advocate General *Sharpston* Case 427/06 – Bartsch [2008] ECR I-7245, para. 69) state this clearly. The predictions made that all knowledge of labour law would be discarded turned out to be unfounded. The opinions are worth reading

because they summarize and analyze the relevant judgments of the *ECJ*. The Court confirmed its decision in Mangold in the case of Kücükdeveci (Case 555/07 – Kücükdeveci [2010] ECR I-365, see also *Thüsing/Horler*, 47 CMLR 2010, 1161).

The state, however, remains the state even when it is an employer, thus there is no question of a horizontal effect in these circumstances (see Case 188/89 – Foster [1990] ECR I-3313; *Fairhurst*, Law of the European Union, 2007, pp. 273 *et seqq.*; *Eady*, Emanation of the State, 26 Industrial Law Journal 1997, 248–252). 32

Mrs. Foster retired at the age of 60 in compliance with British law at that time which did not grant retirement for men until the age of 63. Mrs. Foster argued that this was in conflict with Art. 5 of the Directive 76/207/EEC which at the time was not yet transposed in Great Britain. The *ECJ* approved of a direct effect against the employer, for the gas company which was owned for the most part by the state was considered the state in terms of Art. 288(2) TFEU. 33

The essential reason why the *ECJ* repudiates a direct horizontal effect of directives is the wording of Art. 288 TFEU which assigns such an effect only to regulations but specifically not to directives. This distinction remains even in the event of failure to transpose. The *ECJ* emphasized in this respect that the assumption of a horizontal direct effect would lead to "recogniz[ing] a power in the Community to enact obligations for individuals with immediate effect, whereas it has competence to do so only where it is empowered to adopt regulations" (see Case 91/92 – Faccini Dori [1994] ECR I-3325). 34

The line where a **state** begins and where it ends is blurred. As a result of a submission requesting a preliminary decision by the *Austrian Supreme Court*, the *ECJ* dealt with the question of the effect of directives against private law subjects of which the only shareholder is a state entity (Case 297/03 – Sozialhilfeverband Rohrbach [2005] ECR I-4305). In its decision the *ECJ* puts straight that an individual can also enforce those not yet implemented directives against private law subjects that are governed by the state in sole shareholding. In this context it is immaterial whether the relevant state entity is responsible for transposing the directive. Considering the strong municipal tendencies to privatize duties of public service (e. g. previous municipal undertakings of waste management or municipal facilities like swimming pools) the decision is nevertheless of great significance – the questions with which the *ECJ* will have to deal with in the near future will be questions of demarcation: What applies for not sole but significant state shareholding, what applies for mere lower-level state minority shareholding? 35

Furthermore, conditional for a direct effect is that the **directive is sufficiently precise** to generate legal consequences. A court must be able to apply it (compare in particular Case 6/90 and Case 9/90 – Francovich et al [1991] ECR I-5357; Case 62/00 – Marks & Spencer [2002] ECR I-6325). 36

Sometimes a trick is used. By confirmed judgment of the *ECJ* it is sufficient (Case 6/90 and Case 9/90 – Francovich et al [1991] ECR I-5357) if **minimum sanctions** can be derived from the prescriptions of the directive; these are then directly applicable. This becomes relevant, for instance, for the transposition deficits of the anti-discrimination directives (see on the implementation of these directives: *Bell*, The Implementation of the European Anti-Discrimination Directives: Converging towards a Common Model?, 79 The Political Quarterly 2008, Issue 1, 36–44). Art. 15 of Directive 2000/43/EC and Art. 17 of Directive 2000/78/EC give the Member States the responsibility and the discretion to determine sanctions that are to be imposed for infringements of the national provisions adopted pursuant to the directives and to take all necessary measures to that extent. The only condition is for the sanction to be effective, proportionate and dissuasive. This discretion granted therein is *prima facie* contradictory to the sufficient precision needed for direct effectiveness with respect to the legal consequences. A minimum sanction could however be the voidness of a unilateral declaration of intention in breach of the discrimination ban. This would be true for e. g. – from the 3 December 2003 onwards – the termination of an employment contract in 37 civil service owing to undesirable religious practices (Such as the **German case** of a teacher who insisted on wearing a headscarf in class – see the decisions in *Bundesverwaltungsgericht* (*BVerwG*) of 4 July 2002-2 C 21/01 and *Bundesverfassungsgericht* (*BVerfG*) of 24 September 2003-2 BvR 1436/02). However, caution is advised as a claim for damages is conceivable as a remedy – without the validity of the termination being affected – and would suffice as implementation of the directive, so the invalidity of the dismissal represents a minimum requirement of the directive only if it is to be seen as of a lesser degree compared to an extensive damage claim. This is a matter of judgment and remains to be seen.

38 An increasingly debated question of late is to which extent directives can be implemented by judge-made law. The *ECJ* assumes that the implementation of a directive does not require legislative action, however there must be a guarantee that the legal position under national law is sufficiently clear and precise (Case 144/99 – Commission v Netherlands [2001] ECR I-3541, para. 17). This is disputed at times in labour law.

39 Various anti-discrimination directives allow the Member States to determine objective reasons that justify direct discrimination (see Art. 14(2) of Directive 2006/54/EC; Art. 4(1) of Directive 2000/78/EC; Art. 4 of Directive 2000/43/EC). It is debatable whether these objective reasons can be specified by the courts or whether legislative action is necessary. The *ECJ* – in view of the special control duties prescribed by Art. 9(2) of the Directive 76/206/EEC (now Art. 31(3) of Directive 2006/54/EC) by which the Member States must review at regular intervals whether the set cases of permissible difference of treatment based on gender are to be maintained and must report the results of this review to the Commission – has considered legislative action necessary, albeit merely with respect to evidence of the differences, not of their determination (Case 248/83 – Commission v Germany [1985] ECR, 1474). Currently, there is dispute over to which extent § 14(1) Teilzeit- und Befristungsgesetz, with its generic reference that a fixed-term contract is permissible subject to an objective reason, is a sufficient transposition of Clause 5(1) of the framework agreement on fixed-term employment contracts (contained in Directive 1999/70/EC). There are possibly better arguments in support of it being in conformity with Union law. See in detail § 4 para. 46.

40 If there is no direct application of European Law, then only an **interpretation in conformity with European law** can help (see Chapter 10 Consistent Interpretation in *Prechal*, Directives in European Community Law: A Study on EC Directives and their Enforcement by National Courts, 1995, pp. 200 *et seqq.*).

41 As long as there is room for interpretation, the national courts and authorities are to interpret the national law in light of the adopted but not yet transposed directive (fundamentally: Case 397/01 to 403/01 – Pfeiffer [2004] ECR I-8835; Case 14/83 – von Colson & Kamann [1984] ECR, 1891, 1909; Case 308/89 – di Leo [1990] ECR I-4185). Transposition gaps can thereby be closed by employing a modified understanding of the existing national law. So whereas the direct effect cannot effectuate obligations for private subjects, the interpretation in conformity with the directives affects all legal relations. Its limits are reached when language, system and purpose of the national law do not allow an interpretation in conformity with European provisions: An interpretation in conformity with European law is possible and necessary, any bending of the law to make it conform with European law – i. e. an interpretation *contra legem* – is not permissible (see Case 109/09 – Deutsche Lufthansa; Case 212/04 – Adeneler [2006] ECR I-6057; also against the opinions of Advocate General *Colomer* in the *Pfeiffer* case, Case 397/01 to Case 403/01, ECR I-8835). In the *ECJ*'s opinion, the rule of interpretation of domestic law in conformity with the directives does not apply after transposition of the content of the directive, but with expiry of the transposition deadline without the Member State having needed to have attempted or tackled transposition (see Advocate General *Tizzano* in his opinion to Case 144/04 – Mangold [2005] ECR I-9981 para. 115 with reference to the – though not definitive – decision of the Case 80/86 – Kolpinghuis Nijmegen [1987] ECR I-3969; see also the full statement of reasons of Advocate General *Kokott*, Case 212/04 – Adeneler [2006] ECR I-6057).

IV. To recap: Interpretation of European Law

The rules of interpretation of European law are still a little fuzzy. There is agreement on the rough sketch but the precision drawing in the individual case reveals significant methodical differences. Undisputed is the fact that starting point of every interpretation is the wording of the statute. Attention must be paid to the fact that all versions of the directives have the same validity (Art. 55(1) TEU). Oftentimes it is not enough to just look at one language version, as differences in meaning exist compared to the wording of other versions (see *Werkmeister/Pötters/Traut*, in: Barnard/Odudu (eds.), Cambridge Yearbook of European Studies, Vol. 13, 2010–2011, pp. 314 *et seqq.*). According to the *ECJ*, in the event of conflicting language versions, little weight should be given to the wording at all because all language versions are equally binding (see e. g. Case 511/08 – Heinrich Heine [2010] ECR I-3047). 42

It is equally undisputed that in interpreting a directive the **context of its creation** must be considered. Materials or examples of domestic law can reveal what the language of the directive actually means. Understanding of European (Labour) Law therefore often requires the willingness to review comparative law. Another important aid in interpretation are the recitals contained in the legal acts, as they can provide a useful insight into how the legislators understood a piece of legislation. 43

The right of the agency worker to access the amenities or collective services of the user undertaking, guaranteed in Art. 8 of the proposal for a directive on temporary work (COM 2002 [741] final) was taken directly from French and Spanish law (Art. L. 1251-24 Code du travail; Art. 17(2) Spanish Law 14/1994 of 1 July 1994). If one were to equate the term "Sozialeinrichtung" in German with the same term used in the German statute § 87(1) no. 8 Betriebsverfassungsgesetz, it would have a completely different meaning. This would then also include pension funds whereas the European legislator was thinking more of canteens and shuttle busses as can be seen from the French and Spanish provisions, see Art. 6 Directive 2008/104/EC. 44

The **systematic argument** can also be found in the judgments of the *ECJ*: What do other provisions of the directive or of European law as a whole say? Here too, the recitals of a directive must be considered at all times when interpreting a directive (cf. on this note Case 240/02 – Asempre [2004] ECR I-2461, para. 22; cf. also Case 13/05 – Navas [2006] ECR I-6467). 45

Advocate General *Mazák* draws on this concerning the question whether a collective agreement that regulates compulsory retirement can be examined under direct application of Directive 2000/78/EC (Case 411/05). He answers this in the negative referring to the Recital 14 of the Directive ("This Directive shall be without prejudice to national provisions laying down retirement ages"). (Opinion of Mr Advocate General *Mazák* delivered on 15 February 2007 in the Case 411/05 – Félix Palacios de la Villa v Cortefiel Servicios SA [2007] ECR I-08531). 46

A subset of the systematic argument is the **obligation to interpret in conformity with primary law**. The *ECJ*, admittedly, refers to this only rarely (see though e.g. Advocate General *Kokott* in her opinions of 25 January 2007 – Case 392/05 – Alevizos [2007] ECR I-03505). In labour law the question arises when interpreting the Posting of Workers Directive, see § 9 paras. 17 *et seqq.* Where an interpretation in conformity with primary law is no longer possible, the directive is void for being in violation of primary law (Case 236/09 – Test-Achats). 47

Of particular significance is the **teleological approach**: What does the European primary law aim to achieve? What does the directive want? When in doubt, 48

European provisions are to be interpreted in such a way as to give their objectives the best possible efficacy. The key word here is the ***effet utile.*** This legal principle requires that in the event of several possible interpretations, the interpretation that corresponds with the objective and spirit of the provision in a practical sense must prevail. The principle of "effet utile" applies even if Union law and the national law of a Member State are in conflict with each other: the conflict must be resolved in a way that does not undermine the efficacy or enforcement of Union law. An important application of this principle originating from international law is the Francovich case (Case 6/90 and Case 9/90 [1991] ECR I-5357), in which the *ECJ* established a liability of the Member States regardless of fault when in breach of Community law. In labour law the *ECJ* referred to this for instance when ascertaining the scope of the right to information of national employees' representatives in order to establish a European Works Council as provided in Directive 94/45/EC (now Directive 2009/38/EC), see § 10 para. 24.

V. What can the EU regulate in the field of labour law?

49 The European Union can only enact laws in areas for which it is explicitly authorized. The **principle of conferral** applies (Art. 5(1) TEU). There is a relationship of **subsidiarity** between the European Union and the Member States (Art. 5(3) TEU). Power-giving laws that are particularly relevant for labour law are the following:

50 **Art. 19 TFEU** (ex-Art. 13 EC) was incorporated by the Amsterdam Treaty. It confers upon the Council the power to take appropriate action to combat discrimination based on sex, race, ethnic origin, religion or belief, disability, age or sexual orientation. The Council is required to act unanimously as well as only on proposal by the Commission and – since the adoption of the Lisbon Treaty – only with the European Parliament's consent. The provision is quite contentious as the line between patronizing equalization and necessary protection of disadvantaged groups is difficult to find. The authority does not only apply to labour law but encompasses the entire (private) law.

51 The only secondary laws based on Art. 19 TFEU (ex-Art. 13 EC) so far are the Directives 2000/43/EC, 2000/78/EC and the Directive 2004/113/EC. See on this in detail § 3 paras. 1 *et seqq.*

52 **Art. 46 TFEU** (ex-Art. 40 EC) authorizes setting out measures to bring about freedom of movement. This includes issuing regulations.

53 Regulation (EEC) No. 1612/68 on the freedom of movement for workers within the Community as well as the Directive 68/360/EEC on the abolition of restrictions on movement and residence for workers of Member States and their family members within the Community is based on this.

54 Of principal importance is Art. 153 TFEU (**ex-Art. 13 EC**) which was largely taken from Art. 2 of the Agreement on Social Policy but then redrafted in the Nice Treaty (see further on Art. 137 EC: *Blanpain*, European Labour Law, 2003, pp. 487 *et seqq.*). It marks the **blanket provision for lawmaking** in labour law. Art. 153(1),(2) TFEU stipulate that directives may be issued in the areas listed in (a), (b), (e), (f), (h), (i), (j) by the Council following the procedure stated in Art. 294 TFEU (ex-Art. 251 EC) by qualified majority and consent of the European Parliament or – in the areas listed in Art. 153(1)(c),(d),(f) and (g) TFEU – by a unanimous decision by the Council after consultation with the European Parliament.

Art. 153(1) TFEU contains the following areas:

(a) improvement in particular of the working environment to protect workers' health and safety,
(b) working conditions,
(c) social security and social protection of workers,
(d) protection of workers where their employment contract is terminated,
(e) the information and consultation of workers,
(f) representation and collective defence of the interests of workers and employers, including codetermination, subject to paragraph 5,
(g) conditions of employment for third-country nationals legally residing in Union territory,
(h) the integration of persons excluded from the labour market, without prejudice to Art. 166 TFEU,
(i) equality between men and women with regard to labour market opportunities and treatment at work,
(j) the combating of social exclusion.

How the separate fields in Art. 153(1) TFEU are to be **distinguished** from one 55
another has not yet been settled in detail. In particular, the term working conditions in Art. 153(1)(b) is in many respects ambiguous.

The **exclusion in Art. 153(5) TFEU** is important. According to this, there is no 56
lawmaking authority for "pay, the right of association, the right to strike or the right to impose lock-outs."

The fact that the right to impose lock-outs is mentioned explicitly is remarkable. In the European 57
constitutions one will find numerous guarantees of the right to strike without mention of a right to impose lock-outs. The domestic labour legislations of the different Member States have a inconsistent attitude towards lock-outs: in Portugal it is forbidden (see *Blanpain*, Comparative Labour Law and Industrial Relations in Industrial Market Economies, 2010, p. 707), in its neighbouring country Spain it is allowed, but only unter strict conditions (compare *Alonso/Rodriguez-Saudovon*, Labour Law in Spain, 2010, p. 151 *et seq.*).

The meaning of the **term "pay"** is in dispute. The wording by all means suggests 58
a broad understanding and so it was debated whether, for example, the ban on discrimination of temporary agency workers stipulated in the directive proposal on temporary agency work (COM [2002] 701 final] was covered by a legislative authority or not.

Shortly after presenting the draft, the supposition was raised that the Union lacks the authority to 59
issue the proposed discrimination ban to the extent of it pertaining to pay. In Art. 137(5) EC (now Art. 153(5) TFEU) regulating pay was expressly left out of the scope. This argument was already made in the past by **German scholars** e. g. *Wank and Börgmann.* For the same reasons they were of the opinion that the framework agreement on fixed-term employment contracts (contained in Directive 1999/70/EC) lacked a basis for a discrimination ban regarding pay (*Wank/Börgmann*, 52 RdA 1999, 383, 384 – regarding the predecessing provision Art. 2(2) of Social Policy Agreement). The concerns here, more so than there, are certainly notable, albeit ultimately not crucial. However, the European legislator cannot refer to the enabling provision of Art. 19 TFEU, for temporary work is not mentioned in this provision as a forbidden discriminatory ground. Arguably, he could not do this with respect to the part-time directive and the fixed-term directive either, as they forbid discrimination irrespective of proportional discrimination based on sex which is mentioned – unlike part-time or fixed-term – as a discriminatory attribute. Yet Art. 153(2) TFEU could perhaps be a sufficient basis after all, as the exclusion provision of Art. 153(5) TFEU was created just like its predecessor Art. 2(3) of the Social Policy Agreement principally to prevent a European-wide minimum wage. The part-time directive and the fixed-term directive do not prescribe an absolute

wage but a relative wage. They have provisions pertaining to the distribution of pay, not the amount; that is another matter. The employer may pay as little as he likes as long as he distributes the pay amongst his staff without discrimination. For this reason the finally adopted Directive 2008/104/EC was quite rightly based on Art. 153(2) TFEU.

60 There are other uncertainties as well: In the green paper "Modernising labour law to meet the challenges of the 21st century" (COM [2006] 708 final; see also para. 19), the Commission considers expanding European Labour Law to include **employee-like** workers. European law could not base this on the law-making authorities in Arts. 153 *et seqq.* TFEU as these only have the employee in mind. To include an "employee-like" worker, whatever this is to mean, goes beyond the traditional understanding of this authority provision and opens up the flood gates: How alike must the employment relationship be to let it be regulated by European law? There are no guidelines for this and the danger of extensive – and ultimately: random – interpretation is obvious. The anti-discrimination Directives 2000/43/EC and 2000/78/EC and the commercial agent Directive 86/653/EEC were quite rightly not based on the law-making authorities regarding labour law.

61 All labour law and social law law-making authorities at European level have a common objective: the extension of employee protection. Even in the assigned areas the European legislation cannot lead to a **total harmonisation** in the sense that European law could for instance provide a maximum standard of dismissal protection. This would contradict the purpose of the law-making competences that are set out in Art. 151 TFEU (ex-Art. 136 EC): harmonisation *through improvement*.

VI. Means of reviewing conformity with European Law

62 Under Art. 267 TFEU (ex-Art. 234 EC) the national judge can submit a question to the *ECJ* if he has doubts as to the interpretation of European law relevant to the case; the judge in the last instance has a duty to submit in this event (*Craig/de Búrca*, EU Law: Text, Cases and Materials, 2008, pp. 465 *et seqq.*). German courts obey this readily. They are leading in the current statistics: 71 cases in the year 2010 compared to e. g. only 33 as a result of submissions by **French courts** and 29 **British cases**. The difference can certainly not be explained by any negligence in implementation on the part of the German legislator – for in the number of actions for failure to fulfil obligations **Greece** is leading with 14 new cases in the year 2010. **Germany** ranks near the bottom with 7 actions.

VII. Role of the social partners

63 The role of social partners in the genesis of European Labour Law was legally outlined more closely for the first time in the Social Policy Agreement (on the role of social partners: *Blanpain*, Comparative Labour Law and Industrial Relations in industrialized Market Economies, 2004, pp. 168 *et seqq.*). Previously this had already influenced European legislation through informal contacts and lobbying. Now there was a fixed legal framework, the details of which, however, have not been clarified yet:

64 The question of who is **social partner in terms of Arts. 153 *et seqq.* TFEU** is left unanswered in the TFEU. On the employers' side BUSINESSEUROPE (previously the UNICE) and the CEEP established themselves, on the employees' side the European Trade Union Confederation (ETUC). Others have forced their way onto the playing field but the European Court of First Instance decided that no right of

the social partners' exists within the scope of Art. 155 TFEU (ex-Art. 139 EC, cf. CFI Case T-135/96 – UEAPME [1998] ECR II-2335) to participate in the proceedings instituted pursuant to Art. 138(4) EC (now Art. 154(4) TFEU). This should be applicable to other rights of the social partners. The diversity of European organizations forces the focus on the representative unions.

To be consulted in accordance with Art. 154(3) TFEU (ex-Art. 138(3) EC), the participating organizations must comply with thc following conditions (Resolution of the European Parliament of 7 June 1994 on application of the Agreement on social policy. See also communication concerning the application of the Agreement on social policy presented by the Commission to the Council and the European Parliament, COM 93 (600) final, p. 2): 65

- they must be organized at European level,
- they must be composed of organizations that are recognized in the respective Member State as a social partner, or be included in the consultations by the conventions of the respective Member States,
- they should be representative of most Member States, as far as possible,
- they must be composed of employer or employee organizations,
- their membership unions must have the right to participate in collective bargaining, either directly or through their members, on their respective levels,
- they must have the capacity to represent their members in the joint social dialogue and must certify their representativeness.

These organizations can be part of the private sector or the public sector and can be specialized in the specific problems of employees and employers in small and medium-sized enterprises or industries.

In addition, the CFI emphasized in the **UEAPME case** that the parties of an agreement must be democratically legitimized under Art. 139 EC (now Art. 155 TFEU) and must be representative of the represented fields (CFI Case T-135/96 – UEAPME [1998] ECR II-2335; critical *Franssen/Jacobs*, 35 CMLR 1998, 1295). This can be applied to the consultation under Art. 138(2) EC (now Art. 154(2) TFEU).

Under Art. 154(1) TFEU the Commission has the task to promote the consultation of the social partners at Union level and shall take any relevant measure to facilitate the **dialogue between the social partners** by ensuring balanced support for the parties. This very broad mandate is further substantiated by different participation rights: 66

- **Consultation rights.** Under Art. 154(2) and (3) TFEU the Commission shall consult the social partners before submitting proposals in the social policy field. The latter are not restricted to giving an opinion but may apply for a procedure provided for in Art. 155 TFEU. The Commission is free to decide whether it wishes to follow the proposal. 67
- **Law-making competences.** The procedure provided for in Art. 155 TFEU aims to lead to the adoption of a framework agreement in which, similar to a directive, questions of European Labour Law can be regulated. The agreements themselves are not legally binding however. They need to be implemented. This can be done either in accordance with the procedures and practices specific to the social partners of the Member States or (more importantly), in matters covered by the Art. 153 TFEU, i. e. where the EU has legislative power, at the joint request of the signatory parties by a Council decision on a proposal by the Commission. 68

According to **the *first* alternative**, the contractual agreement adopted in accordance with Art. 155(1) TFEU between the social partners at Union level does not have a direct effect – unlike a Regulation under Art. 288(2) TFEU; the effect *extra partes* is subject to the law of the respective Member States. The European social partners are therefore dependent on the parties to a collective agreement or the Member States to implement their instructions. For the national law of the Member 69

States this means in practice that the responsible parties to a collective agreement repeat the contents of the European agreement in a national "implementation collective agreement" and make additions – as needed for implementation purposes. The obligations of the parties to a collective agreement and the normative effects are exclusively a matter of national law which is set out expressly in Art. 155(2) TFEU. The agreement adopted at Community level is only binding for the European social partners that were involved with the adoption; it is not legally binding for the social partners at member state level, let alone for the Member States. The social partners acting at European Union level lack the mandate – at least at this time – to obligate the social partners of the Member States to implement the adopted agreements, as long as they have not assumed this as a membership duty in the European umbrella organization. The agreement itself having a normative effect is, *a fortiori*, out of the question by national law concerning collective agreements. The fact that the Member States are not obligated to implement the agreement to give it legal effect, arises from the declaration to Art. 4(2), alt. 1 Social Agreement which in itself is not legally binding but can be used as an instrument of interpretation of a recommendatory nature. Agreements that are adopted under Art. 155(2) alt. 1 TFEU serve merely as a coordination of the collective agreements in the Member States; they have the nature of a *gentlemen's agreement*. Indeed the *ECJ* is also competent under Art. 267 TFEU for the interpretation of non-binding legal instruments adopted on the basis of Union law (Case 133/75 – Frescassetti [1976] ECR, 983, 993; Case 322/88 – Grimaldi [1989] ECR, 4407, 4419; Case 188/91 – Deutsche Shell [1993] ECR I-363, 388) if one recognizes the contractual agreement of the social partners at Union level as a permissible object of interpretation. The interpretation however cannot be more binding for the Member States and member state social partners than the object of interpretation itself. A uniform applicability of the agreements in the Member States cannot therefore be guaranteed by this procedure but it can perhaps be promoted.

70 In accordance with **the *second* alternative** of Art. 155(2) TFEU the agreement is implemented by a Council decision on a proposal from the Commission. The nature of such a "decision" is not clear. The interpretation is further complicated by the different terms used in the different authentic language versions (compare Art. 55 TEU). In the English, French, Italian, Spanish and Portuguese version the word "decision" (decision, decision, decisione, decisión and decisão) is used just as in Art. 288(4) TFEU, whereas in the Danish, German and Dutch text the term "resolution" (*afgørelse*, *Beschluss* and *besluit*) can be found. Some **German authors** are therefore of the opinion that the *resolution* is a legal act closely "related" to a decision in terms of Art. 288 TFEU, capable of being directly applicable to the addressees (Member States and those affected in the Member States) (e. g. *Heinze,* 23 ZfA 1992, 331, 338). Other authors wish to leave the choice of specific form, be it regulation, directive, decision or "innominate" *resolution*, to the Council and thereby grant it more flexibility (*Blanpain/Engels,* European Labour Law, 1997, p. 119). Finally, some German scholars suggest that the decision has the nature of a directive according to the system and purpose of Art. 155(2) TFEU (*Buchner,* 46 RdA 1993, 193, 201; *Deinert*, 57 RdA 2004, 211, 225). The latter is probably the case at least as a rule due to the reference to Art. 153 TFEU and corresponds with previous practice.

The **opportunity of implementing framework agreements** has previously only been made use of by employing directives: Directive 1999/70/EC on EGB-UNICE-CEEP-framework agreement on fixed-term employment contracts, Directive 1996/34/EC of the Council on the framework agreement concluded by UNICE, CEEP and EGB on parental leave; Directive 1997/81/EC of the Council on the framework agreement concluded by UNICE, CEEP and EGB on part-time work. On 8 of October 2004 the four big European organizations of the social partners signed a framework agreement on work-related stress (compare http://ec.europa.eu/employment_social/dsw/public/actRetrieveText.-do?id=10402). Unlike the other previous framework agreements (e. g. on fixed-term and part-time work) the social partners do not want this agreement to be implemented by a directive but by their members. As regards content, the only things agreed on were specific procedures to identify and manage problems. The same is true for the agreement on telework (compare http://ec.europa.eu/social/BlobServlet?docId=216&langId=en) as well as the framework agreement on harassment and violence at work (COM [2007] 686 final). 71

- **Implementation competences.** According to Art. 153(3) TFEU a Member State can entrust the social partners at their joint request with the implementation of directives adopted pursuant to Art. 153(2) TFEU. This has not been exercised yet in any European states. 72

§ 2. Freedom of movement for workers

Literature: *Barnard*, The Substantive Law of the EU: The Four Freedoms, 3rd ed., 2010; *Condinanzi/ Lang/Nascimbene*, Citzenship of the Union and Freedom of Movement of Persons, 2008; *Grigolli*, Free Movement of Workers versus Protection of Minorities – Has the European Court of Justice Toppeld one of the "Pillars" of South Tyrolean Autonomy, The European Legal Forum (E), Vol. 3, 2000/01, 171; *Singer*, Free Movement of Workers in the European Economic Community: The Public Policy Exception, 29 Stanford Law Review 1977, No. 6, 1283–1297; *Staples*, The Legal Status of Third Country Nationals Resident in the European Union, 1999; *van der Mei*, Free Movement of Persons within the European Community: cross-border access to public benefits, 2003; *Weiss/ Wooldridge*, Free Movement of Persons within the European Community, 2nd ed., 2007; *White*, Workers, Establishment and Services in the European Union, 2005.

I. Outline

1. Objective

A primary objective of the European Union is to establish a common economic area (common market, Art. 3 TEU and internal market, Art. 26 TFEU). The TFEU contains provisions, the so-called fundamental freedoms, which – along with the related secondary legislation – are to ensure the free movement of economic goods. Free exchange of goods and services is provided for by the freedom of movement of goods (Arts. 28–37 TFEU) and the freedom to provide services (Arts. 56–62 TFEU). The freedom of movement of capital and payments is set out in Arts. 63–75 TFEU. The freedom of movement for workers (Arts. 45–48 TFEU) along with the freedom of establishment (Arts. 49–55 TFEU) constitute the freedom of movement for persons. Whereas the freedom of establishment regulates the exercise of self-employed operations, the **freedom of movement for workers deals with employed work**. The Arts. 45–48 TFEU and the secondary legislation based thereon serve to achieve a European labour market where workers can offer, and employers can request, labour irrespective of national borders (*Barnard*, The Substantive Law of the EU: The Four Freedoms, 2007, pp. 249 *et seqq.*). 1

The development in the European Union has now transcended beyond its economic goals. The citizenship of the Union (Arts. 18–25 TFEU) created a general – albeit not unlimited – right to free movement (Art. 21 TFEU) which is applicable irrespective of any economic objective of the person's stay. It is here that the Union shows that it is evolving into a political and social Community (*Kostakopoulou*, The Evolution of European Citizenship, European Political Science: EPS, Vol. 7, Issue 3, 2008, pp. 285–295). However, the right to freedom of movement for workers remains significant for labour law as the overriding, and in many respects more extensive, special rule. 2

2. Guarantees

3 Freedom of movement for workers can be roughly divided into three different guarantees:

4 – **The right to participate in the labour market of other Member States:** Art. 45(3) TFEU guarantees workers a right to access the labour market and as such the territory of other Member States. These rights are put in concrete terms in secondary legislation by the Regulations (EEC) No. 1612/68 and No. 1251/70 as well as the Directive 2004/38/EC. The Directive 2004/38/EC was to be transposed by the 1 May 2006 and replaces the Directives 64/221/EEC and 68/360/EEC (*Barnard*, EC Employment Law, 2006, pp. 188 *et seqq.*). This aspect of freedom of movement for workers is directed for the most part solely at the Member States. Therefore, it is a question of public law and does not concern the relationships between worker and employer. Nevertheless, a short outline of the public law aspects contained therein will be given (see paras. 25 *et seqq.*).

5 – **Prohibition of discrimination:** Art. 45(2) TFEU and, more specifically, Arts. 7–9 of Regulation (EEC) No. 1612/68, contain the prohibition of any different treatment of workers of other Member States exercising their right to free movement (so-called *migrant workers)* based on citizenship. Besides public law, social law and tax law (see para. 33), the rule of non-discrimination pertains above all to labour law.

6 – **Prohibition of restrictions**: According to decisions of the *ECJ*, a prohibition of restrictions can be found in Art. 45 TFEU beyond its wording prohibiting non-discriminatory barriers to freedom of movement, unless they can be objectively justified (*Barnard*, EC Employment Law, 2006, pp. 192 *et seqq.*).

3. Justification

7 Limitations to the freedom of movement for workers are not prohibited *per se*. Just as in the constitutional laws of many states – where not every infringement on a constitutional right is prohibited as such but can be justified – it is possible to justify limitations of the guarantees in Art. 45 TFEU. One must distinguish between written (Art. 45(3) TFEU) and unwritten justifications. Provisions restricting freedom of movement for workers must always satisfy the principle of proportionality and may not violate the fundamental rights recognized by Union law (Case 100/01 – Ministre de l'Intérieur v. Olazabal [2002] ECR I-10981, para. 43: "It must also be remembered that a measure restricting one of the fundamental freedoms guaranteed by the Treaty may be justified only if it complies with the principle of proportionality. In that respect, such a measure must be appropriate for securing the attainment of the objective which it pursues and must not go beyond what is necessary in order to attain it (Case 55/94 – Gebhard [1995] ECR I-4165, para. 37)"; Case 260/89 – ERT [1991] ECR I-2925, para. 43; Case 368/95 – Familiapress [1997] ECR I-3689, para. 24; both decisions related to freedom of service and freedom of movement of goods, respectively, the principles however can also be applied to the freedom of movement for workers).

4. Direct effect

8 Art. 45 TFEU has a direct effect. This applies absolutely in relation to the state and with respect to state provisions (Case 41/74 – Van Duyn v. Home Office [1974]

ECR 1337). Furthermore, the court acknowledges that the prohibition of discrimination contained in Art. 45 TFEU at any rate applies to the employer-worker relationship as well (Case 281/98 – Angonese [2000] I-4139; Case 94/07 – Raccanelli [2008] I-5939 paras. 43 *et seqq.*). The recent decisions by the *ECJ* allow the conclusion that the prohibition of restrictions also has such a third-party direct effect (cf. Case 325/08 – Olympique Lyonnais [2010] ECR I-02177).

As to secondary legislation, the principles illustrated above apply (§ 1, paras. 28 *et* 9 *seqq.*): Regulations are directly applicable pursuant to Art. 288(2) TFEU, that is to say with respect to the state as well as – as long as the regulation contains such provisions – between the citizens.

Example: Art. 7(4) of Regulation (EEC) No. 1612/68 declares provisions in collective and individual employment agreements void insofar as migrant workers are discriminated against therein. The voidness takes effect directly as a result of the regulation without the need for any sort of directive by the national legislator.

5. Beneficiaries

Not only workers can rely on Art. 45 TFEU, employers can too. Otherwise the 10 Member States could circumvent the prohibitions that are in force for the benefit of workers by simply directing appropriate laws at employers (Case 350/96 – Clean Car Autoservice GmbH v. Landeshauptmann von Wien [1998] ECR I-2521, para. 25).

6. Relationship between secondary and primary law

As portrayed above, the right to freedom of movement for workers consists of the 11 primary law rule in Art. 45 TFEU on the one hand and of a number of secondary legal instruments on the other. The question of the relationship between primary law and secondary law, in particular Regulation (EEC) No. 1612/68, has not quite been settled. The *ECJ* seems to consider the secondary legislation to be a substantiation and elaboration of Art. 45 TFEU that does not preclude the right to rely on the fundamental primary law rule directly (Case 15/69 – Württembergische Milchverwertung Südmilch AG v. Ugliola [1969] ECR 363; cf. also Case 36/74 – Walrave and Koch v. Association Union Cycliste Internationale [1974] ECR 1405, where the *ECJ* draws on the secondary legislation of Art. 7(4) of Regulation (EEC) No. 1612/68 as an argument when interpreting Art. 45 TFEU).

II. Scope of free movement for workers

1. Workers

The **term 'worker'** is not defined in Art. 45 TFEU. It is clear, however, that the 12 term must be determined by Community law (consistent practice of the *ECJ* since the judgment of 19 March 1964: Case 75/63 – Unger [1964] ECR 1977). Thus, there is a definition of 'worker' that is unique to European law. Were one to leave the definition to the national legal systems, the Member States would have the power to deprive groups of persons at will of the protection of free movement for workers. The practical efficacy of the free movement provisions would no longer be guaranteed.

This is different in the case of directives concerning labour law. They frequently refer to the 13 definition of employee applied by national law (see e. g. Art. 3(1)(a) of Directive 2008/104/EC [agency workers directive]; Art. 2 No. 1(d) of Directive 2001/23/EC [transfer of undertakings]; Art. 2(d) Directive 2002/14/EC (Works Council/"Renault-Directive"); Directive 1999/70/EC in conjunction with Section 2 No. 1 EGB/UNICE/CEEP framework agreement [fixed-term/part-time]. For many this difference in approach does not make sense. Essentially, it reflects the principle of subsidiarity and it is for this reason that the Member States insist upon it time and time again.

14 Subsequently, a worker is any person who for a certain period performs services under the direction of another person in return for which he receives remuneration (Case 66/85 – Lawrie-Blum [1986] ECR 2121; whether unpaid interns or trainees fall within the definition of worker under Art. 45 TFEU is a matter of debate. Only employed work falls within the definition of worker. If a self-employed person wishes to work permanently in another Member State, then the scope of protection for freedom of establishment (Art. 49 *et seqq.* TFEU) is applicable. The amount of remuneration and the extent of the work is of no importance; notably part-time workers fall within the definition of worker within the meaning of Art. 45 TFEU (Case 53/81 – Levin [1982] ECR 1035), as long as the work is not purely marginal and ancillary (Case 357/89 – Raulin [1992] ECR I-1027). It must be considered a "genuine and effective" economic activity. An activity that merely serves their social rehabilitation does not fall within the scope (Case 344/87 – Bettray [1989] ECR 1621). In contrast, it does not matter if the activity is in some way related to non-economic goals, for instance of a cultural or sportive nature. Even professional footballers are workers under Art. 45 TFEU (Case 415/93 – Bosman [1995] ECR I-4921; Case 325/08 – Olympique Lyonnais [2010], ECR I-02177).

15 There are some significant differences to the definition of workers and employees in the national legal systems. The most significant difference to **German labour law** lies in the fact that civil servants, judges and soldiers also fall within the definition of worker under Art. 45 TFEU (Case 152/73 – Sotgiu [1974] ECR 153). Under German law these persons are not considered workers because their work is based on a special legal relationship under public law and not based on a private law contract (*Dütz/Thüsing*, Arbeitsrecht, 18th ed., 2013, chapter 2, para. 34).

16 To include civil servants, judges and soldiers in principle in the protective sphere of the freedom of movement for workers makes sense: Whether an employment relationship under domestic law is governed by public or private law lies in the power of the national legislator. Were one to primarily use this as a point of reference, then the Member States would ultimately have the power to define the scope of freedom of movement for workers. Consequently, the fundamental right of Art. 45 TFEU also affects civil service law, which however will not be further elaborated upon within the context of this text book on labour law.

17 Under **English law**, more weight is placed on the employment contract than in EU law, where there is more focus on the activity exercised. The Employment Rights Act 1996 sets out in section 230(1) that an employee – belonging to the broader category of workers – is "an individual who has entered into or works under (or, where the employment has ceased, worked under) a contract of employment" (*Honeyball/Bowers*, Textbook on Labour Law, 2004, pp. 18 *et seqq.*). There are three criteria which have to be fulfilled to have the status of an employee: "1. There must be 'mutuality of obligation' between the parties to the contract; 2. there must be a relationship of employer and employee; and 3. the contract must not contain any terms inconsistent with the relationship of employer and employee" (*Davies*, Perspectives on Labour Law, 2nd ed., 2009, p. 84). Furthermore,

there are two levels which have to be taken into consideration to determine whether an employment contract exists and hence a person is an employee. One level is described as the 'wage-work bargain', i. e. that the employee does work for an employer and in return receives remuneration, which is similar to EU law. The other level is the 'global contract'. Here, the employer must make a promise to the employee to provide for future work, and this in turn has to be accepted by a promise of the employee (*Davies*, Perspectives on Labour Law, 2nd ed., 2009, pp. 84 *et seqq.*). If these levels can be found there is mutuality of obligations between the parties (see further Nethermere (St Neots) Ltd v Taverna and Gardiner [1984] IRLR 240; O'Kelly v Trusthouse Forte plc [1983] 369). Regarding the second requirement to be fulfilled there are various tests established by case law: the control test (Ready Mixed Concrete v Minister of Pensions [1968] 2 QB 497), the integration test (Stevenson, Jordan, and Harrison Ltd. v MacDonald and Evans [1952] 1 TLR 101) and the most recent economic reality test (Market Investigation Ltd v Minister of Social Security [1969] 2 QB 173). The last test essentially considers whether the person in question was performing business on his own account. If the employer takes account for the business conducted than the person in question can be regarded as an employee. Concerning the last requirement – the contract must not contain any terms inconsistent with the relationship of employer and employee – the British courts pointed out that an employee is a person performing work on a personal basis for an employer (see further Express and Echo Publications Ltd. v Tanton [1999] IRLR 367; MacFarlane v Glasgow CC [2001] IRLR 7).

Another difference of **UK law** as opposed to EU law is the difference made **18** between employee and worker. A worker is understood as being a category in between employee and self-employed. The worker as such is defined as "an individual who has entered into or works under (…) (a) a contract of employment, or (b) any other contract, whether express or implied and (if it is express) whether oral or in writing, whereby the individual undertakes to do or perform personally any work or services for another party to the contract whose status is not by virtue of the contract that of a client or customer of any profession or business undertaking carried on by the individual" (ERA 1996, section 230(3)). Again it becomes clear that the focus is on the contract rather than on the activity exercised.

2. The exception of Art. 45(4) TFEU

One must distinguish between the definition of worker and the exclusion in **19** Art. 45(4) TFEU pursuant to which the freedom of movement for workers is not applicable to **activities in the public service**. The idea behind this is that certain official activities are so delicate that the state reserves them for persons that are tied to the state by the special bond of nationality. The *ECJ* and the prevailing opinions in legal academic literature rightly define this exception in terms of European law. The inherent prerogative of interpretation therefore does not lie with the national legislator (Case 152/73 – Sotgiu [1974] ECR 153). The same considerations that apply to the European definition of worker also apply here: just as the Member States cannot positively define the term "worker", they cannot negatively determine the exception. The ***ECJ* adopts a narrow interpretation** of Art. 45(4) TFEU in accordance with its basic rules of interpretation and the purpose of the exception. Only activities involving the exercise of sovereign authority or the exercise of duties that focus on preserving the interests of the state or other public bodies are classified as the public service (Case 225/85 – Commission v. Italy [1987] ECR 2625; see also *Barnard*, EC Employment Law, 2006, pp. 261 *et seqq.*; *Barnard*, The Substantive Law of the EU: The Four Freedoms, 2007, pp. 481 *et seqq.*). This includes, for example, the work of the police but not the care provided by nurses in public hospitals (Case 307/84 – Commission v. France [1986] ECR 1725) or the research at a governmental science institute (Case 225/85 – Commission v. Italy [1987] ECR 2625).

3. Family members of migrant workers

20 Freedom of movement would only be a right on paper if the migrant worker could not take his family along with him to another Member State or if his family could travel with him but is discriminated against in the host country. The Directive 2004/38/EC therefore obligates the Member States to grant family members of migrant workers (see Art. 2 no. 2 Directive 2004/38) a right of entry (see Art. 5 Directive 2004/38) and residence (see Arts. 6 *et seqq.* Directive 2004/38) as well as a right to take up employment (Art. 23 Directive 2004/38). These rights apply specifically also to family members that are not Union citizens. Art. 12 of Regulation (EEC) No. 1612/68 grants the children of migrant workers a right of admittance to the host state's education and vocational training. The Commission has proposed a codification of these scattered rules and consequently a revocation of the Regulation (COM [2010] 204 final). Art. 24(1) second sentence of Directive 2004/38 generally extends the right to equal treatment also to family members. Provided that the family members are not Union citizens enjoying their own rights to free movement, the aforementioned rights are derived rights that are subject to the existence and exercise of the migrant worker's rights (see also *Barnard*, The Substantive Law of the EU: The Four Freedoms, 2007, pp. 416 *et seqq.*; *Condinanzi/Lang/Nascimbene*, Citzenship of the Union and Freedom of Movement of Persons, 2008, pp. 75 *et seqq.*)

4. Cross-border situation

21 As with all fundamental freedoms the freedom of movement for workers requires a cross-border situation (*Condinanzi/Lang/Nascimbene*, Citzenship of the Union and Freedom of Movement of Persons, 2008, pp. 71 *et seqq.)*. This however should not be misunderstood to mean that a worker may not rely on Art. 45 TFEU against his home state. The Member States may not, for instance, hinder their own citizens from leaving the country in order to take up employment in another Member State (cf. Art. 4 of Directive 2004/38). A cross-border situation also exists where a migrant worker returns to his home state after having exercised his right to free movement (Case 370/90 – R. v. IAT and Surinder Singh, ex parte Secretary of State for the Home Department [1992] ECR I-4265).

22 Purely domestic cases, for example when a worker wishes to change jobs within his own Member State, are not covered by Art. 45 TFEU. This can lead to the **problem of discrimination of nationals** (*discrimination à rebours* or reverse discrimination) when European law stipulates non-application of certain provisions in cross-border situations whereas the provision is applicable in purely domestic cases. Under European law such unequal treatment is not unlawful (*van der Mei*, Free Movement of Persons within the European Community: cross-border access to

public benefits, 2003, pp. 80 *et seqq.*; Case-Law: Case 175/78 – R v. Saunders [1979] ECR 1129, para. 11; Joined Cases 35 & 36/82 – Morson and Jhanjan v. the Netherlands [1982] ECR 3723, para. 16; but: Case 370/90 – The Queen v Immigration Appeal Tribunal et Surinder Singh, ex parte Secretary of State for Home Department [1992] ECR I-04265, para. 19).

5. Transitional provisions for nationals of the acceding states

In the course of the accession of certain East European countries to the EU, eight Middle and East European states as well as the Republic of Malta and the Republic of Cyprus acceded to the EU on the 1 May 2004. Fearing a large influx of workers from these states and a subsequent strain on the labour market of many old Member States, transitional periods pertaining to full effectiveness of free movement for workers for nationals of the acceding states were agreed upon in the accession agreements. Consequently, workers from the acceding states, unlike workers from the old Member States, needed work permits. The same is true for the accession of Rumania and Bulgaria (see on Association Agreements *White*, Workers, Establishment and Services in the European Union, 2004, pp. 12 *et seqq.*; *Weiss/Wooldridge*, Free Movement of Persons within the European Community, 2007, chapter 9). The transition period for the Member States that acceded in 2004 ended on the 30 April 2011, for Rumania and Bulgaria it will end on the 31 December 2013. 23

6. Freedom of movement for nationals of other states

In contrast, nationals of certain states enjoy limited rights to free movement solely on the basis of international agreements. These are in particular, the Association Agreement (see Art. 217 TFEU) with Turkey and the Association Agreement on the European Economic Area (EEA) which affects Iceland, Norway and Liechtenstein. More information on these and other agreements can be found in pertinent commentary literature and handbooks, see e. g. *Staples*, The Legal Status of Third Country Nationals Resident in the European Union, 1999, pp. 46 *et seqq.*). 24

III. Right to participate in the labour market (Art. 45(3) TFEU)

1. Guarantees

Art. 45(3) TFEU grants workers the right to (a) accept employment offers actually made, (b) to move freely within the territory of Member States for this purpose, (c) to stay in other Member States for the purpose of employment and (d) also to remain in the relevant Member State even after conclusion of employment. These specifications set out in primary law are substantiated by secondary law based on Art. 46 TFEU. 25

Arts. 1 to 6 of Regulation (EEC) No. 1612/68 grant migrant workers in principle unlimited access to the labour market of another Member State. Laws containing special provisions regarding access to, and pursuance of, employment of foreign nationals do not apply to migrant workers (Art. 3 of Regulation (EEC) No. 1612/68). The same is true for laws regulating access restrictions by number or percentage (Art. 4 of Regulation (EEC) No. 1612/68). Even as regards governmental support in seeking employment, migrant workers are entitled to the same assistance by the employment office as that afforded to nationals (Art. 5 of Regulation (EEC) No. 1612/68). Here, too, the Commission has proposed recodification (COM [2010] 204 final). 26

The possibility of taking up employment in another Member State would, in effect, be deprived of its value if unhindered entry and residence in another Member State were not guaranteed. Art. 45(3)(b), (c) and (d) TFEU therefore guarantee these rights directly. Details, in turn, are regulated by secondary legislation. The general right to reside is regulated in the Directive 2004/38/EC. Regarding those 27 entitled to remain in the territory (Art. 45(3)(d) TFEU) the Directive 2004/38/EC applies as well.

28 This was implemented in **Germany** by the Freizügigkeitsgesetz/EU which not only serves the implementation of the right to freedom of movement for workers (section 2(2) no. 1 and 5) but also refers to freedom of establishment (no. 2), freedom of service (no. 3 and 4) and to persons that exercise their general right to freedom of movement as a Union citizen as provided for in Art. 21 TFEU (no. 6). The issuance of a certificate of residency as set out in section 5(1) Freizügigkeitsgesetz/EU is merely declaratory and is therefore entirely different to the residence permits issued to other foreigners (Case 8/77 – Sagulo [1977] ECR 1495).

In the **United Kingdom**, Directive 2004/38/EC was implemented by the Immigration (European Economic Area) Regulations 2006 of 30 April 2006. However, even though most of the Directive is deemed to have been correctly implemented, there are some debatable provisions: the rights of residence and entry of third country nationals being family members of an EU citizen and the right of equal treatment as such (European Citizen Action Service, Comparative Study on the Application of Directive 2004/38/EC of 29 April 2004 on the Right of Citizens of the Union and their Family Members to move and reside freely within the territory of the Member States: Executive Summary, available at: www.statewatch.org/news/2009/feb/ep-free-movement-report.pdf). As regards the rights of third country nationals, the Commission found that with regard to Art. 5 of Directive 2004/38/EC the UK has not implemented it correctly, since it makes the "right of residence of third country family members conditional upon their prior lawful residence in another Member States" as it follows from *Akrich*. (Case 109/01 – Secretary of State for the Home Department v. Akrich [2003] ECR I-9607; Report from the Commission to the European Parliament and the Council on the application of Directive 2004/38 on the right of citizens of the Union and their family members to move and reside freely within the territory of the Member States, COM (2008) 840/3, Brussels). In the aftermath the *ECJ* ruled in the case Metock that a requirement of prior lawful residence in another Member State would be contrary to Community Law (Case 127/08 – Blaise Baheten Metock and Others v Minister for Justice, Equality and Law Reform [2008] ECR I-06241, para. 41). Therefore the Immigration (European Economic Area) (Amendment) Regulations 2012 came into force, especially setting out the rights of EEA nationals and their family members to enter and reside in the UK and also confirming the criteria for rights to permanent residence.

2. Public Policy Exception

29 The guaranteed rights set out in Art. 45(3) TFEU can be limited on grounds of **public policy, security and health**. The terms public policy, security and health as terms of European law are subject to review by the *ECJ* (Case 41/74 – van Duyn [1974] ECR 1337, paras. 18 *et seq.*). Under general European principles of interpretation and as a derogation from a fundamental principle, they are to be interpreted strictly (see Case 41/74 – Van Duyn [1974] ECR 1337, para. 18; Case 441/02 – Commission v. Germany [2006] ECR I-3449, paras. 32–35; Case 348/96 – Criminal Proceedings against Calfa [1999] ECR I-11, para. 23; the Court held in *Orfanopulous* that "a particularly restrictive interpretation of the derogations from that freedom is required by virtue of a person's status as a citizen of the Union". Joined Cases 482/01 & 493/01 – Orfanopoulos [2004] ECR I-5257, para. 65). There must be a genuine threat to public policy affecting fundamental interests of society (Case 30/77 – R. v. Bouchereau [1977] ECR 1999, para. 35). Substantiations in secondary legislation of the public policy exception are contained in Arts. 27 *et seqq.* of Directive 2004/38, with regards to content as well as procedure. In the event of the public policy exception taking effect, it will be possible to adopt measures limiting residence to the point of refusing entry or deportation (see also *Barnard*, The Substantive Law of the EU: The Four Freedoms, 2007, pp. 466 *et seqq.*; *Singer*,

Free Movement of Workers in the European Economic Community: The Public Policy Exception, 29 Stanford Law Review 1977, No. 6, 1283–1297).

IV. Prohibition of discrimination (Art. 45(2) TFEU)

1. The basic idea and purpose of the prohibition of discrimination

Under Art. 45(2) TFEU, freedom of movement includes the elimination of any unequal treatment of workers based on their nationality. Art. 45(2) TFEU is a special rule to the general rule of non-discrimination on grounds of nationality set out in Art. 12(1) EC with respect to free movement for workers (*Craig/de Búrca*, EU Law: Text, Cases and Materials, 2008, p. 744). In secondary law the prohibition of discrimination is substantiated in Arts. 7 *et seqq.* of Regulation (EEC) No. 1612/68 (which the Commission has proposed to revoke in the course of recodification, COM [2010] 204 final). The scope of the non-discrimination rule goes beyond specific employment regulations and also includes any discrimination in the person's surroundings. It suffices that the relevant provision affects the activity either directly or indirectly. 30

Example: In case 137/84 – Mutsch [1985] ECR 2681 a German man working in Belgium was charged with a crime in Belgium. A Belgian law for the protection of the German-speaking minority in east Belgium stipulated that Belgian defendants could request usage of the German language in a trial in particular districts of east Belgium. The German defendant requested application of this law in his case. On submission of the question of the Belgian court, the *ECJ* held that the right to use his own language fell within the scope of the prohibition of discrimination of Art. 45 TFEU (ex-Art. 39 EC) and was a social advantage in terms of Art. 7(2) of Regulation (EEC) 1612/68. As a result, the German defendant could request the use of the German language. 31

The **purpose of the prohibition of discrimination** is obvious: A European labour market where workers can search for and take up work irrespective of borders cannot be created by a guarantee of free entry and residence alone. The outlook of remaining a "second class" worker and resident due to discrimination dissuades people from working in another Member State not less than formal restrictions do. 32

2. Types of discrimination

First of all, Art. 45(2) TFEU prohibits regulations that discriminate directly by reason of nationality (direct or overt discrimination). However, according to consistent practice of the *ECJ*, discrimination also exists if a regulation applies other criteria of differentiation than nationality but this application in fact leads to migrant workers primarily suffering disadvantages; alternately referred to as indirect or covert discrimination (*Barnard*, The Substantive Law of the EU: The Four Freedoms, 2007, pp. 254 *et seqq.*). A classic example of this are regulations that differentiate by residence because this criterion predominantly, albeit not necessarily, affects foreigners (consistent practice since Case 152/73 – Sotgiu v. Deutsche Bundespost [1974] ECR 153). 33

Other examples of indirect discriminatory regulations are: not taking account of previous employment abroad (Case 419/92 – Scholz v. Opera Universitaria di 34

Cagliari and Cinzia Porcedda [1994] ECR I-505; cf. more recently Case 195/98 – Österreicher Gewerkschaftsverbund, Gewerkschaft öffentlicher Dienst v. Republik Österreich [2000] ECR I-10497; payment of tideover allowances only to students having completed secondary education in that Member State (Case 278/94 – Commission v. Belgium [1996] ECR I-4307). Language requirements typically constitute indirect discrimination, though these are explicitly lawful under Art. 3(1) of Regulation (EEC) No. 1612/68 as far as job particularities require them.

35 To begin with, the inclusion of indirect or covert discrimination serves to prevent circumvention of the prohibition of direct discrimination. However, a discriminatory intention is not necessary. It suffices that the measure has a discriminatory effect (cf. Art. 3(1) of Regulation (EEC) No. 1612/68). The prohibition of covert discrimination can therefore also be seen as a means to achieve actual equality for migrant workers. On the concept of covert discrimination see also § 3, paras. 18 *et seqq.*

3. Addressees of the prohibition of discrimination

a) Member States

36 The prohibition of discrimination first of all addresses the Member States as a public authority. Laws enacted by the government must not disadvantage migrant workers compared to domestic workers unless justified by way of exception (hereunto below, paras. 50 *et seqq.*).

37 Due to the wide scope of application (see para.30), indicated in particular by the inclusion of "social advantages" by Art. 7(2) of Regulation (EEC) No. 1612/68, this affects a large amount of provisions that are not of a labour law nature yet grant advantages to natives on account of their being workers or because of their domestic residence.

Examples: Fare discounts for families with many children; (Case 32/75 – Fiorini (née Christini) v. SNCF [1975] ECR 1085) Income support; (Case 249/83 – Hoeckx v. Openbaar Centrum voor Maatschappelijk Welzijn [1985] ECR 973) Use of German language before court (see above, para. 31, Mutsch case).

38 The prohibition of discrimination is significant also in tax law (cf. Art. 7(2) of Regulation (EEC) No. 1612/68) (*Barnard*, EC Employment Law, 2006, 197 *et seqq.*). Laws that relate to circumstances with domestic or foreign elements are particularly problematic. Above all, the Member States are bound to the prohibition of discrimination when forming their labour law as part of private law.

39 To the extent to which the state itself is an employer, it is bound to the prohibition of discrimination in this capacity.

b) Associations

40 It has been recognized in the case law of the *ECJ* for a long time that the prohibition of discrimination in Art. 45(2) TFEU is directly applicable to collective agreements (see Case 15/96 – Kalliope Schöning-Kougebetopoulou v Freie und Hansestadt Hamburg [1998] ECR I-00047). This affects collective agreements (Case 234/97 – Teresa Fernández de Bobadilla v Museo Nacional del Prado, Comité de Empresa del Museo Nacional del Prado and Ministerio Fiscal [1999] ECR I-04773) but also, for instance, the rules and regulations of sports associations.

Case 36/74 – **Walrave and Koch v. Association Union Cycliste Internationale** [1974] ECR 1405

The two Dutchman Walrave and Koch participated in cycling championships, so-called "stayer-races" as pacemakers on motorbikes. The cyclists ride in their slipstream. The races they participated in included the world championship for which the rules of the Union Cycliste Internationale applied. These rules contained a provision according to which the pacemaker and the stayer must be of the same nationality. The plaintiffs fought this clause before a Dutch court which submitted the question, inter alia, to the *ECJ* whether such a clause is incompatible with the right to free movement for workers.
The *ECJ* held that the plaintiffs' activity comes within the scope of Art. 39 EC as long as it constitutes an economic activity and not just one of a purely sportive nature. This depended above all on whether the pacemaker and the stayer constituted a (national) team. The precise determination of this though was incumbent on the national court. In the following, the *ECJ*, with reference to Art. 7(4) of Regulation (EEC) No. 1612/68, supported a third party effect of the primary law rule of non-discrimination set out in Art. 39(2) EC (now Art. 45(2) TFEU). The objective of abolishing obstacles to freedom of movement for persons would be compromised if the abolition of state barriers could be neutralized by private law organizations and institutions constructing such obstacles by virtue of their legal autonomy. What is more, in some Member States the working conditions are governed by collective agreements and in others by state laws. The uniformity of the rule of non-discrimination would be in danger if actions of public authorities and of associations were to be treated differently.

The principles of this decision were confirmed and perpetuated in the following 41
years (Case 13/76 – Donà v. Mantero [1976] ECR 1333; Case 415/93 – Union Royale Belge de Société de Football Association v. Bosman [1995] ECR I-4921; Case 325/08 – Olympique Lyonnais [2010] ECR I-02177 para. 30). In these decisions the *ECJ* held, inter alia, that rules of football associations that restricted the employment of foreign players are not compatible with Art. 45 TFEU (for another aspect of the Bosman decision see below, paras. 55 *et seqq.*). This line of judgments makes sense: Private associations are indeed different to the state in that they enjoy the constitutionally guaranteed right of collective autonomy. From an individual's point of view though, collective rules can have the same compulsory effect as law laid down by the state. It is therefore justified to apply the prohibition of discrimination directly to association rules. The *ECJ*'s argument that a uniform application of the prohibition is only ensured if state and association rules are treated equally, is also convincing since comparable substantive regulations are sometimes laid down by associations and sometimes by public authority as a result of different traditions amongst the Member States. The *ECJ* applied the rule of non-discrimination with respect to the freedom to provide service in the not undisputed decisions Laval and Viking Line (see Case 341/05 – Laval un Partneri Ltd v Svenska Byggnadsarbetareförbundet and Others [2007] ECR I-11767; Case 438/05 – International Transport Workers' Federation and Finnish Seamen's Union v Viking Line ABP and OÜ

Viking Line Eesti [2007] ECR I-10779) to not only collective agreements but further to collective industrial action. If one agrees with this, the same must apply to the prohibition of discrimination and freedom of movement for workers.

c) Individual private persons

42 Whether, in what way and to what degree private persons are bound by the prohibition of discrimination is a somewhat contentious issue. It makes sense to address the separate problems step by step.

aa) As addressees of Member State laws

43 First of all, private persons are bound – in a manner of speaking indirectly – to the prohibition of discrimination as addressees of state laws because the labour laws laid down by the state must be designed to be non-discriminatory (see above, para. 36). This effect of the European rule of non-discrimination poses no problem.

44 Problems arise when labour law provisions grant advantages in a discriminatory manner.

Case 15/69 – **Württembergische Milchverwertung Südmilch AG v. Ugliola** [1969] ECR 363

Mr. Ugliola, an Italian national, was employed by a private employer in Germany. He fulfilled his obligation for military service in Italy and thus interrupted his employment. On his return he demanded the period of military service to be taken into account in the calculation of the duration of his service with his employer. Under section 6(2) first sentence of the Arbeitsplatzschutzgesetz, military service periods are to be taken into account in calculating the duration of the service with the employer. The Arbeitsplatzschutzgesetz, according to the system and the spirit of the legislation, refers only to obligations for military service with the *Bundeswehr* (German army).
The *ECJ* decided on submission by the *Bundesarbeitsgericht* (German Federal Labour Court) that the employer must also take periods of military service into account when the obligation for military service is fulfilled by a migrant worker in his home country. This results from the prohibition of discrimination as set out in Art. 39(2) EC (now Art. 45(2) TFEU) and Art. 7 of Regulation (EEC) 1612/68 (see most recent reform COM [2010] 204 final).

45 In its appellate decision following the *ECJ* judgment the *Bundesarbeitsgericht (BAG)* ruled in favour of Mr. Ugliola (*BAG* of 5 December 1969 – 5 AZR 215/68). It is interesting that the BAG expressly noted that the claim cannot be based on section 6(2) first sentence of Arbeitsplatzschutzgesetz but is directly based on the right to equal treatment as set out in Art. 45(2) TFEU or Art. 7 of Regulation (EEC) No. 1612/68. In contrast, the *ECJ* had stated in its reasons that a rule of national law protecting workers from the unfavourable consequences for working conditions arising out of absence through obligation for military service must also be applied to migrant workers who fulfil their obligation for military service in their home country. Of course, the result is the same despite different reasoning; the approach of the *ECJ* though illustrates more strongly that the source of the unequal treatment

that needs correcting lies not in the employer's behaviour but in the provision in the Arbeitsplatzschutzgesetz. The scope of the employer's duties is not determined just by the – when considered in isolation discriminatory – national law but by the interplay with the directly effective European legislation.

bb) Autonomous action under private law

The extent of the prohibition of discrimination with respect to freedom of movement for workers is uncertain on the subject of autonomous action under private law. In a free market economy the principle of freedom of contract is predominant. Private persons have the authority within the limits of peremptory law laid down by the state to decide if and with whom (freedom to contract) and with what content (freedom of contractual content) they wish to enter into a contract. In any case, they are not directly subject to the obligations to which the state is bound as an authority under public law. **46**

It is undisputed that the prohibition of discrimination applies directly to the extent to which it is substantiated by secondary law. Art. 7(4) of Regulation (EEC) No. 1612/68 declares all discriminatory provisions in collective agreements or individual employment contracts void. The fact that this rule is directly applicable in contracts between private persons is clearly set out in Art. 288(2) TFEU. Whether the primary law norm of Art. 45(2) TFEU has a direct effect vis-à-vis third parties, is in dispute. The *ECJ* applies Art. 45(2) TFEU **to private relationships between private persons** and even to hiring decisions. **47**

Case 281/98 – **Angonese** [2000] ECR I-4139

A private savings bank in the Italian city of Bolzano required its employees to be bilingual in German and Italian due to the language peculiarities of the region. It demanded a certain certificate as proof of bilingualism ("patentino") which was issued only by public offices in Bolzano. Obtaining this was considerably more difficult for those persons living outside of the province of Bolzano than for residents. The plaintiff in the initial trial, an Italian citizen, was verifiably completely bilingual, yet not in possession of the "patentino". He was thus not considered in the selection procedure.

After confirming a link to Community law contrary to the Advocate General's reservations (Opinions of Advocate General *Fennelly* in the Case 281/98 – Angonese [2000] ECR I-4139), the *ECJ* decided that the requirement was unjustified indirect discrimination based on nationality. As Art. 7(4) of Regulation (EEC) No. 1612/68 was not applicable because it pertained to a hiring decision, the *ECJ* deduced its conclusion directly from Art. 39 EC (now Art. 45 TFEU). Following its judgments in Walrave and Bosman, it confirmed the application of the prohibition of discrimination to relationships between private persons. With reference to case law regarding Art. 141 EC (now Art. 157 TFEU) whose direct effect against singular measures by private persons is recognized, the *ECJ* then extended the prohibition to the hiring decision in this case. It held that this had an indirectly discriminatory effect and was not justified because proof of bilingualism could be produced other than by means of the "patentino".

48 The decision was partially met with **criticism** from legal scholars (Streinz/*Franzen*, EUV/AEUV, 2012, Art. 39 EC Treaty, paras. 97 *et seqq.*; *Grigolli*, Free Movement of Workers versus Protection of Minorities – Has the European Court of Justice Toppeld one of the "Pillars" of South Tyrolean Autonomy, 3 The European Legal Forum (E), 2000/01, 171): An indirect third party effect is a disproportionate infringement upon private autonomy and does not take into account that autonomous action is the basis for exercising the right to free movement. It is suggested instead to recognize an indirect effect vis-à-vis third parties of the fundamental rights. The duty of protection approach is based chiefly on an *ECJ* decision regarding free movement of goods (Case 265/95 – Commission v. France (Spanish strawberries) [1997] ECR I-6959). That case involved the violent obstruction of fruit and vegetable imports from other countries in the Community by French farmers, against which the French state did not intervene in a sufficient manner. The *ECJ* ruled that the Member States have an obligation under Art. 34 TFEU along with Art. 4(3) TEU to take appropriate measures to protect the free movement of goods from obstructions by private individuals. It stated that when applying general provisions of private law, a proportional balance between the demands of the fundamental rights and opposing private interests can be found.

49 One must **agree with this criticism** on the point that different standards must be applied to private infringements on free movement for workers than those applied to state infringements. This can certainly be achieved more appropriately by assuming a mere indirect third party effect (the *ECJ* does not distinguish between indirect and direct third party effect). In European law though, a direct third party effect is decreed to a very large extent by the positive law of Art. 7(4) of Regulation (EEC) No. 1612/68. Assigning a direct third party effect to the primary law norm in agreement with the *ECJ* therefore corresponds more with the system of the freedom of movement for workers. The substantive issue of taking private autonomy into account can be resolved in the context of justification even with this approach.

4. Justification possibilities

a) Discrimination by the state

50 The **public policy exception** (see on this: *Barnard*, The Substantive Law of the EU: The Four Freedoms, 2007, pp. 461 *et seqq.*) in Art. 45(3) TFEU permits special rules for foreign nationals and thereby allows nationality to be used as a governing factor. Consequently, the *ECJ* (Case 350/96 – Clean Car Autoservice GmbH v. Landeshauptmann von Wien [1998] ECR I-2521, para. 25) classifies it as a justification for direct and indirect discrimination. This classification is debatable: the public policy exception systematically relates to the special rights in paragraph 3. It pertains above all to the subject area of the law concerning aliens and right of residence. The nationals are not affected by this due to the nature of the subject matter so even the term 'discrimination' is not quite right in this context. It would be clearer therefore not to generally consider the public policy exception as a justification for discrimination but – in accordance with the systematic structure of Art. 45 TFEU – as a possibility to limit the rights set out in paragraph 3 (*Calliess/Ruffert/Brechmann*, EUV/AEUV, 4th ed., 2011, Art. 39 EC, para. 89). Beyond this, direct discrimination cannot be justified. The opinion voiced – mainly with regard to other fundamental rights – that direct discrimination can be justified on grounds of overriding reasons of the general public (cf. *Weiß*, 9 EuZW 1999, 493) should not be applied to the right to free movement for workers. In a European labour market where nationality is meant to be irrelevant with respect to employment relationships, nationality as such cannot represent an objective reason for unequal treatment.

51 This is not true for **indirect discrimination**. Although there are some who argue – including the *ECJ* – that this can only be justified on the strict grounds set out in Art. 45(3) TFEU (Case 10/90 – Masgio v. Bundesknappschaft [1991] ECR I-1119, para. 24). Considering the broadness of the term 'indirect discrimination', this

restriction is too narrow. Therefore, in cases of indirect discrimination one must resort to the unwritten justification rule of "overriding reasons of the general public" developed by the *ECJ*. Measures that are not linked to nationality but still predominantly affect cross-border cases are subsequently not unlawful discrimination if they are suitable to pursue a legitimate aim in protecting overriding interests of the general public and their effects do not exceed the necessary degree. Examples of such reasons are, say, the protection of public health, the coherence of the national tax system or the proper administration of universities. In its more recent decisions the Court also seems to want to apply a more generous standard (Case 138/02 – Collins [2004] ECR I-2703). Regarding the indirectly discriminatory requirement of knowing certain languages, Art. 3(1) of Regulation (EEC) No. 1612/68 contains a justification criterion. However, mere economic or fiscal considerations cannot justify unequal treatment (see e.g. Case 264/96 – Imperial Chemical Industries plc (ICI) v. Colomer (re freedom of establishment) [1998] ECR I-4695, para. 28).

b) Discrimination by private persons

To begin with, unequal treatment by private persons can be justified on the same 52 grounds as that perpetrated by the state (Case 415/93 – Union Royale Belge de Société de Football Association v. Bosman [1995] ECR I-4921, para. 86; Case 325/08 – Olympique Lyonnais [2010] ECR I-02177, paras. 38 *et seqq.*). The question is whether private individuals can rely on other grounds of justification beyond this. There is a need for this: private individuals are simply not obligated to look out for the interests of the general public but are in fact exercising their constitutional rights when they pursue economic activities. This is exactly the reason why some of the legal scholars object to Art. 45 TFEU having a direct effect vis-à-vis third parties (see above, para. 48; concurring *Grigolli*, Free Movement of Workers versus Protection of Minorities – Has the European Court of Justice Toppeled one of the "Pillars" of South Tyrolean Autonomy, 3 The European Legal Forum (E), 2000/01, 171). If one supports a direct third party effect and thereby classes private individuals on a par with the state, then the objective disparity between the state's duty of care towards the general public and private individuals' exercise of freedoms must at least have an impact at justification level. One must especially allow private individuals – unlike the state (see above, para. 51) – to rely on economic reasons. The *ECJ* has made this quite clear. In Olympique Lyonnais the Court held that restrictions on transfers of professional footballers can be justified if they aim to secure the clubs' return of training fees if the player leaves the club (Case 325/08 – Olympique Lyonnais [2010] ECR I-02177, paras. 38 *et seqq.*, especially 42). The Court already expressed in the Angonese case that the indirectly discriminating requirement could be justified if it were "based on objective factors unrelated to the nationality of the persons concerned and if it were in proportion to the aim legitimately pursued" (Case 281/98 – Roman Angonese v. Cassa di Risparmio di Bolzano [2000] ECR I-4139, para. 42). There was no talk of their needing to be a connection to the interests of the general public.

In the specific case however, the *ECJ* considered the condition imposed by the savings bank that 53 the language skills must be certified by the "patentino", which is only obtainable in South Tyrol, to be disproportionate and at the same time referred to a case in which the language requirement was laid down by a state institution (Case 379/87 – Groener v. Minister for Education [1989] ECR 3967, para. 23). The reasons behind this judgment could be the fact that the "patentino" itself originated from a public office. The Bolzano savings bank perpetuated a "national framework of order" (*Forsthoff*, 10 EWS 2000, 389, 394) by which foreigners by nature could not abide easily. But dismantling such traditional structures that tend to disadvantage migrant workers is exactly what the right to free movement for workers serves to do. In this respect, the strict standard that the *ECJ* applied in the Angonese case is in effect justified.

54 Unlike state measures, private measures that are directly discriminatory can indeed be justified.

V. Prohibition of restrictions

1. Basics

55 The *ECJ* not only deduces a prohibition of direct and indirect discrimination from Art. 45 TFEU but also – closely related – a prohibition of restrictions. So this is not about provisions that directly apply the forbidden criterion of nationality or criteria that usually have something to do with nationality (e. g. residence) but provisions that restrict the exercise of the right to free movement either factually or legally without an evident connection to nationality. The *ECJ* decision in the Bosman case illustrates what is meant by this. It represents the leading case on the interpretation of Art. 45 TFEU as a prohibition of restrictions.

Case 415/93 – **Bosman** [1995] ECR I-4921

Jean Marc Bosman was a professional footballer of Belgian nationality who was employed by a Belgian football club. After his contract expired he wanted to switch to a French club. His intentions failed owing to the transfer rules laid down by national and European (UEFA) football associations by which the French club had to pay the Belgian club a transfer fee. These rules applied not only to transfers abroad but also to transfers within Belgium.
The *ECJ* viewed the transfer rules as a violation of Art. 39 EC (now Art. 45 TFEU). Although the rule does not discriminate either directly or indirectly on grounds of nationality, it affects the players' access to the labour market of another Member State in a direct way. As a result the rules needed justification which the *ECJ* found was not the case regarding the specific rules in question.
Despite winning the lawsuit before the *ECJ* and the fame he achieved in doing so, Jean Marc Bosman's good fortune ended there: Although the *ECJ* considered the transfer rules to be in violation of Art. 39 EC (now Art. 45 TFEU), this did not change the fact that Bosman's career came to an end. After the transfer to the French second league club USL Dunkerque failed on account of the transfer rules, no football club would have him. It took nine years after the lawsuit for him to be awarded compensation for the premature conclusion of his career in the amount of 780 000 EUR. In spite of this, he is now penniless and dependent on welfare.

56 Classifying Art. 45 TFEU as a prohibition of restrictions is indicated by its wording (Opinions of Advocate General *Lenz* in the Bosman case, para. 193. The reasoning of the Advocate General is overall considerably more extensive than the court decision and well worth reading). Its paragraph 1 guarantees the freedom of movement for workers. Only in paragraph 2 is there talk of a prohibition of

discrimination. One can easily see paragraph 2 as – a substantial – part of a comprehensive provision of freedom of movement. The decisive argument is ultimately the aim of freedom of movement for workers to create a European labour market. If workers are prevented from leaving their past place of employment and accepting work in another European country, one cannot speak of a Europe-wide labour market. The realisation that a worker would have the same trouble regarding an intended change of work within the same Member State would not alter these findings in the slightest. The presence of discrimination is therefore irrelevant (Case 415/93 – Union Royale Belge de Société de Football Association v. Bosman [1995] ECR I-4921, para. 103).

The classification of Art. 45 TFEU as a prohibition of restrictions exhibits distinct 57 parallels to the law regarding the other fundamental freedoms. These too were initially classed as prohibitions of discrimination and were then developed into general prohibitions of restrictions by the *ECJ*. This is true for free movement of goods since the path-breaking **"Cassis de Dijon"** judgment (Case 120/78 – Rewe Zentrale v. Bundesmonopolverwaltung für Branntwein (Cassis de Dijon) [1979] ECR 649). A similar development took place with respect to freedom of service (cf. Case 43/93 – Vander Elst v. Office des Migrations Internationales [1994] ECR I-3803, para. 14) and freedom of establishment (cf. Case 107/83 – Ordre des Avocats au Barreau de Paris v. Klopp [1984] ECR 2971).

Expanding the scope of guarantee of freedom of movement for workers raises 58 the issue that practically every domestic provision can in some way or other affect the exercise of fundamental rights. A worker may for example be dissuaded from seeking employment in a Member State by its high income tax rates (cf. the remarks by Advocate General Mischo in Case 255/97 – Pfeiffer Großhandel GmbH v. Löwa Warenhandel GmbH [1999] ECR I-2835, para. 58). The range of provisions that are potentially capable of deterring workers from exercising their right to freedom of movement is extremely broad and could constitute almost the whole legal system. Were all these provisions to be regarded as prohibitions of freedom of movement for workers, they would be subject to needing European justification and the control of the *ECJ*. The sovereignty of the Member States would be substantially restricted. This neither corresponds to the character of the EU as a confederacy nor to the purpose and spirit of the fundamental freedoms. Art. 45 TFEU simply does not guarantee a general liberty of action but freedom of movement. Not every provision that indirectly influences the decision for or against employment abroad in the EU constitutes a restriction.

As much as the necessity to limit the term 'restriction' makes sense in principle, 59 its classification and finally the concrete ascertainment of what rules qualify as restrictions pose difficulties. In the context of free movement of goods the *ECJ* differentiates with the **so-called "Keck"-formula** between product-related regulations which constitute a restriction and mere selling arrangements which do not need justification under EU law as long as they are not discriminatory (Joined Cases 267 & 268/91 – Criminal Proceedings aginst Bernard Keck and Daniel Mithouard [1993] ECR I-6097, para. 16). In the context of free movement of persons, i. e. also the free movement for workers, there is in principle a consensus that the definitive differentiation criterion is access to the labour market (Case 190/98 – Graf v. Filzmozer Maschinenbau GmbH [2000] ECR I-493, para. 23; *Barnard*, The Substantive Law of the EU: The Four Freedoms, 2007, pp. 276 *et seq.*). Provisions that neither differentiate between nationalities nor discriminate against cross-border actions must only be assessed with regard to the prohibition of restriction if they can be classified as access barriers. The same applies to leaving restrictions (Case 325/08 – Olympique Lyonnais [2010] ECR I-02177, para. 34).

60 **Access barriers** must be distinguished in particular from the general framework conditions for dependent work which, notwithstanding the relevance these have for the decision to work in another Member State, do not affect the transfer itself. Framework conditions include in particular *regulations regarding the exercise of profession.* These cannot restrict access to the labour market as their application presupposes that access has already been gained. This applies equally to leaving restrictions.

61 In view of these standards the obligation to pay transfer fees in the Bosman case was correctly regarded as a restriction of free movement for workers in need of justification. Mr. Bosman had decided after consideration of all relevant location factors, including not only pay and professional prospects but also without a doubt the legal framework conditions, to work in France and therefore to exercise his right to free movement. The implementation of this decision was considerably complicated by the obligation to pay transfer fees. This implementation is protected against disproportionate complications by Art. 45 TFEU. It does not matter whether the exercise of the right to free movement for workers is restricted by regulations on the host Member State's side (restrictions on establishment of residence) or the home Member State's side (leaving restrictions).

62 In the Graf case the *ECJ* tried to narrow down the prohibition of restrictions.

Case 190/98 – **Graf v. Filzmozer Maschinenbau GmbH** [2000] ECR I-493

Mr. Graf, a German national, was employed by an Austrian company. As he wished to accept employment in Germany, he resigned. There is a rule in Austria that in the event of the employment relationship ending after a certain period of time, employees are entitled to a severance indemnity, the amount of which is determined by the duration of the employment. In the event of resignation, inter alia, the claim became extinct under previous Austrian law. The Austrian court submitted the question to the *ECJ* whether Art. 39 EC (now Art. 45 TFEU) precludes a national provision which stipulates that an employee loses his severance indemnity claim at conclusion of the employment relationship only because he terminated the relationship himself through resignation in order to take up employment in another Member State.

The *ECJ* answered the submitted question in the negative. The provision is clearly not capable of dissuading the employee from ending his previous employment to take up employment in another Member State. For the severance indemnity claim is not subject to the employee's decision whether he wants to remain with his employer but instead is subject to a hypothetical future event that is the subsequent termination of the employment relationship without the employee's doing. Such an event is too uncertain and its effects too indirect as to consider the severance indemnity rule a restriction

63 The *ECJ*'s pursuit to limit the prohibition of restrictions must be welcomed in principle. The judgment may ultimately be correct in its result because even if the Austrian severance indemnity system were declared contrary to European law, Mr.

Graf still would not necessarily have been entitled to a severance indemnity. Yet the reasons given in the decision are not quite convincing. Criteria like "too uncertain" or "too indirect" are not suitable for deciding future cases in a predictable rational way (critical therefore *Streinz*, Europarecht, 2011, para. 809a).

A more **precise analysis of how the severance indemnity system works** would have been appropriate. Severance pay in the event of a dismissal initiated by the employer for operational reasons, i.e. compensation for the loss of employment arising from the employer's sphere of influence, would definitely not constitute a restriction within the meaning of Art. 45 TFEU. Because such a payment merely represents compensation for a blameless misfortune. Advocate General *Fennelly* in his opinion for the Graf case in paragraph 34 compares the severance indemnity with entitlements following an industrial accident. An employee would undoubtedly miss out on such entitlements if he were to give up his employment. In his opinion, this does not however represent a restriction of free movement as it is completely uncertain if an industrial accident will ever occur. One must certainly agree with the Advocate General regarding entitlements following industrial accidents – it is questionable though whether this claim and the severance indemnity claim are even comparable. The fact that compensation is not awarded if the employee resigns voluntarily is not, a priori, capable of negatively influencing the employee's decision to implement his wish to change employment. In contrast, a provision obligating an employee to pay compensation to the employer in the event of voluntary resignation would definitely be classed as a restriction. If such a provision were lawful, then it would be feasible that an employee would prefer to take up employment in another Member State but refrains from doing so simply because it would involve costs for the compensation fee. In modified form this was the case in the Bosman matter and also in Olmpique Lyonnais (Case 325/08 – Olympique Lyonnais [2010] ECR I-02177). The Austrian provision cannot be classed as either one or the other definitively but it is more closely related to the latter, restrictive rule. The severance indemnity is not granted only in the event of a dismissal by the employer but also in the event of a mutual agreement to terminate, a lapse of contract, termination for the purpose of retirement (but then only for long-term employment, section 14(4)no1 Betriebliches Mitarbeitervorsorgegesetz) and even in case of death (section 14(5) Betriebliches Mitarbeitervorsorgegesetz). So the severance indemnity can be seen as a sort of saved up pay that is not paid until the conclusion of the employment (in Austrian academic literature the severance indemnity is referred to as extraordinary pay by reason of dissolution of the employment relationship. There is a dominant welfare aspect but it has elements of a "loyalty bonus", see *Floretta/Spielbüchler/Strasser*, Arbeitsrecht I [Individualarbeitsrecht], 1998, p. 234). Not receiving the severance in the event of resignation or employer initiated dismissal by fault of the employee presents a loss of "prospective entitlement" to the saved up pay. He, who is "disloyal" to his employer in order to work elsewhere, is punished by the loss of severance indemnity. It would have been preferable to class the Austrian severance indemnity system as a restriction of free movement for workers which could then have been justified on sufficiently significant grounds. **64**

2. Addressees of the prohibition of restrictions

a) Member States

It is without question that the prohibition of restrictions is directed at the Member States in their capacity as legislators. National provisions therefore that restrict access to, or departure from, the labour market need to be justified. 65

This affects, e.g., regulations that forbid pursuit of occupation in more than one location (cf. Case 96/85 – Commission v. France [1986] ECR 1475; Case 351/90 – Commission v. Luxembourg [1992] ECR 3954. In both cases the specific regulations were also discriminatory as well). 66

b) Associations

Furthermore, the prohibition of restrictions applies to collective agreements. The fundamental Bosman judgment as well as quite a few decisions that followed involved such agreements (Case 176/96 – Lehtonen and Castors Canada Dry 67

Namur-Braine ASBL v. Fédération royale belge des sociétés de basket-ball ASBL (FRBSB) [2000] ECR I-2681; cf. also Joined Cases 51/96 & 191/97 – Deliège v. Ligue Francophone de Judo et Disciplines Associés ASBL (re freedom of services) [2000] ECR I-2549). This was confirmed most recently in the Olympique Lyonnais case. The arguments for including private association agreements are the same as those that attest to indirect third party effect of the prohibition of discrimination.

c) Private individuals

68 To what extent the prohibition of restrictions applies to private autonomous measures by individuals has not yet been settled in case law and legal academic literature. The *ECJ* has only ever had cases to rule upon involving association agreements. The matter of Angonese involved indirect discrimination and not a mere restriction even if the differentiation is difficult in this case. Whether at least one or two fundamental freedoms have a direct third party effect, is still unclear. In her Opinion of 8 September 2011 – C-282/10 on the Dominguez case, Advocate General *Trstenjak* adopted a restrictive position regarding the fundamental rights of the EU Charter and rejected a direct third party effect. The court concurred in its judgement and merely pointed out that the employer in that particular case might be regarded as an entity of the state under its Foster-doctrine (of case C-188/89 – Foster vs. British Gas plc. [1990] ECR I-3313).

69 If one were to attribute a third party effect to the prohibition of restrictions, a vast number of measures would need justification. Something as simple as concluding a fixed-term employment contract without the possibility of termination leads to the employee being bound to a certain employer and therefore to a restriction of his (cross-border) mobility. To subject such private autonomous decisions to a test under the prohibition of restrictions would not only raise (constitutional) concerns – to a greater extent than in the case of the prohibition of discrimination – regarding private autonomy. The intention of the freedom of movement for workers would be exceeded: **Art. 45 TFEU ensures freedom of mobility, but does not force the exercise of this right.** If a private law subject decides for itself to forgo mobility in favour of other advantages (e. g. job security for a certain period of time or a higher salary), there is no cause to correct this decision or even to review it. Therefore, private autonomous decisions are not subject to the prohibition of restrictions.

70 The persuasiveness of this reasoning based on private autonomy vanishes to the extent that legal autonomy yields to factual superiority and heteronomy, as can be the case especially with the relationship between employee and employer. At this point the **concept of a state duty of care,** or rather indirect third party effect, which was rejected with respect to discrimination in favour of the direct third party effect recognized by the courts, gains importance. The state is not only obliged to dispense with mobility restrictions as far as possible. It is also its duty to protect employees from too extensive mobility restrictions emanating from the employer.

3. Justification possibilities

71 State restrictions of free movement for workers can be justified on grounds of overriding interests of the general public. The standard is therefore the same as with

indirect discrimination. This synchronization is reasonable because in practice it is often difficult to distinguish between restrictions and indirect discrimination.

72 Association rules that restrict free movement can be justified on the same grounds as state regulations can be. Moreover, one must acknowledge interests specific to associations as grounds for justification (cf. Case 415/93 – Union Royale Belge de Société de Football Association v. Bosman [1995] ECR I-4921, para. 79; Case 25/08 – Olympique Lyonnais [2010] ECR I-02177, para. 38).

73 In the **Bosman case** (see above, para. 55) the *ECJ* found the interests of the association, namely the financial and competitive balance between the clubs as well as promoting talent, notwithstanding reference to the "considerable social importance of sporting activities and in particular football in the Community", to be creditable (Case 415/93 – Union Royale Belge de Société de Football Association v. Bosman [1995] ECR I-4921, para. 106). This approach poses a problem. Associations have legitimate self-interests that demand consideration irrespective of overall social importance.

VI. Recognition of training and other qualifications

74 The chances of gaining access to sought-after employment are largely influenced by vocational training and other qualifications. There is a considerable inclination in this area to favour conventional national qualifications. This applies first of all to professions that require certain minimum qualifications prescribed by the state, like for instance the medical profession and that of lawyers, teachers and architects. But even where no such state regulations exist foreign qualifications are frequently placed at a disadvantage compared to the familiar and, from the point of view of employers, reliable domestic qualifications (cf. Case 281/98 – Roman Angonese v. Cassa di Risparmio di Bolzano [2000] ECR I-4139).

75 The **different treatment of domestic and foreign qualifications** is therefore capable of infringing upon free movement for workers. As far as foreign workers in possession of certificates of qualification from their home country are affected, this problem can be considered indirect discrimination as migrant workers will typically have foreign certificates of qualifications. But nationals that obtained their vocational qualifications abroad can also be affected. The *ECJ* confirms in settled case-law that there is a cross-border link in these cases (Case 115/78 – Knoors v. Secretary of State for Economic Affairs [1979] ECR 399, para. 24; Case 246/80 – C. Broekmeulen v Huisarts Registratie Commissie [1981] ECR 2311, para. 20).

76 In the area of regulated professions the Community took action at secondary level. The regulations do not need to be laid down by the state but can also be laid down for example by a collective agreement, as long as it has a certain general applicability (Case 234/97 – Fernández de Bobadilla v. Mueseo Nacional del Prado [1991] ECR I-4773, para. 20). Requirements made by individual employers do not represent regulations (cf. Case 234/97 – Fernández de Bobadilla v. Mueseo Nacional del Prado [1991] ECR I-4773, para. 23).

77 The factual problem of different treatment of domestic and foreign qualifications can be approached from two angles. For one thing, the difference in the qualifications can be reduced by harmonisation. Specific minimum conditions have been determined obliging the home state to recognize foreign qualifications in compliance thereof. This path was taken originally in the area of medical professions in particular (cf. Directive 77/452/EEC, for nurses; Directive 78/686/EEC and 78/687/EEC for dentists; Directive 78/1026/EEC and 78/1027/EEC for veterinarians; Directive 85/432/EEC and 85/433/EEC for pharmacists; Directive 93/16/EEC for doctors). The disadvantage of

this solution lies particularly in the fact that a harmonisation has to be created for every single profession which has proved to be barely feasible in practice not least given the interests of the affected professional groups and the growing number of Member States (cf. H/S/W/*Hanau*, chapter 15, para. 398). Therefore, the EU since the 1980s has resorted to create a general framework for the recognition of qualifications (Directive 89/48/EEC, 92/51/EEC and 99/42/EC).

78 The law contained in a number of directives has now been consolidated into the Directive 2005/36/EC which had to be transposed into national law pursuant to Art. 63 by the 20 October 2007 (see on the Directive itself *Tayleur*, Qualified Approval, 157 New Law Journal 2007, 1494–1495). Outside the scope of the Directives, in particular for those professions not regulated (the Directive applies only to regulated professions, cf. Art. 1 of Directive 2005/36/EC), the qualification requirements must have regard to Art. 45 TFEU (Case 234/97 – Fernández de Bobadilla v. Mueseo Nacional del Prado [1991] ECR I-4773, para. 28; Case 281/98 – Roman Angonese v. Cassa di Risparmio di Bolzano [2000] ECR I-4139).

VII. Social law coordination and its effects on labour law (Art. 48 TFEU)

79 The subject of freedom of movement for workers also includes the **coordination of the social security systems** pursuant to Art. 48 TFEU. It is however not a matter of harmonizing the social systems: (Case 340/94 – E.J.M. de Jaeck v Staatssecretaris van Financiën [1997] ECR I-461, para. 18) Social policy is principally the Member States' affair. But the exercise of free movement for workers would be largely jeopardized if a worker had to fear the loss of acquired rights or other disadvantages in the event of a change of employment to another Member State. The necessity of coordination in order to achieve free movement was taken into account in Art. 48 TFEU which confers upon the European Parliament and Council the power to adopt relevant measures (see with regard to Art. 42 EC *Pennings*, Introduction to European Social Law, 2003, 20 *et seqq.*). Art. 48 TFEU does not however have a direct effect between private persons (*ECJ* of 10 March 2011 – Case 379/09 – Casteels v British Airways plc). The Council and Parliament made use of these legislative powers by issuing the Regulation (EEC) No. 1408/71 (for more detailed info on R 1408/71 see *Pennings*, Introduction to European Social Law, 2003, especially chapters 4–7.) and the implementing Regulation (EEC) No. 574/72. The Regulation (EEC) No. 1408/71 is superseded by the new Regulation (EC) No. 883/2004 which will apply as soon as an implementing Regulation (see Art. 89 of Regulation (EC) No. 883/2004) enters into force (Art. 91 of Regulation (EC) No. 883/2004). Regulation (EC) No. 987/2009 represents such an implementing Regulation and entered into force on 16 September 2009. Regulation (EC) No. 883/2004 has since been amended many times, most recently by Regulation (EU) No. 1244/2010. Further amendments are intended.

80 **Details** on this subject matter are appropriately placed in the field of European social law and are discussed in relevant legal academic literature there. Coordination of the social systems can also have direct consequences for labour law as two *ECJ* judgments show, which led to some publicity regarding continued payment of wages during illness.

Case 45/90 – **Alberto Paletta and others v Brennet AG (Paletta I)**
[1992] ECR I-3423
Case 206/94 **Brennet AG v Vittorio Paletta (Paletta II)**
[1996] ECR I-2357

Four members of the Italian family Paletta were employed by a German employer. As in previous years all four Palettas reported sick for several weeks at the end of their summer vacation which was attested by an Italian doctor. The employer suspected the alleged illness to be a welcome extension of their annual vacation and refused payment of wages. Mr. Paletta sued for payment of outstanding wages.

During the lawsuit the *ECJ* had to rule twice on questions submitted by German courts. The results were as follows: payment in the event of illness constitutes a cash benefit of social security (Art. 4(1)(a) of Regulation (EEC) No. 1408/71 – equivalent to Art. 3(1)(a) of Regulation (EC) No. 883/2004). The *ECJ* held in the first Paletta judgment that this also applied to continued payment of wages by the employer. With that the employer was an "institution" of the cash benefit for the purpose of Art. 18 of Regulation (EEC) No. 574/72 (Art. 27 of Regulation (EC) No. 987/2009). Consequently, he was bound by the findings of the Italian doctor unless he took advantage of the possibility provided by Art. 18(5) of Regulation (EEC) No. 574/72 to have the employee examined by a doctor of his own choice. The *ECJ* did not allow the correct objection that this possibility was often barred in practice. Practical difficulties cannot put the interpretation of provisions into question. On submission by the German *Bundesarbeitsgericht*, the *ECJ* ruled (Paletta II) that employers are not barred from adducing evidence to support abuse or fraudulent conduct on the part of the worker concerned, in that, although he may claim to have become incapacitated for work, such incapacity having been certified in accordance with Art. 18 of that Regulation, he was not sick at all and on these grounds may deny payment of cash benefits. But, this reversal of the burden of proof which would force the employee to provide additional evidence of his illness in case of doubt of the veracity of the certification of incapacity for work would not be compatible with Community law. Such a rule would put those employees that fall ill in another Member State at a disadvantage, a situation which the Community rule seeks to eliminate.

The judgments illustrate on the one hand at what hidden points the right to free **81**
movement for workers can become significant for labour law. On the other hand they demonstrate the importance of the right to free movement for workers even with respect to procedural questions of burden of proof and producing evidence.

§ 3. Protection against discrimination

Literature: *Baudet-Caille*, Harcèlement et discrimination au travail, 2010; *Bell*, The Implementation of the European Anti-Discrimination Directives: Converging towards a Common Model?, 79 The Political Quarterly 2008, 36–44; *Bourn/Whitmore*, Anti-Discrimination Law in Britain, 3rd ed., 1996; *Brown*, The Race Directive: Towards Equality for All the Peoples of Europe?, 21 Yearbook of European Law 2001, 195; *Bryan*, Equality and Freedom from Discrimination: Art. 13 EU Treaty, 24 Journal of Social Welfare and Family Law 2002, 223–238; *Castillo*, Igualdad y no discriminacion: la proyeccion sobre el tratamiento laboral de la discapacidad, 2010; *Cichowski*, Judicial Rulemaking and the Institutionalization of European Sex Equality Policy, in: Stone Sweet/Sandholtz/Fligstein, The Institutionalization of Europe, 2001, Chapter 6, 113–137; *Fredman*, Discrimination Law, 2nd ed. 2011; *Gold*, A Tale of Two Amendments: The Reasons Congress Added Sex to Title VII and Their Implication for the Issue of Comparable Worth, 19 Duquesne Law Review 1981, 453–458; *Honeyball*, Pregnancy and sex discrimination, 29 Industrial Law Journal 2000, 43–52; *Hosking*, A High Bar for EU Disability Rights: Case C-13/05, Chacón Navas v Eurest Colectividades SA, 36 Industrial Law Journal 2007, 228–237; *Kenner*, EU Employment Law: from Rome to Amsterdam and beyond, 2003; *Laborde*, Observations à propos de la loi du 12 juillet 1990, 1991, 615; *Lewis/Norman*, Employment Discrimination Law and Practice, 2nd ed., 2004; *Macnicol*, Age Discrimination: An Historical and Contemporary Analysis, 2006; *Martinez-Vivot*, Discriminacion Laboral: Despido Discriminatorio, 2000; *Note*, Employment Discrimination Against the Handicapped and Section 504 of the Rehabilitation Act: An Essay on Legal Evasiveness, 97 Harvard Law Review 1984, 997; *Putz*, Discrimination au travail, 2010; *Rawls*, A Theory of Justice, 1971; *Rothstein/Craver/Schroeder/Shoben*, Employment Law, 4th ed., 2009; *Sargeant/Lewis*, Employment Law, 6th ed., 2012; *Schiek*, Torn between Arithmetic and Substantive Equality? Perspectives on Equality in German Labour Law, 18 International Journal of Comparative Labour Law and Industrial Relations 2002, 149 *et seqq.*; *Seifert*, Federal Labor Court strengthens religious freedom at the workplace, 4 German Law Journal 2003, No. 6, 549–569; *Sen*, The Idea of Justice, 2011; *Smith/Craver/Clark*, Employment Discrimination Law, 2000; *G. Thüsing*, Following the US Example: European Employment Discrimination Law and the Impact of the Council Directives 2000/43/EC and 2000/78/EC, International Journal for Comparative Labour Law and Industrial Relations, Vol. 19, 2003, 187–218; *G. Thüsing/Horler*, Case note on Kücükdeveci, 47 Common Market Law Review (CMLR) 2010, 1161 *et seqq.*; *Tobler*, Indirect Discrimination: A Case Study into the Development of the Legal Concept of Indirect Discrimination under EC Law, 2005; *Waddington*, Testing the Limits of the EC-Treaty Art. on Non-Discrimination, 28 Industrial Law Journal 1999, No. 2, pp. 133 *et seqq.*; *Waddington/Bell*, More Equal than Others: Distinguishing European Union Equality Directives, 38 Common Market Law Review (CMLR) 2001, 587–611; *Wintermute*, When is pregnancy discrimination indirect sex discrimination?, 27 Industrial Law Journal 1998, 23–26; *Zimmer/Sullivan/White*, Cases and Materials on Employment Discrimination, 7th ed., 2008.

I. Introduction

The equality principle has been part of the **foundation of every judicial culture** 1
since the ancient world. Equality and justice seem inseparable; they presuppose and affect each other. In his book "The law of society" the German sociologist *Niklas Luhmann* put it this way: "The equality principle is the most abstract preference of the legal system, the last criterion for assigning disputes to right and wrong. In this capacity it assumes the name 'justice'" (Law as a Social System, 2004). This may be the reason why protection against discrimination has been a fixed institution in many labour law systems for many years already and is slowly starting to take root in civil law. Even those who know that freedom of contract is a highly valued good which may not be infringed upon recklessly neither by legislators nor by judges, and

Discrimination prohibitions in European Law

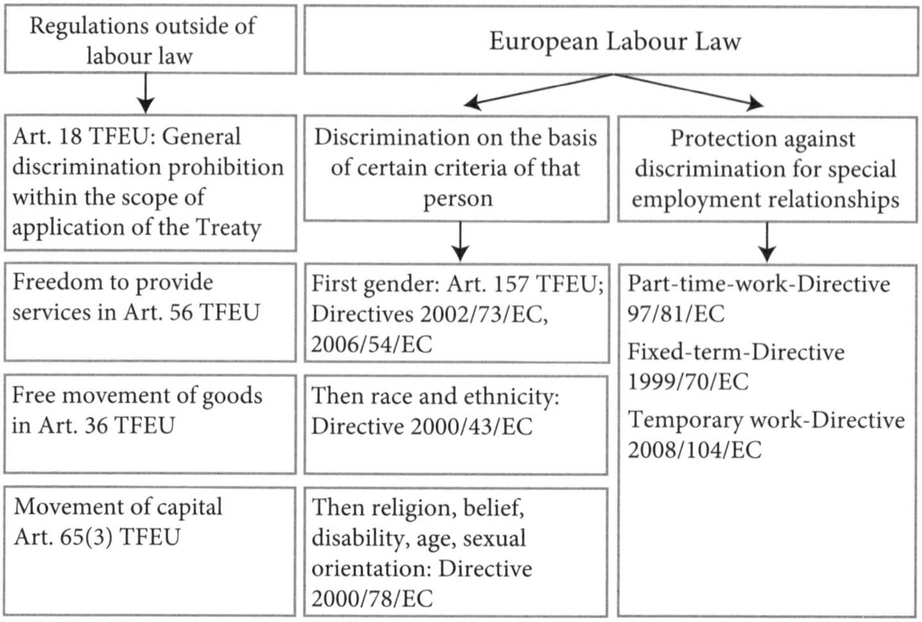

also those who support a virtually unregulated labour market in order to preserve the utmost flexibility and employment, can agree that unjustified affronts and ostracizing of individual population groups and worker groups must not exist.

2 Admittedly: one could argue at length about what justice is; and one will hardly arrive at a consensus. The more different the culture, the more difficult it will be to reach an agreement. This agreement will have to be confined to a minimum consensus (very worth reading *Kelsen*, What is justice?: Justice, Law and Politics in the Mirror of Science: Collected Essays, 2000; *Rawls*, A Theory of Justice, 1971 and his former student *Sen*, The Idea of Justice, 2009). This minimum consensus will no doubt include the phrase that **alike must be treated alike**. This is the basic idea of discrimination prohibitions, which is why it is not surprising that they are an important instrument for the harmonization of European law. Their standardization is arguably only a first step towards approximation; for even they leave the crucial judgment open as to what is equal.

3 **Discrimination prohibitions in European law are numerous**. Outside of labour law there is a general prohibition of discrimination in Art. 18 TFEU within the scope of application of the Treaty: "Within the scope of application of this Treaty, and without prejudice to any special provisions contained therein, any discrimination on grounds of nationality shall be prohibited". Alongside this there is the freedom of movement of goods laid down in Art. 36 TFEU and the freedom of capital in Art. 65(3) TFEU. The freedom to provide a service laid down in Art. 45 TFEU is of significance to employment law. As set out in paragraph 2 it includes "the abolition of any discrimination based on nationality between workers of the Member States as regards employment, remuneration and other conditions of

work and employment". The *ECJ* has dealt with these freedoms on numerous occasions; and some of the doctrinal patterns tested on them were later applied to labour law.

The **concept of indirect discrimination** (see e. g. *C. Tobler*, Indirect Discrimination: A Case Study into the Development of the Legal Concept of Indirect Discrimination under EC Law, 2005, Part Two: The Development of the Legal Concept of Indirect Discrimination in EC Law, A.I.2. The foundational cases: introducing the idea of indirect discrimination, pp. 104 *et seqq.*) where seemingly neutral provisions, criteria or procedures put persons with a particular characteristic at a particular disadvantage compared to other persons and these provisions, criteria or procedures are not justifiable by a legitimate aim and the means to achieve the aim are not appropriate and necessary (definition Art. 2(2) of Directive 2000/78/EC), was first established for the freedom to provide a service (leading case: Case 152/73 – Sotgiu [1974] ECR 153; recently Case 350/96 – Clean Car Autoservice GmbH v. Landeshauptmann von Wien [1998] ECR I-2521) before it was applied to sex discrimination in the Jenkins case (Case 96/80 – Jenkins [1981] ECR 911). To this day the *ECJ* has not succeeded in giving similarly precise specifications for justifying indirect discrimination with regard to Art. 45(2) TFEU (see hereunto also *Marlene Schmidt*, Das Arbeitsrecht der Europäischen Gemeinschaft, 2001, section III, para. 34). At least the *ECJ* recently made a step in the right direction in the Petersen case (Case 228/07 – Petersen [2008] ECR I-6989). According to this decision, unless it is objectively justified and proportionate to the aim pursued, a provision of national law must be regarded as indirectly discriminatory if it is intrinsically liable to affect migrant workers more than national workers and if there is a consequent risk that it will place the former at a particular disadvantage. 4

II. Development

The more different the cultures and societal framework conditions are, the more difficult it will be to reach an agreement on a fair employment law. The minimum consensus is that alike must be treated alike. But what is equal and what is only similar? 5

The discrimination prohibitions in European Labour Law can be roughly divided into **two groups**. At the outset there was the prohibition of discrimination on grounds of particular characteristics of a person. This began with the prohibition of sex discrimination under Art. 119 EC Treaty (now Art. 157 TFEU), the Directives 75/117/EEC (now Directive 2006/54/EC) and 76/207/EEC (amended by Directive 2002/73/EC and now replaced by Directive 2006/54/EC) and was continued in more recent times with the Directive 2002/73/EC on sex discrimination and the prohibition of discrimination on grounds of race and ethnic origin under Directive 2000/43/EC and of religion, belief, disability, age and sexual orientation under Directive 2000/78/EC. In addition, there is anti-discrimination protection for special employment relationships. The discrimination prohibitions of the temporary agency work Directive 2008/104/EC, the part-time-work-Directive 97/81/EC, the fixed-term-work-Directive 99/70/EC and also the framework agreement on telework (2002) are different to the first group in as much as they do not refer to a characteristic or criterion of the worker but subject particular employment contracts to a rule of non-discrimination. The protection is linked to the contract, not to the worker; this constitutes a considerable development of anti-discrimination protection (see on the Directives also *Waddington/Bell*, More Equal than Others: Distinguishing European Union Equality Directives, 38 CMLR 2001, Issue 3, 587–611). 6

III. The implementation of Directives 2000/78/EC, 2000/43/EC and 2002/73/EC

7 An important development of discrimination prohibitions in employment law were the directives adopted in the year 2000 and were followed by the revised directive on equal treatment of the sexes. In simple terms the provisions from Brussels can be illustrated as follows:

Directive	Transposition deadline	Protected criterion	Scope of application
Anti-racism-Directive 2000/43/EC of 29 June 2000	19 July 2003	• Race/ethnic origin	• Employment and occupation (especially employment law) • Education, health and social services (main area public law) • Access to goods and services available to the public (especially private law)
Framework-Directive 2000/78/EC of 27 November 2000	2 December 2003 (based on age 2 December 2006)	• Religion/ belief • Disability • Age • Sexual identity	• Employment and occupation (especially employment law)
Revised Equal Treatment-Directive 2002/73/EC of 23 September 2002	5 October 2005	• Gender	• Employment and occupation (especially employment law)
Directive on equalization of the sexes 2004/113/EC of 14 September 2004	21 December 2007	• Gender	• Access to mass market goods and services available to the public; private insurances (especially private law, particularly private insurance law)

Directive	Transposition deadline	Protected criterion	Scope of application
Revised Directive on equal opportunities of men and women 2006/54/EC of 26 July 2006	15 August 2008	• Gender	• Employment and occupation (especially employment law)

Both these directives – as well as the Directive 2004/113/EC which does not apply to employment law – are based on Art. 13 EC (now Art. 19 TFEU) which was created by the Amsterdam Treaty and constitutes the enabling power for taking broad action to protect against discrimination in not only employment law. It confers the power upon the Council to "take appropriate action to combat discrimination based on sex, racial or ethnic origin, religion or belief, disability, age or sexual orientation" (see hereunto *Bryan*, 24 Journal of Social Welfare and Family Law 2002, 223–238; *Kenner*, EU Employment Law: from Rome to Amsterdam and beyond, 2003, chapter 9, pp. 393 *et seqq.*; *Waddington*, Testing the Limits of the EC-Treaty Art. on Non-Discrimination, 28 Industrial Law Journal 1999, No. 2, 133–152.). Since the Lisbon Treaty the Council now needs the European Parliament's consent (see Art. 19(1) TFEU). 8

To implement the Directives in **France** two statutes were passed in 2001: *Egalité professionelle entre les femmes et les hommes* and the *Loi relative à la lutte contre les discriminations* which amended several provisions of the *Code du travail* and the *Code pénal* extending the existing discrimination protection. French law forbids discrimination on grounds of origin, gender, family situation, health, disability, conventions and morals, political opinion, trade union activities and actual or presumed belonging or not belonging to a race, nation or religion in its Arts. 225-1 to 225-3 *Code pénal* under penalty of prison and a fine. The *Code du travail*, in L 1132-1, contains provisions prohibiting discrimination on the aforementioned grounds as well as for reasons of sexual orientation, age, pregnancy, genetic characteristics, religion, physical appearance and surname which in part go beyond the requirements of the Anti-Discrimination Directives. An independent administrative authority was also created to monitor compliance with the French anti-discrimination legislation. 9

In the **United Kingdom** there was considerable protection against discrimination in place before the implementation of the Anti Discrimination Directives, including the Equal Pay Act, the Race Relations Act, the Sex Discrimination Act and the Disabilities Discrimination Act. These were amended to fully meet the requirements set out by the Directives. In addition, the Employment Equality (Religion or Belief) Regulations 2003 and the Employment Equality (Sexual Orientation) Regulations 2003 were enacted. Protection against age discrimination was finally achieved by the enactment of the Employment Equality (Age) Regulations 2006. The UK has recently enacted the Equality Act 2010 as a consolidating and harmonising measure. 10

In **Germany**, the Anti-Discrimination Directives were implemented by the Allgemeines Gleichbehandlungsgesetz (AGG) which came into force on the 14 August 2006. It draws a distinction between the forbidden distinguishing factors of "race", ethnic origin, sex, religion or belief, disability, age and sexual orientation. Even before the enactment of the AGG, German law had certain discrimination prohibitions in place (e.g. § 611 a BGB, Art. 3(3) GG, § 75(1) BetrVG, § 81(2) SGB IX), but protection against discrimination did not play a significant role in German labour law. An explanation for the lack of a developed system of discrimination protection before 11 the AGG is the fact that Germany has a highly developed system of dismissal protection which offered a level of protection that other countries achieved using discrimination legislation.

IV. The different forms of unlawful discrimination

1. In general – the term "discrimination"

12 The different kinds of discrimination are defined in Art. 2(2) of the Directives 2000/43/EC, 2000/78/EC and 2006/54/EC. Pursuant to this, **unequal treatment** of employees in itself does not necessarily constitute discrimination. Different work clothes for male and female employees, anniversary presents or job titles are not covered by the discrimination prohibitions as long as the differentiation between the sexes is not a manifestation of attributing different value. The law does not apply to giving different shifts to Turkish and Kurd employees and different opening hours for a swimming pool for men and women because it is undetermined who is being advantaged and disadvantaged. There may also be no case of discrimination if a disadvantage in one respect is offset by an advantage in another area. European law allows for a comparison of benefits between groups; this has been stipulated explicitly by the British legislator for less favourable treatment of fixed-term workers, see § 4 para. 16. If however there is no benchmark to be able to compare advantages and disadvantages, then the benefit in one area does not call the disadvantage in another area into question in the event of an employee or customer challenging less favourable treatment in a lawsuit. The plaintiff has to provide full evidence of a disadvantage, but it suffices to prove a disadvantage with respect to individual work or contract terms. So the employee or customer does not have to undertake a comprehensive comparison of the relevant contract terms in his claim. But the employer and offeror have the opportunity to extend the frame of comparison and prove the equivalence of the different treatment.

13 In principle the **comparison group in employment law** means all employees of a single employer. Additionally, there are cases where a comparison is undertaken with employees beyond the boundaries of a single employer, e. g. when collective agreements cover several companies or a parent company centrally lays down the work conditions for all its affiliates (see opinions of Advocate General *Geelhoed* of 14 March 2002 in Case 320/00 – Lawrence and Others [2002] ECR I-7325; see also Case 256/01 – Allonby [2004] ECR I-873; hereunto also *Thüsing*, 55 DB 2002, 2601). It always includes the entire scope of regulation. The comparison group is significant especially for determining indirect discrimination (see paras. 18 *et seqq.)*. The comparison group for a collective agreement is its entire scope of application.

14 When disadvantageous consequences can be linked to a forbidden criterion, then this already constitutes discrimination based on forbidden grounds which has to be justified. An additional subjective component in terms of intent to discriminate is not necessary. This means that even if men and women or younger and older employees are treated differently for the sake of their wellbeing, this is discrimination if it is so perceived by that person. Even if the discriminatory decision on the employer's part is based on a number of motives, it will be considered discrimination if any of the motives is based on grounds of sex, age, ethnic origin etc. of the candidate. If there is intent to discriminate, then it does not matter that the decision could have been justified by legitimate non-forbidden grounds.

2. Direct discrimination

Direct discrimination happens when a person is treated less favourably than another is, has been or would be treated in a comparable situation. This applies in equal measure to all reasons for unequal treatment mentioned in the various directives. Discrimination can also occur in the form of an omission. The disadvantage lies in an affront. 15

In the **borderline area between direct and indirect discrimination** lie the differentiations that are not linked explicitly to a forbidden criterion but to a criterion that is connected to one of the reasons mentioned in the directives. For these cases European law has expressly stipulated a rule that discrimination based on pregnancy is seen as direct discrimination based on gender (s. Art. 4 (1) (a) of the Directive 2004/113/EC) but: the *ECJ* hold in Case 177/88 – Dekker [1990] ECR I-03941, para. 11: "… only women can be refused employment on grounds of pregnancy and such a refusal therefore constitutes direct discrimination on grounds of sex.") and this was also included specifically in Title VII Civil Rights Act after the Supreme Court had previously decided differently (General Electric Co. v. Gilbert, 429 U.S. 125 (1976)). The question remains as to what extent this is a rule that allows the drawing of an analogy – or quite the contrary: an exception to the rule that does not. There are strong arguments in favour of direct discrimination being the case when subgroups of a group with a particular protected characteristic are discriminated against: Muslims are only affronted if they wear a head scarf, women only when they are overweight, homosexuals only if they wear "gay pride" stickers, older candidates only if they look their age. Such discrimination represents something in between direct and indirect discrimination: the differentiation is not based on a characteristic that is always related to a forbidden discrimination criterion – that would be covert direct discrimination – and it is also not based on a characteristic that, while normally linked to a forbidden discrimination criterion, can still arise in both comparison groups – this would be indirect discrimination. It is a characteristic that only arises in connection with the forbidden discrimination criterion but not always. One cannot therefore class it with the one side or the other; the wording of the European discrimination directives does not help with this issue. In US-American law this is referred to as **sex plus-discrimination** because the discrimination is subject to belonging to one sex or another plus another characteristic cumulatively. American courts lean towards indirect discrimination in these cases (hereunto Phillips v. Martin Marietta Corp., 400 US 542, 544 [1971]). A US-American court also judged the decision of a college only promoting Jesuits to certain positions as being direct discrimination based on religion – because while not all Catholics are Jesuits, only Catholics are Jesuits (Pime v. Loyola University of Chicago, 803 F2 d 351). 16

To devise an **acceptable compromise** for this issue, one will arguably not be able to class all cases of subgroup-specific discrimination as direct discrimination, as in that case discrimination against Muslims for wearing a head scarf would be direct sex discrimination too – because the Islam only commands women to wear head scarves. Rather, the decisive factor must be whether a subgroup's certain characteristic is representative for the forbidden discrimination criterion. If it is an expression of the religion, then it is discrimination of religion, even if not every follower of this faith chooses this expression. It cannot however be direct but rather indirect 17 discrimination when bald women are rejected as sales persons whereas bald men are not, because not having hair is not an expression of being female.

3. Indirect discrimination

a) Structure

18 Indirect discrimination is doctrinally more difficult to grasp. **A final definition has not yet been found**. Art. 2(1)(b) of Directives 2000/43/EC and 2000/78/EC, states that indirect discrimination occurs when provisions, measures, criteria or practices that appear to be neutral particularly put persons or groups who have one of the discrimination characteristics at a disadvantage compared to other persons or groups who do not have one of these discrimination characteristics. This does not apply to cases where an objective reason justifies the unequal treatment and the applied means are necessary and appropriate. The prohibition of indirect discrimination is contained in essence in every discrimination prohibition. It is meant to prevent people from seeking a pretext of differentiating by apparently neutral criteria in order to ultimately implement the forbidden decision. This is not a prohibition that pursues a justice of its own but merely an auxiliary instrument to enforce the actual prohibition of direct discrimination.

19 The protection against indirect discrimination can be a **method** to **protect against discrimination on the basis of other reasons** where direct discrimination is not forbidden. This is demonstrated quite clearly in British judgements. Where claims regarding discrimination against older employees were able to be brought in Great Britain in the past, these had to rely on indirect discrimination on the basis of sex (women often had less seniority due to the typical breaks in employment for parenting purposes) or ethnicity (immigrants came to Great Britain and into the British employment market at a later time in life and could therefore only achieve minimal seniority), because the former was forbidden by the SDA, the latter by the RRA, and a prohibition of age discrimination did not exist till 1st October 2006 (see also *Glass*, The British Resistance to Age Discrimination Legislation: Is it time to follow the U.S. Example, 11 Comparative Labour Law Journal 1995, pp. 491 *et seqq.*).

b) Definition

20 The definition of indirect discrimination is identical in Art. 2(1)(b) of Directive 2006/54/EC and Arts. 2(2) (b) of Directive 2000/43/EC and Directive 2000/78/EC. Using variant language Art. 2(2) of Directive 97/80/EC determined that indirect discrimination occurs "where an apparently neutral provision, criterion or practice disadvantages a substantially higher proportion of the members of one sex unless that provision, criterion or practice is appropriate and necessary and can be justified by objective factors unrelated to sex". The percentage of persons affected was the decisive factor in previous case law; the wording of the provision no longer bases indirect discrimination on this.

21 It is questionable whether and to what extent the **change in wording** has actually brought about a change in substantive law. Indeed, several opinions make this assumption without exactly defining the extent of the change. They argue, with reference to decisions of the *ECJ* regarding free movement for workers, where no distinction is made, that proof of statistical unequal treatment will in future be dispensable with respect to discrimination in terms of the discrimination directives as well (*Schiek*, 18 International Journal of Comparative Labour Law and Industrial Relations 2002, iss. 2, pp. 149 *et seqq.*). This is supported by the explanatory

memorandum in the draft proposal of the directive which refers to this case law expressly (COM [1999] 565 final with reference to Case 237/94 – O'Flynn [1996] ECR I-2617). In recent case law too the *ECJ* has continued this approach and perhaps even gone further. In the opinions of Advocate General *Stix-Hackel* of 5th February 2004 in the Merida case (Case 400/02 – Merida [2004] ECR I-8471) it says: "Indirect discrimination arises through the application of different rules to comparable situations or the application of the same rule to different situations and where the measure concerned cannot be justified by an objective difference or as a measure proportionate to its aim". Precisely this second alternative is the big step beyond the previous rule and it is questionable if this step is reflected in the new choice of words. This would mean that equal treatment and not just unequal treatment by the employer would be covered by the discrimination prohibitions. The equal treatment would require justification if it was particularly disadvantageous for a certain group of workers. This particular disadvantage can in effect only be a judgment call; statistical evidence will be of no use in the case of prohibitions against substantive discrimination.

Objective justification by a legitimate aim achieved by appropriate and necessary 22 means is a standard that falls short of the one applied to direct discrimination under Art. 4 of Directive 2000/43/EC and Directive 2000/78/EC by far. It is suppose to simply ensure that any other criteria other than those mentioned in the Directive are not used simply for the purpose of achieving unlawful discrimination circuitously.

4. Harassment

Art. 2(3) of Directive 2002/73/EC stipulates that harassment and sexual harass- 23 ment are deemed to be discrimination and in so far are subject to the discrimination prohibition as well. To accomplish **protection against harassment** by means of the equality principle is nevertheless quite a new approach for European Law and is **inconsistent**, see paras. 86 *et seqq*.

5. Instruction to discriminate as discrimination

Under Art. 2(4) of Directives 2000/43/EC, 2000/78/EC and Art. 2(2)(b) of Direc- 24 tive 2006/54/EC the instruction to discriminate is also deemed to be discrimination. The instruction must be issued with intent. It is however not necessary for the instructor to be aware of the unlawfulness of his actions, for the legislative prohibition of discrimination comprises all forms of discrimination without the requirement of fault. For the existence of an instruction it is not necessary for the instructed person to actually carry out the discrimination.

This had **even before the European directive were enacted its examples in national law** (for 25 Great Britain see the former sec. 30 RRA; sec. 111 EA 2010). In European Law this does not include – unlike anti-discrimination laws of several Member States – the assistance to discriminate. Someone who willingly and knowingly enables sexual harassment is not liable under discrimination law as long as he is not an employer. Someone who disposes of women's or blacks' job applications or suggests pretexts to the employer in order to reject candidates is not liable under European provisions. This is the same in **German** anti-discrimination law. **British law** is different (Sec. 33 [1] former RRA – hereunto Hallam v. Avery and Another ICR 408 HL [2001]; sec. 112 [1] EA 2010).

The **reason for this extension** lies in the protection against discrimination itself. It does not 26 pursue a separate and independent protective purpose. By deeming the instruction to discriminate as discrimination in the European prohibitions it is guaranteed that discrimination itself is protected against even more securely. It is building a **"fence around the Torah"**: a prohibition is extended beyond its original intention and meaning to make sure that at least the core area of this prohibition is not touched (see the Talmud, Mishnah: Abbot I 1 for the relevant interpretation doctrines and legislation genesis in Jewish law).

V. The beginnings: sex discrimination

1. Development

The beginnings: Sex discrimination

- Originally Article 119 EC-Treaty, now Article 157 TFEU 4; Transposition by 31st Dec 1961; important amendments through Amsterdam Treaty: equal work and promotion of one sex
- Directive 75/117/EEC: specification of the primary law; purpose: acceleration of implementation of prohibition of pay-discrimination
- Directive 76/207/EEC: Extension beyond pay
- Directive 97/80/EC: Regulation of burden of proof particularly for indirect discrimination: Accomplishment of discrimination protection
- Sexual harassment as sex discrimination, Directive 2002/73/EC.

27 The prohibition of sex discrimination was contained in the European Treaties from the very beginning (for the background see *Cichowski*, Judicial Rulemaking and the Institutionalization of European Sex Equality Policy, in: Stone Sweet/ Sandholtz/Fligstein, The Institutionalization of Europe, 2001, Chapter 6, pp. 113–137). Ex-Art. 119 EC-Treaty ordered the principle of equal pay for men and women for equal work to be realized by the 31 December 1961. This however did not happen everywhere and was more or less condoned by the Commission (see comments in the decision Case 43/75 – Defrenne II [1976] ECR 455, paras. 69–75; see also Case 246/96 – Magorrian and Cunningham [1997] ECR I-7153; for background to Art. 119 see also the opinion of Advocate General *Dutheillet* in Case 80/ 70 – Defrenne I [1971] ECR 445.) For more efficacy of this principle the Directive 75/117/EEC was adopted which was designed to state the primary law obligation of Art. 119 EC-Treaty more precisely. The development was not concluded with this; by virtue of the Amsterdam Treaty in the year 1997 Art. 119 EC-Treaty became Art. 141 EC and the principle of equal pay for men and women for equal work as set out by the Directive was extended to work of equal value; by inserting paragraph 4 the contentious question regarding the permissibility of measures in favour of

women was answered in the affirmative. Up until then the rule was solely contained in Art. 2(4) of Directive 76/207/EEC and its compatibility with European primary law was questionable (see also the preceding proposal by the Commission for a Directive on an interpretative amendment of Art. 2(4) COM [1996] 93 final). Shortly beforehand the Directive 97/80/EC was adopted on the burden of proof in cases of sex discrimination. It applies to all situations that are covered by Art. 157 TFEU, the Equal Pay Directive, the Equal Treatment Directive and, as far as it pertains to questions of discrimination based on sex, the Maternity Directive as well as the Directive on parental leave. It covers indirect and direct discrimination and for the latter in particular it remains politically controversial.

The most recent advance in terms of sex discrimination was the extension of 28 protection against unequal treatment to include **sexual harassment** by the Directive 2002/73/EC. Sexual harassment was now classified as discrimination which corresponds, for example, with US-American discrimination laws.

2. Current problems of sex discrimination

The quite abundant case law of the *ECJ* and the literature dealing with the 29 prohibition of sex discrimination is difficult to classify into groups. Some classic and current problems of sex discrimination can however be mentioned:

For cases beyond these ones, see http://ec.europa.eu/justice/gender-equality/rights/case-law/index_en.htm for a **complete and always up-to-date overview on sex-discrimination.**

- For one thing, the **relationship between promotion and equal treatment** is 30 unclear, i. e. to what extent women in particular can be favoured over men. Art. 157(4) TFEU states that, with a view to effectively ensuring full equality between men and women in working life, the principle of equal treatment shall not prevent any Member State from maintaining or adopting measures providing for specific advantages in order to make it easier for the underrepresented sex to pursue a vocational activity or to prevent or compensate for disadvantages in professional careers. This raises many questions: To what extent must the sex be underrepresented? How far can the preference go? In this context the *ECJ* had to decide mainly on quota rules of various equal treatment laws of German federal states (Case 450/93 – Kalanke [1995] ECR I-3051; Case 409/95 – Marschall [1997] ECR I-6363; Case 158/97 – Badeck and Others [2000] ECR I-1875). It accepted quotas that did not force an automatic preference for the one sex when both are equally qualified; for details on this see the new discrimination directives at the relevant provisions. This promotion of the underrepresented sex seemed to be a specific German concern; it was only introduced into English law by the Equality Act 2010 (cf. sec. 158 *et seqq.*). More recent decisions have failed to establish clear guidelines (see in particular Case 476/99 – Lommers [2002] ECR I-2891). Nowadays, sec. 159 Equality Act 2010 gives vague hints, how far positive action is allowed.
- It also seems open to dispute when **sex can be regarded as a justification** within 31 the meaning of Art. 2(1)(b) of Directive 2006/54/EC and, accordingly, when it represents a forbidden criterion for differentiation. The *ECJ* has previously only acknowledged this in one decision regarding British armed forces (Case 273/97 – Sirdar [1999] ECR I-7403) but there are probably more cases of this kind. In a recent decision regarding Directive 2004/113/EC the *ECJ* held that unequal

treatment of men and women when calculating insurance tariffs (men and women have different life expectancies) is not justified (Case 236/09 – Association Belge des Consommateurs Test-Achats and Others).

32 Unequal treatment on grounds of sex is justified if the sex constitutes a genuine and occupational requirement. Actually, not a single job exists where sex is truly essential, except maybe the job of a wet nurse. It was agreed though that the scope of justification is not exhausted there, and so the **German government** named several other examples in a consultation paper to the European Commission that it wants to (not legally bindingly) also include: Occupational activities where the authentic fulfilment of a role or a task depends on a certain sex, for instance, actors or models; activities in the church, e. g. a priest in the Catholic church; activities outside the EU where only one sex is accepted by reason of legal rules, religious convictions or cultural particularities; activities in a women's shelter insofar as the care concept of the institution requires women exclusively. On the other hand this list also contained "activities in the field of internal and external security", e. g. the Bundeswehr (German Armed Forces); this has been rendered mute by the *ECJ* decision (Case 285/98 – Kreil [2000] ECR I-69). In correlation to American case law one may differentiate between a substantive and a crucial vocational requirement in a narrow and wide sense. In the narrow sense this encompasses all cases where it is actually or legally impossible for an employee of a certain sex to perform the gender-neutral task, in the wide sense this can include cases where one sex cannot perform the task as well as the other due to biological differences, and the public has a particular interest in the optimal performance of the job (e. g. security personnel at a prison). Mere customer preferences can usually not justify a difference in treatment (at length *Thüsing*, Arbeitsrechtlicher Diskriminierungsschutz, 2nd ed. 2013, para. 343; see also *Seifert*, Federal Labor Court strengthens religious freedom at the workplace, 4 German Law Journal 2003, No. 6, 549–569).

33 **British case law on the Equality Act 2010 and its predecessor, the SDA,** is particularly profuse (legislation and cases are available at www.bailii.org). It is justified to only hire women for a *live girls chat 1-2-1* (Cropper v. UK Express Limited, ET case no. 25757/91); the mere wish to staff a radio show with a female and a male host will not suffice (Mitchelson v. Essex Radio PLC, ET case no. 3201226/96). A security guard can be a woman (Barker v. Goodwave Security Ltd, ET case no. 2406811/97). Even a fashion salesman, who measures trouser lengths on men, can be a woman (Wylie v. Dee & Co (Menswear) Limited [1978] IRLR 103; see though a different result for the sale of women's clothing in the Austrian decision OGH of 12th January 2000, 9 Ob AS 318/99 a; rightly critical Rebhahn/*Rebhahn*, GlbG, 2005, sec. 3 at 81). A lavatory attendant of a men's room must be male (Lowthorpe v. Atlas Trailer Co Limited, ET case no. 24949/89).

34 To some extent the question is also unresolved when **work is of equal value in terms of Art. 157(1) TFEU.** In distinguishing between equal work and work of equal value, the former is considered work of basically equal kind. The decisive factor is that the usual activities of the compared persons are identical or, taking workload, responsibility, work conditions and qualifications into account, are of equal kind, so that the employees can substitute each other when required. With work of equal value such substitutability is not necessary. The term can also be found in other legal systems, e. g. in the US-American *Equal Pay Act* (29 USC, sec. 206 [d]), the Swiss Federal Constitution (*Schweizer Bundesverfassung*) (Art. 4(2)), the former United Kingdom Equal Pay Act 1970 (section 1(1) & (2)) or in the convention 100 of the ILO of 1951. The *ECJ* has not had to take a stand on the equal value of two jobs in a judgement so far (see in particular recently Case 236/98 – Jämställdhetsombudsmannen [2000] ECR I-2189; Case 96/80 – Jenkins [1981] ECR 911). The more different the work, the more difficult it becomes to establish reliable standards for assessing equal value (at length see *Thüsing*, NZA 2000, 570; *Barnard*, EC Employment law, 2006, 345 *et seqq.*). It is not necessary for the employees to work for the same employer for Art. 157(1) TFEU to apply (Case 320/00 – Lawrance and Others [2002] ECR I-7325).

- The *ECJ* has occupied itself many times with regulations that set out **a different retirement age for women and men**. The most famous example was the decision *Barber*: 35

Mr. Barber challenged the fact that when he was dismissed for operational reasons at the age of 52, he was given a lower redundancy pay on account of his sex compared to what a woman of the same age would have been entitled to, and that he did not receive a company pension which a woman of the same age would have been entitled to (Case 262/88 – Barber [1990] ECR I-1889). The *ECJ* considered this unlawful discrimination; this was one of the few decisions from which mainly men profited (the cases about pensions are abundant: Case 262/88 – Barber [1990] ECR I-1889; Case 110/91 – Moroni [1993] ECR I-6591; Case 256/01 – Allonby [2004] ECR I-873; Case 351/00 – Niemi [2002] ECR I-7007; the most recent case is Case 356/09 – Kleist [2011]). 36

- Of current significance is the **unequal treatment because of pregnancy**. According to Art. 2(2)(c) of Directive 2006/54/EC this is unequal treatment based on sex. Consequently, **French law** absolutely forbids asking about pregnancy, Art. L. 1132–1 in conjunction with Art. L. 1221-6 Code du travail. In a decision in 2001 the *ECJ* declared that in the cases of fixed-term employment, even if an applicant will not be able to perform the task for a considerable period of time due to the pregnancy, the unequal treatment because of the pregnancy is unlawful sex discrimination (Case 109/00 – Tele Danmark [2001] ECR I-6993). Previously it was generally assumed that this strict prohibition of unequal treatment only applied to open-ended employment relationships. Now the Court declared: "Since the dismissal of a worker on account of pregnancy constitutes direct discrimination on grounds of sex, whatever the nature and extent of the economic loss incurred by the employer as a result of her absence because of pregnancy, whether the contract of employment was concluded for a fixed or an indefinite period has no bearing on the discriminatory character of the dismissal. In either case the employee's inability to perform her contract of employment is due to pregnancy" (Ibid., para. 31). This discrimination protection was further extended in the Danosa case. There the *ECJ* held that officers of capital companies can be considered employees with the result that the removal of a Board member based on pregnancy constitutes direct discrimination based on sex (Case 232/09 – Danosa [2010]). 37

The ***ECJ*'s approach can certainly be questioned** (see *Wintermute*, When is pregnancy discrimination indirect sex discrimination?, 27 Industrial Law Journal 1998, opposed *Honeyball*, Pregnancy and sex discrimination, 29 Industrial Law Journal 2000, 43–52). If a pregnancy is treated the same way as any other "illness-related" absence from work, then this does not constitute unequal treatment, but equal treatment which is merely de facto, though not legally, disadvantageous to women. Precisely this is the approach of US-American law, even though the equal treatment principle there, *Title VII of the Civil Rights Act* (42 US Code 20002 [k]), was expressly extended to include unequal treatment because of pregnancy as discrimination (the express reference proves that this is not a matter of course). 38

In contrast, taking the *ECJ*'s judgments into account, the conclusions of the Court seem to stand to reason but are nevertheless not imperative. Under Art. 14(2) of Directive 2006/54/EC a difference of treatment which is based on a characteristic related to sex shall not constitute discrimination where, by reason of the nature of the particular occupational activities concerned or of the context in which they are carried out, such a characteristic constitutes a genuine and determining occupational requirement, provided that its objective is legitimate and the requirement is proportionate. This is not the case for long-term employment but if an employee is hired specifically as a replacement for a pregnant person, then the pregnancy would 39 frustrate performance, and from the employer's perspective there is no difference to other cases of non-performance. The sentence "the application of provisions concerning the protection of pregnant women cannot result in unfavourable treatment regarding their access to employment" (Case 207/98 – Mahlburg [2000] ECR I-549, para. 27) formulated so unconditionally is not accurate; at any rate this cannot be followed from the structure of discrimination protection and the implementing directives.

VI. The Anti-Discrimination Directives 2000/43/EC and 2000/78/EC

40 By means of the discrimination Directives 2000/43/EC and 2000/78/EC, European discrimination protection gained a new dimension. The provisions had to be transposed by the 19 July 2003 (for racial and ethnic discrimination), by the 2 December 2003 (for the other criteria except disability) and by the 2 December 2006 (disability) respectively.

1. Directive 2000/43/EC – Race and ethnicity

41 There seem to be no problems in assessing the discrimination prohibitions based on race and ethnic origin. These are criteria which as a rule have nothing to do with work performance, so that formal equal treatment and a decision based on objective, performance-related criteria will bring about the desired result of actual equal opportunity.

42 Indeed, this does not answer the question as to what race and ethnic origin actually mean. The **term "race"**, documented in Romanic languages since the 13th century, did not refer to biological, but to social categories up until the 17th century. Race described the affiliation or origin of a family, a "house" in terms of "noble family", right up to being a synonym for "dynasty". In the discovery and travel reports of the 17th century "race" describes, along with "genre", "espèce", "classe", "kind" and "sort", unknown human populations of foreign countries. In the past, the *ECJ* has only once taken a view on the employment law prohibition of race discrimination (Case 328/04 – Vajnai [2005] ECR I-8577). The *ECJ* declared that the Hungarian prohibition of wearing a five-point red star did not clash with the prohibition of race discrimination. This was not particularly surprising ("It is clear that Mr Vajnai's situation is not connected in any way with any of the situations contemplated by the provisions of the treaties and the Hungarian provisions applied in the main proceedings are outside the scope of Community law.", para. 14). The public statement made by an employer that he will not employ persons of a certain ethnic origin or race constitutes indirect discrimination, according to the operative part of the decision in Feryn (Case 54/07 – Feryn [2008] ECR I-5187), which also means that the burden of proof lies with the employer. A glance into Directive 2000/78/EC, to determine the meaning of race does not help either: according to the grounds stated in the government draft the term "race" is used in the same way as in the Directive 2000/43/EC and Art. 13 EC-Treaty – now Art. 19 TFEU – in order to highlight the link to "racism" and keep the signal effect of the word. This is not meant to acknowledge any existence of different human races, for Recital 6 of Directive 2000/43/EC reads: "The European Union rejects theories which attempt to determine the existence of separate human races. The use of the term 'racial origin' in this Directive does not imply an acceptance of such theories." (see however *Levi-Strauss*, Structural Anthropology: Volume 2, 1983, p. 325: "One should not assume to have thus settled in a negative way the problem of inequality of human *races*, if one considers at the same time the problem of the inequality – or diversity – of human *cultures* which – de facto if not de jure – is closely linked to it in public opinion"). The term "race" insofar is not an "actual characteristic". Nevertheless, the French *Code du travail* simply refers to belonging to a race (Art. L. 1132-1 Code du travail *"appartenance à une race")*, as does the English *Equality Act 2010,* whereas Belgian law speaks of "alleged" race ("*une race prétendue*", [*Loi du 20 janvier 2003 relative au renforcement de la législation contre le racisme*]) showing much more clearly that they do not presume an existence of human races.

For this reason in the practice of the courts the prohibition of discrimination will most likely be resolved in future using the **term 'ethnic origin'**. This term too though is difficult to define. It is certainly not to be equated with the term nationality; Recital 13 of Directive 2000/43/EC states expressly: "This prohibition of discrimination [...] does not cover differences of treatment based on nationality" (hereunto in detail § 2 at para. 30 *et seqq.*). A positive description however cannot be found in the Directive. Extra-juridical understanding of ethnicity is the fact or state of belonging to a social group that has a common national or cultural tradition (this as an example, the definition in the Oxford dictionary, under ethnicity). Modern ethnology defines ethnicity as the greatest identifiable sovereign unity that is known and wanted by the relevant people themselves. But this is hardly tangible. 43

British courts have been more precise in the reading of the **Race Relations Act (which is now consolidated in the Equality Act 2010)**. There, ethnic origin is defined as "a long shared history, of which the group is conscious as distinguishing it from other groups; a cultural tradition of its own, including family and social customs and manners, often but not necessarily associated with religious observance; a common religion different from that of neighbouring groups or from the general community surrounding it"; or – as a fourth – "the characteristic of being a minority or being an oppressed or a dominant group within a larger community" (Lord *Fraser* in Mandla v. Lee, 2 AC 548 [House of Lords 1983]). 44

All this can be adopted as a **starting point in the interpretation of European law**. Indeed, caution is in order with respect to the fourth criterion. As an alternative requirement it has become too wide to only cover ethnic groups; as a cumulative criterion on the other hand it is not needed in order to distinguish an ethnic group. This classification hits the target course of the discrimination prohibition, yet it cannot be seen as more than an auxiliary criterion. On the whole what is definitive is the awareness as "a different group" in traditions, origin and occurrence. Skin colour, appearance, language and religion can be important criteria here to describe the archetype of the ethnicity (similarly *Ford*, 47 UCLA L. Rev. 1803 [2000]). The correlations here to the prohibition of discrimination on the basis of religion are striking. As this can be a significant and formative criterion for ethnic origin, British courts in the past have recognized religious groups as ethnic groups (e. g. in Mandla v. Lee, 2 AC 548 [House of Lords 1983] – Sikhs; rejected in Dawkins v. Department of Environment, ICR 583 [EAT 1991] – Rastafarians; see hereunto also *Fredman*, Discrimination Law, 2002, 70 *et seqq.*; on overlap of race discrimination and religious discrimination see also *Brown*, 21 Yearbook of European Law 2002, 195; using the example of the head scarf prohibition also *Thüsing/Wege*, 11 ZEuP 2004, 404). 45

It is forbidden to treat an employee less favourably compared to others, just because the employer dislikes, examples given enough, people of colour or Sinti. Where this criterion is significant for the employment relationship however, then the employer may consider this, for under Art. 4(1) of Directive 2000/43/EC the Member States can provide that unequal treatment based on a characteristic related to race or ethnic origin does not constitute discrimination if, by reason of the nature of a particular occupational activity, this is a determining and genuine occupational requirement, and as long as there is a legitimate objective and a proportionate requirement. It is notable that US-American law does not recognize the possibility of justification in *Title VII Civil Rights Act*. 46

Comprehensive references of case law where "**customer preferences**" can justify a difference in treatment of sex or race can be found in *Adamitis*, Appearance matters: a proposal to prohibit appearance discrimination in employment, 75 Wash. L. Rev. 2000, p. 95 *et seqq.*; *Sidhu*, Out of sight, out of legal recourse: Interpreting and revising title VII to prohibit workplace segregation based on religion, 36 N.Y.U. Rev. L. & Soc. Change 2012, p. 103, 127 *et seqq.*; *Smith/Craver/Clark*, Employment Discrimination Law, 2009, p. 561; *Zimmer/Sullivan/White*, Cases and Materials on Employment Discrimination, 2008, p. 278, 308. As an example Fernandez v. Wynn Oil Co., 653 F.2 d 1273 (9th Cir. 1981). The British Race Relations Act once made an exception for actors and waiters in an ethnic restaurant ("genuine occupational 47 qualification" in sec. 5(2)(b) and (c)) but this exception cannot be found in the Equality Act 2010.

48 This corresponds essentially with the standard that is already applied to sex discrimination. One will have to apply the same stringency as with sex discrimination, just as Title VII of the Civil Rights Act or Art. L. 1131-1 *Code du travail*, the central discrimination prohibition of French employment law, applies the same standard to both. So in this respect, this is not really a new concept, the only extension is the sphere of impermissible discrimination characteristics. There should be no debate about the justification of the discrimination prohibition as such. It was the starting point of US-American discrimination law which was adopted precisely to prevent discrimination due to race.

49 Indeed, rules on sex discrimination were already included when the *Civil Rights Act* was enacted. But, these were incorporated into the text of the Act at a very late stage of the process. It was initiated – as rumour has it – by a Southern delegate's motion who wanted to take the prohibition of race discrimination *ad absurdum* in an attempt to defeat the bill: if you want to forbid race discrimination, then you would have to forbid discrimination against women, too. Whether this story is true, is admittedly uncertain (see the detailed analysis of *Gold*, 19 Duquesne Law Review 1981, 453, 458).

2. Directive 2000/78/EC – disability

50 The other discrimination prohibitions provided for by Directive 2000/78/EC are just as difficult to grasp. The first difficulties arise with the interpretation of disability as grounds for discrimination.

a) Who is disabled?

51 Even the question, what disability means, poses a problem. European law gives no answer to this; the national legal systems offer very diverse ones. Which one is more likely to be correct, can only be conjectured: **German constitutional law** has had a prohibition of discrimination since 1994 in Art. 3(3) 2nd sentence Grundgesetz: "No-one shall be discriminated against by reason of their disability". Unlike, on the other hand, Art. L. 1132-1 ***Code du travail*** (see para. 57); there it says: No-one shall be excluded from a hiring process and no employee shall be reprimanded or dismissed due to his health or a disability. As no distinction is made between health and disability, no efforts are made to distinguish them; a certain threshold of disability is not required (similarly sec. 2 of the Irish Employment Equality Act, by which a disability means "the total or partial absence of a person's bodily or mental functions, including the absence of a part of a person's body, the presence in the body of organisms causing, or likely to cause chronic disease or illness, a condition or malfunction which results in a person learning differently from a person without the condition or malfunction, a condition, illness or disease which affects a person's thought processes, perception of reality, emotions or judgement or which results in disturbed behaviour and shall be taken to include a disability which exists at present, or which previously existed but no longer exists, or which may exist in the future or which is imputed to a person"). This perception corresponds with the *Americans with Disabilities Act*, where disability means a physical impairment which substantially limits one or more "major life activities". Sec. 6 of the **British Equality Act 2010** has a similar view in that disability means someone who has a physical or mental impairment which has a substantial and long-term adverse effect

on his ability to carry out normal day-to-day activities. In **Dutch law**, on the other hand, there is no definition of disability included in the Act on Equal Treatment on the Grounds of Disability or Chronic Illness 2003 (*Wet gelijke behandeling op grond van handicap of chronische ziekte*, Staatsblad van het Koninkrijk der Nederlanden, 2003, 206), since instead of discrimination the term distinction (*onderscheid*) is used which renders the Act applicable to both disabled and not-disabled persons (*Waddington*, Dutch Summary Report on the Implementation of the Disability Provisions of the Framework Employment Directive, 2004).

Against the background of national legal systems one can assume that the **term** 52 **disability** in the draft directive is also meant **to be understood in a broad sense**. But then the same difficulties exist in determining what a disability is, just like in the aforementioned laws: Is a symptomless HIV-infection a disability? **German academic literature** says no (*Hueck/v. Hoyningen-Huene*, KSchG, 2007, § 1 at 188; see also *Lepke*, 53 RdA 2000, 93), the French scholars say yes (says at any rate – though without giving any reasons – *Laborde*, Dr. soc. 1991, 615, 616), the **American courts** were divided until the *Supreme Court* decided it authoritatively and answered the question in the affirmative (Bragdon v. Abbott 524 U.S. 624 (1998); unlike previously in Runnebaum v. NationsBank of Maryland, 7 AD Cases 216 [15.8.1997]). Is a person also disabled if he is an alcoholic? American courts say this is the case (cf. Mararri v. WCI Steel Inc., 7 AD Cases 978 [2.12.1997]), yet the traditional sense of the word "disability" most likely does not allow such a conception.

More than five years after the judgment in *Navas* a Danish court has sought a preliminary ruling 53 (Case C-337/11 and C-335/11 – 1 July 2011) and has thereby given the *ECJ* the opportunity to further develop its case-law on the term 'disability'. With specific reference to the *Navas* decision, the Danish court *Sø- og Handelsretten* has referred the question to the *ECJ* whether any person who, because of physical, mental or psychological injuries, cannot or can only to a limited extent carry out his work in a period that satisfies the requirement as to duration specified by the *ECJ* (in paragraph 45 of the judgment in the *Navas* case) is covered by the concept of disability within the meaning of the directive. The answer was expectable broad: The Court explained that the concept of 'disability' must be interpreted as including a condition caused by an illness medically diagnosed as curable or incurable, if that illness entails a limitation which results in particular from physical, mental or psychological impairments which in interaction with various barriers may hinder the full and effective participation of the person concerned in professional life on an equal basis with other workers, and the limitation is a long-term one. The Court noted that the concept of 'disability' does not necessarily imply complete exclusion from work or professional life. In addition, a finding that there is a disability does not depend on the nature of the accommodation measures to be taken by the employer, such as the use of special equipment. It will be for the national court to assess whether, in the present cases, the workers were persons with a disability. The Court also noted that the directive requires the employer to take appropriate and reasonable accommodation measures in particular to enable a person with a disability to have access to, participate in, or advance in employment. Even if it were not covered by the concept of 'pattern of working time' expressly mentioned in the directive, a reduction in working hours may be regarded as an appropriate accommodation measure in a case in which the reduction makes it possible for the worker to continue in his employment. It is, however, for the national court to assess whether, in the present cases, a reduction in working hours, as an accommodation measure, represents a disproportionate burden on the employers.

The *Americans with Disabilities Act* also excludes certain impairments from 54 being disabilities, even though these are also occasionally referred to as mental disablements, *inter alia* paedophilia, exhibitionism, kleptomania and pyromania (§§ 508, 511 ADA). Would such exceptions also be necessary for European law? These problems can only be hinted at here.

55 The decision in Coleman (Case 303/06 – Coleman [2008] ECR I-5603) has outlined the extent of the prohibition of discrimination based on a disability. The *ECJ* held that the prohibition of direct discrimination based on disability is not limited only to people who are themselves disabled but also applies to persons who are indirectly affected by the disability and therefore suffer a disadvantage. In the specific case an employer had treated an employee who cared for a disabled child less favourably. The Court convincingly argues that Directive 2000/78/EC does not protect the disabled person but forbids less favourable treatment on grounds of a disability. This also applies to harassment within the meaning of Directive 2000/78/EC.

b) When is a disabled person being discriminated against?

56 More important in our context is the answer to the question, when a disabled person is being discriminated against. The former Advocate General *Lenz* – before implementation of the Directive 2000/78/EC – wrote in his commentary on Art. 13 EC (now Art. 19 TFEU): "[O]ne need not fear that a disabled person will be given the right to lay claim to a job position for which he is unfit" (*Lenz*, in: Lenz, EGV, 1999, Art. 13 EC at 14). This is probably a little too bold in view of the now undertaken exercise of legislative powers, for in Art. 5 the Directive 2000/78/EC has clearly decided in favour of substantial equality, not just equal treatment: In order to guarantee compliance with the principle of equal treatment in relation to persons with disabilities, reasonable accommodation shall be provided. Though the version of the original draft was unclear as to towards whom this obligation is directed – the employer or the state – the text of the adopted directive is unambiguous: "This means that employers shall take appropriate measures, where needed in a particular case, to enable a person with a disability to have access to, participate in, or advance in employment, or to undergo training, unless such measures would impose a disproportionate burden on the employer." How far exactly this obligation goes is difficult to say. The wording of the English version of the draft proposal corresponds exactly to that of the *Americans with Disabilities Act* ("reasonable accommodations; undue hardship", § 102 (b) (5) (A) ADA), and so the same problems in defining the limits of the obligation to treat equally that have arisen there can be pointed out here: one agrees that not only the costs of the measure, the size and financial power of the company, the degree of disability and the influence on other employees are decisive factors, but also e. g. outside financing possibilities or tax benefits – all in all a not easily ponderable amalgam. The criticism of legal scholars is probably correct in seeing the criterion of "undue hardship" as a standard that is "so vague as to amount to no standard at all" (*Cooper*, Overcoming Barriers to Employment: The Meaning of Reasonable Accommodation and Undue Hardship in the Americans with Disabilities Act, 139 U. Pa. L. Rev. 1991, pp. 1423, 1450; similarly *Note*, Employment Discrimination Against the Handicapped and Section 504 of the Rehabilitation Act: An Essay on Legal Evasiveness, 97 Harv. L. Rev. 1987, pp. 997, 1011: "Rather than provide a clear criterion for decision by designating some limit on the burden that may be imposed on employers, 'undue hardship' seems in practice to have served simply as a label for accommodations that courts have refused to require in particular cases"). The uncertainty is no different in English law, where there is a similar duty to achieve equality by taking "reasonable adjustments" to the workplaces to overcome barriers experienced by disabled people, despite there being no mention of the limitation of

"undue hardship" in the text of the Act (sec. 20 Equality Act 2010 (Disability Regulations)). The legislator itself names several factors at this point (sec. 20 Equality Act 2010 (Disability Regulations)) that are to be taken into account in the consideration process, but without prescribing a particular emphasis for one or the other. This was no different under sec. 6 Disability Discrimination Act 1995 which was applicable before the Equality Act 2010 came into force. The Equality Act 2010 has transferred the Disability Discrimination Act among others into a uniform anti-discrimination code but this has not brought about any significant changes. The statute is still no more than a skeleton which needs to be fleshed out with statutory instruments and case law; a legal consultant is advised to own a comprehensive library (*Fredman*, Discrimination Law, 2011, p. 214 *et seqq.* or the standard text book about the former law under the Disability Discrimination Act from 1995: *Bourn/ Whitmore*, Anti-Discrimination Law in Britain, 1996, chapters 3–04, 3–05, 3–12).

Considering these **difficulties**, it would have been appropriate to take a look around at other European legal systems. The explanatory memorandum of the proposal of the directive refers only to the British, Irish and Swedish legislation of that time (Employment Equality Act of 1998 [Ireland]; Disability Discrimination Act 1995 [UK]; Act on discrimination of people with disabilities [Sweden]). This needed explaining at least with regard to Irish law, for therein the extent of an employer's obligation to equalize was much smaller. Under sec. 16(3)(c) Employment Equality Act he only needed to make such adjustments that did not incur costs. Moreover, sec. 34(3) stated expressly that it is not a case of discrimination on grounds of disability if equal treatment – even without accommodations – would result in significantly increased costs (An employer's obligation has however been extended by the new legislation: Under the now applicable Employment Equality Act 2004, which is closely moulded on the British example, employers may take financial costs into consideration but may be obligated to employ appropriate measures to accommodate disabled employees as long as this does not impose a *disproportionate* burden (sec. 16 Employment Equality Act 2004)). This approaches more the notion of a formal equality. French law saw the prohibition of disability discrimination even more plainly as a duty to formal equality: If a doctor can confirm the unfitness of an employee, then he does not have to be hired or can be dismissed. This only prevents discrimination of employees that are suitable as such but whose performance is underestimated solely on account of their disability. This too is a significant amount of protection, in addition easily conceivable for the courts, even if the duty to consult a doctor in cases of obvious unsuitability seems superfluous (this is criticized by *J. Savatier*, Dr. soc. 1996, p. 971 prompted by a decision of the Tribunal Administratif de Besancon of 11 July 1996, ibid., which ruled that a town may not demand of a commissioned cleaning company that only their "valid" and "robust" employees be assigned the task of cleaning). At the same time, the *Code du travail* – there is a similar rule in German law – puts an obligation on the employer to hire disabled persons to a certain extent (Art. L. 5212-2: 6 % for companies with more than 20 employees). Promotion beyond equal treatment, as set out in Art. 5 of the Directive, takes place here irrespective of the principle of equal treatment, without vague distinctions within the scope of reasonableness. The advantage of the French and German solution in a legal sense is obvious; it is not obvious that the approach in the directive proposal is more effective (Britain also had such a quota system until 1996, cf. *Bourn/Whitmore*, 57

Anti-Discrimination Law in Britain, 3rd ed. 1996, paras. 1–29). In transposing Directive 2000/78/EC French law now stipulates simply: "Les différences de traitement fondées sur l'inaptitude constatée par le médecin du travail en raison de l'état de santé ou du handicap ne constituent pas une discrimination lorsqu'elles sont objectives, nécessaires et appropriées" in Art. L. 1133-3 Code du travail.

3. Directive 2000/78/EC: Religion and belief

58 Very similar questions arise with respect to the prohibition of discrimination on grounds of religion and belief.

a) What is religion?

59 Here too the directive does not provide a legal definition of the discrimination characteristic. This is understandable considering that the open term 'religion' is hardly suitable for a definition and considering the fact that in most cases one intuitively knows whether a certain conviction or world view is a religion or not. But here too there remains significant potential for conflict, e. g. with respect to Scientology: whether this is a religion is debatable. German and English courts reject this notion, French and US-American courts answer in the affirmative (*BAG* of 22 March 1995-5 AZB 21/94, NJW 1996, 143; Regina v. Registrar General, Ex parte Segerdal [1970] 2 QB 697; Hernandez v. Commissioner 109 S.Ct. 2136 [1989]; Cour d'appel de Lyon of 28 July 1997, D. 1997, IR, p. 197 *et seq.* Extensively on this *Thüsing*, Was ist eine Religionsgemeinschaft? – Eine rechtsvergleichende Darstellung am Beispiel der Scientology Church, Memorial Publication for Hartmut Krüger, 2001; *Sargeant/Lewis*, Employment Law, 2006, Chapter 8 – Discrimination on the Grounds of Religion, Belief, Sexual Orientation and Age, 234 *et seqq.*)). If it were a religion, perhaps the current practice of many Federal States of asking civil service applicants about their Scientology membership would be regarded as unlawful discrimination.

60 **US-American law** offers numerous cases of possible borderline cases of religion: Is it a religious creed when an employee only eats cat food (Brown v. Pena, F.Supp. 1382, 1384 (S.D.Fla. 1977), or if he staples his body from top to bottom with piercings (Cloutier v. Costco Wholesale No. 04–1475, 1st Cir. 2004)? Is the First Church of Marihuana a religion or just an excuse to smoke weed (Meyers v. U.S., 95 F.3 d 1475, 10th Cir. 1996)?

b) When is it a case of discrimination on grounds of religion?

61 Again in our context it is more important to determine when a person is being discriminated against. The directive proposal opted clearly for equal treatment, not substantial equality, for there is no obligation to accommodate comparable to Art. 2(4) with respect to religion. This neither makes immediate sense nor is it indicated by the issue at hand, bearing in mind that American law was familiar with an employer's duty to provide reasonable accommodations with regard to religious discrimination years before the corresponding obligation with respect to disabled employees (§ 701 (j) Title VII Civil Rights Act. "The term 'religion' includes all aspects of religious observance and practice, as well as belief, unless an employer demonstrates that he is unable to reasonably accommodate an employee's or prospective employee's religious observance or practice without undue hardship on the conduct of the employer's business"). In actual fact, most cases of conflict involving an employee's religious convictions will not arise in the event of –

probably quite rare – unequal treatment but rather equal treatment that has an unequal effect: All employees must work on Saturdays: Even a Seventh-Day-Adventist or a Jewish employee? All employees must wear a helmet at work: even a Sikh, whose religion requires him to wear a turban in public? All employees receive free catering at the canteen: Must a cook offer kosher food and meat-free meals on Fridays?

German employment law for example is quite familiar with certain duties to take 62 employees into consideration whose faith or conscience forbids them to perform certain tasks. An employee can insist upon being given another task to the extent that it is possible to do so than the one that conceivably burdens his conscience. Only if this is not possible or unreasonable for the employer to do so, the employee can be dismissed on person-related grounds (*BAG* of 24 February 2011-2 AZR 636/09 regarding the dismissal of a warehouse employee of Muslim faith who refused to stock alcohol). In view of this background of existing European law the question arises why equality protection should go as far as equalization for disabled employees, though not the protection of religious convictions.

Nevertheless, **distinguishing** remains difficult. The cases of indirect discrimination on grounds of 63 religion will also be more numerous than those of direct discrimination. The fundamental question here is, whether also equal treatment resulting in *de facto* unequal effects falls under the prohibition of indirect discrimination (see also para. 21). Assuming this, then refusing a Muslim a break for prayer constitutes indirect discrimination even when no employees are granted any short breaks during working hours. **French courts** allowed the employer to lay down such guidelines to a large extent: "Even though the employer is obliged to respect his employees' faiths, unless expressly agreed, they have nothing to do with the employment contract and the employer is not making a mistake when he asks an employee to perform a task which he was hired for, as long as it does not go against public policy." (*Cass. Soc.* of 24 March 1998, Droit social 1998, p. 614 commented on by *Savatier*; similar to the case of an employee who refused to work on a high Islamic holiday, see *Cass. Soc.* of 16.12.1981, Bull. V. Nr. 968). This line must be followed according to our understanding of indirect discrimination. But if an employer sometimes makes exceptions of the general rules then it could constitute indirect discrimination if he does not do so for his employee's religious reasons. This would require justification: if he allows breaks for smoking, then he must give a reason for not allowing the same for praying.

4. Sexual identity

Discrimination based on sexual identity can occur in particular in cases involving 64 soldiers, in church employment and with linking benefits to marital status.

In accordance with the wording of the provision, the prohibition of discrimination includes 65 every **sexual identity**. The explanatory memorandum contains no limitations hereto and even the Directive 2000/78/EC is not able to make a contribution as to any specifications of this differentiation characteristic. Other countries were more cautious in this respect. There, "sexuality involving minor children" is expressly excluded from the prohibition of discrimination due to sexual orientation (e. g. the anti-discrimination law of the state of Massachusetts, G.L. c. 151B, § 4). The fact that such a rule is missing in European law conflicts with the value judgments in criminal law which forbids and sanctions certain forms of practiced sexuality. If one does not want to arrive at a restrictive interpretation, then an employee can indeed be convicted of child abuse, but the employer cannot reject an applicant because of the very same conviction. The justification provided by Art. 4 of Directive 2000/78/EC does not apply as a rule because occupational skills are not affected by sexual dispositions (for exceptions see paras. 66 *et seqq.*). The result seems to be absurd: an applicant could be rejected because he was convicted of theft (because European law contains, unlike the anti-discrimination legislation of many Member States, no prohibitions of discrimination based on criminal records, see *Louks/Lyner/Sullivan*, The Employment of People with Criminal

Records in the European Union, 6 European Journal on Criminal Policy and Research 1998, No. 2, 195–210), but not because he was convicted of sex crime involving minors.

66 Pursuant to settled case law in **Germany** (German Federal Administration Court (*BVerwG)* of 30 July 1991, BVerwGE 93, 143; *BVerwG* of 8 May 1994 – 2 WD 28/94; BVerwGE 103, 192) homosexual behaviour within the *Bundeswehr* (German armed forces) cannot be tolerated. The solidarity within the troops would be severely disturbed if homosexual relationships between individual soldiers with all the emotional implications were to be condoned. So even if one were to regard discrimination based on homosexual behaviour as direct discrimination based on sexual identity, such discrimination would be justified. This is true despite the fact that in the *Bundeswehr* this practice has since changed. Prejudices of the heterosexual majority against a homosexual minority are however by no means sufficient justification for interferences with someone's private life, just as similar negative attitudes towards persons of other race, descent or skin colour are not either (ECHR, *Smith and Grady v. United Kingdom*, Applications Nos. 33985/96 and 33986/96).

67 The dismissal of **employees in church employment** based on practiced homosexuality was accepted in an unbroken line of case law in **German law** (see *inter alia BAG* of 30 June 1983 – 2 AZR 524/81). These authorities still apply, for the forsaking of homosexual practices is a genuine and determining occupational requirement in view of the ethos of church employment (for **Dutch law** see the decision 93/2006 of the equality commission with respect to Muslim teachers at Christian community schools, available at: www.mensenrechten.nl).

68 Various collective agreement rules **take the existence of marriage or same-sex life partnerships into account**. In this context, the question arises as to what extent within an employment relationship it is permissible to differentiate between marriage on the one hand and a heterosexual as well as homosexual life partnership on the other hand. The *ECJ* in the *Grant* case (Case 249/96 – Grant [1998] ECR I-621) ruled that the employer need not grant travel concessions to an employee who had applied for the same concession as is provided for spouses and heterosexual life partners. According to the opinion of the *ECJ*, an employee is not entitled to travel concessions for same sex partners. The *ECJ* determined that Community law does not require the employer to regard stable relationships between two persons of the same sex as equivalent to stable non-marital relationships between persons of the opposite sex. Of course, back then the prohibition of discrimination on grounds of sexual identity was not in force. Under the new law the distinction made by the employer between heterosexual and homosexual life partnerships, as was the case in the *Grant* matter, must be regarded as a violation of the equal treatment principle. Privileging marriage is nevertheless still permissible. This view can rely on the 22nd Recital of Directive 2000/78/EC according to which the national laws on marital status remain unaffected. The exception of a rule governing marital status in the 22nd Recital corresponds with the European legislator's lack of authority to adopt regulations in the area of marital and family law. EU law leaves it up to the Member States to design their family and marital status law according to their national customs. Where the Member States have given equal rights to certain forms of same-sex partnerships, unequal treatment of same-sex partners and married couples violates Directive 2000/78/EC and is not justified (cf. Case 267/06 – Maruko [2008] ECR 2008, I-1757). This decision does not affect the Member States' sovereignty to determine family law, as

the *ECJ* expressly states that a violation of Directive 2000/78/EC only occurs if the Member State decided to put same-sex partnerships on equal footing. If an employer privileges marriage compared to life partnerships outside marriage, then this does not constitute direct discrimination of homosexual employees because heterosexual, unmarried employees are also excluded. Usually this will not constitute indirect discrimination of homosexual life partnerships either because one cannot assume that life partnerships are predominantly homosexual. To sum up: it must be noted that an employer will in future still be able to **privilege marriage** (expressly also sec. 13 [4] Equality Act 2010; hereunto confirming conformity with European law, the House of Lords in the *Amicus* case [2004] IRLR 430) as long as same-sex partnerships have not been assimilated to marriage.

A transsexual's application for the position of a police officer of higher rank 69 **cannot be rejected** (according to the House of Lords in A. v. Chief Constable of West Yorkshire Police [2004] UKHL 21). The possible reservations the public may have do not weigh as heavy in order to justify an affront to a sex-changed employee.

5. Age

The form of discrimination probably most difficult to judge the nature of is, finally, 70 age. Cases of unequal treatment based on age are usually easy to detect. The answer to the question when these cases of unequal treatment are justified is, however, laden with problems.

a) Justification of discrimination based on age

Applicable first of all is the general justification standard laid down in Art. 4(1) of 71 Directive 2000/78/EC. This is a narrow scope and will cover those cases too that are classed under the term "bona fide occupational qualification" in US-American law: Air traffic controllers and bus drivers can be pensioned off even against their will after a certain age, because their physical resilience is crucial for their occupation (cf. the references on case law on § 4 [f] [1] ADEA in *Notestine*, Fundamentals of Employment Law, 2000, pp. 29 *et seqq.*; *Zimmer/White*, Cases and Materials on Employment Discrimination, 2008, pp. 426 *et seqq.*; *Macnicol*, Age Discrimination: An Historical and Contemporary Analysis, 2005). For firemen and policemen there is even an express exemption from the scope of application of the ADEA, cf. § 4 [j] [1] ADEA. More important though are the special provisions on justifiable unequal treatment based on age in Art. 6 of Directive 2000/78/EC. The wording of the norm varied considerably during the individual stages of creation. Under the final version, a row of expressly mentioned differences of treatment do not constitute direct discrimination based on age, "if … they are objectively and reasonably justified by a legitimate aim … and if the means of achieving that aim are appropriate and necessary".

In the US-American *Age Discrimination in Employment Act* too, one can find a 72 difference in justification standards for age discrimination and discrimination based on other criteria. Since 1967 this act has forbidden discrimination of older employees as a basic principle. The possible grounds for justification however are drawn wider here than for other discrimination prohibitions. Aside from "bona fides occupational qualification", "reasonable factors other than age" can also justify a difference in treatment. What seems more generous than the European directive is, however, interpreted very much narrower: Some see this as a justification only for indirect discrimination because a "reasonable factor other than age" is not at all conceivable in cases of direct discrimination. The courts do not go this far, but do not accept a justification in cases when the submitted reason is in close connection with age – e.g. the possibility of drawing a pension (cf. White v. Westinghouse Electric Co., 862 F2 d 56 [3rd Cir. 1988]; EEOC v. Bordens Inc. 724 F2 d 1390 [9th Cir. 1984]). For instance, a mandatory health check for civil servants over 70 years of age is not permitted (EEOC v. Commonwealth of Massachusetts, 987 F2 d 64 [1st Cir. 1993]), and a compulsory retirement age is not possible for most professions (extensively *Suk*, From antidiscrimination to equality: stereotypes and the life cycle in the United States and Europe, 60 Am. J. Comp. L. 2012, p. 75 *et seqq.*; *McMorrow*, Retirement and Worker Choice: Incentives to Retire and the ADEA, 29 Boston College L. Rev. 1988, p. 347 *et seqq.*).

73 In the well-known case Palacios de la Villa the *ECJ* did not specify when discrimination on grounds of age is justified (Case 411/05 – Palacios de la Villa [2007] ECR I-8531). The more recent decisions do not provide an general benchmark of justification either, the Court decides this on a case-by-case basis (cf. Case 152/11 – Odar [2012]; Case 141/11 – Hörnfeldt [2012]; Case 132/11 – Tyrolean Airways [2012]; Case 447/09 – Prigge [2011]; Case 297/10 – Hennigs [2011]; Cases 250/09 and 268/09 – Georgiev [2010], 42; Case 45/09 – Rosenbladt [2010]; Case 499/08 – Andersen [2010]; Case 246/09 – Bulicke [2010]; Case 341/08 – Petersen [2010]; Case 88/08 – Hütter [2009] ECR I-5325; Case 388/07 – Age Concern England [2009] ECR I-1569; Case 427/06 – Bartsch [2008] ECR I-7245).

b) Particular issues: Remuneration levels

74 Remuneration for work performed tends to rise with the years. Therein lies a social benefit which is often justified by reasons such as higher living standards and greater health costs in old age. This is usually unsuccessful. Rather, age-related remuneration levels are oftentimes discriminatory because they are compensatorily based on the life work cycle: As the peak of work performance in most professions is reached many years before reaching retirement, yet pay increases in many cases towards the end, in a long-term employment relationship the too low pay at the time of higher performance is compensated with increased pay at the time of lower productivity. Employees that begin work in a certain company must – without contractual or legislative protection against age discrimination – take into account that the employer may want to part from them towards the end of the employment relationship, in order to avoid the increased remuneration obligations. The age discrimination prohibition prevents such opportunistic behaviour on the employer's part – first of all by forbidding dismissal on grounds of age alone, but also by not allowing, and if so, then only to a very small extent, age-related remuneration. This is reason enough to welcome such protection. However, a higher financial need on account of the social environment (age, family status) has so far been a recognized element of remuneration at least to some extent (*Wiedemann*, Die Gleichbehandlungsgebote im Arbeitsrecht, 2001, p. 47; *Schiek*, Torn Between Arithmetic and Substantive Equality? Perspectives on Equality in German Labour Law, 18 International Journal of Comparative Law and Industrial Relations, 2002, No. 2, 149 *et seqq.*).

75 The employer who bases granting a benefit to an employee on **company loyalty**, does not differentiate by age, however he does differentiate by a criterion that is

typically more likely to occur in older employees. Thus, the rules on justification of indirect discrimination apply. Remuneration for company loyalty certainly represents a legitimate aim and so only the extent of possible differentiations remains open to debate. The employer's freedom of discretion should not be too constricted in this case. For instance, even the framework agreement on fixed-term work (contained in Directive 99/70/EC) recognizes that the wish to make certain benefits subject to length of service is a sufficient justification for a difference in treatment. However, proportionality must be taken into account (see also the opinion of Advocate General *Maduro* in Case 17/05 – Cadman [2006] ECR I-9583 regarding indirect sex discrimination). Some legal systems prescribe this sometimes explicitly. For the differentiation of remuneration based on length of service, which is considered indirect discrimination by age, Schedule 9, Part 2, sec. 10 Equality Act 2010 states that "It is not an age contravention for a person (A) to put a person (B) at a disadvantage when compared with another (C), in relation to the provision of a benefit, facility or service in so far as the disadvantage is because B has a shorter period of service than C". This is also true in essence for German law and probably for the law of other countries too. In which cases a differentiation by length of service shall not be considered unreasonable pursuant to this is difficult to say in the abstract. Particularly when the issue is not basic pay but additional social benefits, a differentiation is probably legal. Yet, differentiation of pay based on length of service may not simply be a **circuitous way to discriminate by age**. That would be the case for example if an employer were to take past service from which the employer did not benefit into account – without substantive reason. Collective agreements in particular must be reviewed with regard to this.

This is also the line that the *ECJ* followed in the **Cadman decision** (Case 17/05 – Cadman [2006] ECR I-9583). The *ECJ* ruled that employers were allowed to take recourse to the criterion of length of service in principle in order to determine remuneration level without needing to provide special justification ("recourse to the criterion of length of service is appropriate to attain the legitimate objective of rewarding experience acquired which enables the worker to perform his duties better [...]"). A remuneration system based on length of service is in general not at variance with the principle of equal pay for men and women. Where a worker doubts such a system and provides evidence capable of giving rise to serious doubts, the employer has to prove specifically that recourse to that criterion is appropriate. The same then applies not only to indirect discrimination based on sex but also indirect discrimination based on age. 76

This decision was confirmed and substantiated by the *ECJ* on 8 September 2011 with regard to two references for a preliminary ruling (Case 297/10 – **Sabine Hennigs v Eisenbahn-Bundesamt** und Case 298/10 **Land Berlin v Alexander Mai**). Even a rule on pay in a collective agreement (specifically, the case regarded collective agreements in the public sector) that determines the basic pay of an employee within a salary group according to age categories, constitutes discrimination against younger employees and infringes the prohibition of age discrimination in EU law. The Court did not accept the argument that older employees have greater financial needs which justifies age discrimination. It called into question that the financial needs of employees increase with age. At any rate this assumption would not suffice to justify age discrimination. The fact that Art. 28 of the Charter recognizes the right of collective bargaining and to conclude collective agreements does not change the approach to be taken to the issue. 77

Where the distinction is made by length of service this will not constitute unjustified age discrimination because the length of service represents professional experience which justifies the distinction. Therefore, only where the length of service – not the age of the employee – is the distinguishing factor in a pay system will this not constitute unlawful discrimination. However, the *ECJ* also held that Arts. 2 and 3(1) of Directive 2000/78/EC as well as Art. 28 of the Charter do not preclude a rule in a collective agreement that maintains, for a transitional period limited in time, some of the discriminatory effects of the earlier system in order to ensure that employees in post are transferred to the new system without suffering a loss of income.

c) Particular issues: Age limit in hiring

78 As the age of a person is classified as a forbidden distinguishing factor by Art. 1 of Directive 2000/78/EC, the question arises whether age limits can be justifiable in the hiring situation: In principle, they are justifiable (see e. g. § 10 No. 3 of the German Allgemeines Gleichbehandlungsgesetz (AGG)), because an extensive familiarization at the workplace must be accompanied by an economically reasonable minimum period of productive performance which is not the case with older workers whose retirement is foreseeable. Here too though, the **principle of proportionality** applies which draws stricter limits around such restrictions than can often be found in practice. When personnel fluctuation is so high that a large portion of employees leave the company before reaching retirement age then this argument is not effective, in the same way it is not effective when a considerable portion of younger employees change employers in that amount of time: if only few employees in actual fact stay with the company for ten years then 55-year-old applicants cannot be rejected with the argument that an extensive familiarization would not be reasonable. This does not apply in companies where personnel fluctuation is low. Where companies keep their employees for a long time, the costs invested in familiarization and training are recouped to a much larger extent. The answer to the question of which age limit is justified therefore depends on the case at hand. Nevertheless, it would be wise to develop some guidelines in order to guarantee a certain level of legal certainty.

79 When looking for **successors for executive positions** it can be justified to even set a very young age limit. What is significant is how much time it usually takes in that company to achieve the executive position strived for and how much time is then reasonable to be able to carry out this position in the company. Generally speaking, age limits are more acceptable where they are phrased as soft targets with the possibility of individual assessment, compared to hard exemption criteria that exclude an applicant from the selection pool even when he or she only slightly exceeds the limit ("The applicant should be in his/her early 40s" is therefore preferable to "We are looking for applicants no older than 45").

80 Indirect discrimination based on age that has a similar effect as setting an age limit or requiring a minimum age, is the requirement of a certain amount of years of **work experience**. As a minimum requirement this can be justified by the demands of the job and can also be permissible as a maximum limit in order to keep away overqualified applicants ("We are looking for applicants with 3 to 6 years of experience"). With respect to avoiding overqualifications it may be appropriate in all probability to apply stricter standards than in the case of a minimum period of work experience. The danger of circumvention of the prohibition of age discrimination is evident.

d) Particular issues: dismissal and age; mandatory retirement

81 The consequences of the prohibition of age discrimination with respect to dismissals are still unsettled to a large extent.

82 **Limiting** or **prohibiting termination** of the employment relationship after a certain age is already covered by the possibility of positive measures under Art. 7 of

Directive 2000/78/EC. The courts do not have to intervene where collective agreement provisions render older employees interminable or prescribe longer notice periods with increasing length of service. The older employee as a rule bears a higher risk of dismissal and has less chance of reintegration into the labour market. Employers and parties to collective agreements can compensate for this disadvantage. It is therefore justified to extend notice periods for employees that have been in service for a longer period – which as a rule applies to older employees (constituting indirect discrimination against younger employees).

The ECJ rulings concerning forced retirement were difficult to predict. Now some questions are settled: In Fuchs v Land Hessen [2011] 077 PBLR – (Case C-159/10), the ECJ ruled that a mandatory retirement age can be objectively justified on the grounds of "establishing a balanced age structure in order to encourage the recruitment and promotion of young people, [and] to improve personnel management." In Hörnfeldt (Case C-141/11) the court interpreted the European law as not precluding a national measure, which allows an employer to terminate an employee's employment contract on the sole ground that the employee has reached the age of 67 and which does not take account of the level of the retirement pension which the person concerned will receive, as that measure is objectively and reasonably justified by a legitimate aim relating to employment policy and labour-market policy and constitutes an appropriate and necessary means by which to achieve that aim. On the other hand: In Prigge v Deutsche Lufthansa (Case C-447/09) the ECJ held that mandatory retirement of pilots at the age of 60 was contrary to Directive 2000/78/EC, mainly because the fact that international and German legislation permitted pilots to work to the age of 65 provided certain conditions were met. 83

A national provision that provides that a notice period increases progressively with the length of the employee's employment relationship but does not allow the length of employment periods prior to the completion of the employee's 25th year of age to be taken into account in calculating the length of the employment relationship violates European law (Case 555/07 – Kücükdeveci [2010]). According to the *ECJ*, this inherent discrimination of younger employees cannot be justified by objective reasons and constitutes a violation of the primary law prohibition of age discrimination which has a direct effect vis-à-vis private parties. As the Court derives the prohibition from primary law, it does not matter that the Directive 2000/78/EC has no direct horizontal effect. This doctrinal conception received some criticism (see *Thüsing/Horler*, 47 C.M.L.R. 2010, 1161 *et seqq.*). 84

VII. Common problems in the directives

Aside from defining the individual discrimination criteria, one may seize upon common issues relevant to all anti-discrimination directives. 85

1. The forms of discrimination – Harassment

Here, the Directives 2000/43/EC, 2000/78/EC and 2006/54/EC have supplied direct and indirect discrimination with a third form, the effects of which are very difficult to predict. Under Art. 2(3) of Directives 2000/43/EC and 2000/78/EC "Harassment shall be deemed to be discrimination within the meaning of paragraph 1, when an unwanted conduct related to racial or ethnic origin takes place with the purpose or effect of violating the dignity of a person and of creating an intimidating, hostile, degrading, humiliating or offensive environment". A similar definition is contained in Art. 2(1)(c) of Directive 2006/54/EC. 86

a) Harassment as discrimination

87 To implement protection against harassment by means of an equal treatment principle is quite a new concept for European law. The directive on discrimination against women did not contain such a provision and consequently the German, French and English discrimination prohibitions did not include harassment protection. Existing protection of employees against sexual harassment at work is achieved by the enactment of independent laws. This alone seems to suggest that the one thing has little to do with the other.

88 This is confirmed by an intuitive evaluation: Intimidations, hostility and insults are to be eliminated not because they constitute a difference in treatment but because it is an **infringement upon the dignity and personal rights** of the affected employee. These actions do not become more acceptable if the employer were to insult all his employees indiscriminately. This is almost self-explanatory and the structure of the equal treatment principle shows why: discrimination prohibitions are intended to avoid the injustice created when otherwise legitimate behaviour becomes unjust through inequitable differentiation. The father who makes his son a gift of a car on his reaching maturity does not act inequitably, nor does the father who gives a more modest present. But if a father gives one son a car and the other son a bicycle on the same occasion, then this is unequal treatment which strikes us as inequitable. With regard to insulting behaviour, as with any inappropriate behaviour against an employee, we need no comparison with other employees to identify the inequity. **The injustice lies in the behaviour itself, not in a comparison with other behaviours**. Precisely this is the reason why it is not immediately clear why an employer should be judged differently according to whether he insults employees in terms of their age or their taste in music. Equally, why should derogatory references to a homosexual be assessed differently to insulting remarks about the employee's nationality? In all these instances the employer has engaged in insulting behaviour and he must desist from it whatever its form.

89 How relying on discrimination protection can be problematic, can be shown in a US-American decision: In that case an employer who was attracted to both sexes had sexually harassed male and female employees. There was no difference in treatment towards the sexes in his behaviour and so the protection of Title VII Civil Rights Act could not be applied. A certainly questionable result (of this opinion is in any case the Court of Appeals for the 7th Circuit: Hohlman v. Indiana, 82 Fep. Cases 1287, 1 May, 2000; on this issue *Thüsing*, NZA 2001, 939; from a British perspective on the so-called **"equal opportunity harasser"** see the winding arguments of Lord *Nicholls of Birkenhead* in Pearce v. Governing Body of Mayfield School [2003] IRLR 512. "Degrading treatment of this nature differs materially from unpleasant treatment inflicted on an equally disliked male colleague, regardless of equality of overall unpleasantness[…]. Because the form of the harassment is gender specific, there is no need to look for a male comparator. It would be no defence to a complaint of sexual harassment that a person of the opposite sex would have been similarly treated […].").

90 Nevertheless, it is possible in theory to class such behaviour as discrimination even if this goes beyond the specific concerns of the equality principle: If an employee is insulted because he is black, therein lies less favourable treatment of the coloured person compared to other employees, precisely because he is a black employee. The difference here between this and other cases of discrimination lies only in the fact that the employee suffers no financial disadvantage; his disadvantage is of a non-pecuniary nature.

b) Why hostile environment?

91 It may initially strike us as surprising that the Directive does not regard every insult towards an employee by an employer as impermissible treatment, but only those which impinge on the working environment. The concept of equal treatment implies no such limitation, seeing not the gravity and range of the insult as decisive, but the prejudicial treatment when compared with the treatment of those not

insulted. Here too, examination of US employment law is helpful, where for over 30 years courts have consistently held that insulting behaviour can constitute discrimination, leading case: Vinson v. Meritor Savings Bank (477 U.S. 57 [1986]). With regard to this, two types of cases may be distinguished from one another. Firstly, there is the so-called *quid pro quo* harassment in which advantages are promised or disadvantages threatened in order to illicit a specific behaviour relating to grounds of prohibited discrimination. Secondly, there is hostile environment harassment which is culpable behaviour on the part of an employer which creates or permits a working environment in which harassment based on grounds of prohibited discrimination is rendered more likely to occur. While the first alternative is gaining importance exclusively in the sexual harassment area, the second alternative is also applicable to other grounds of discrimination. In practice, apart from sexual discrimination, the cases almost always concern racial discrimination, and these were also the first in which the legal concept of the hostile environment was developed by the courts. This requirement was inferred from the wording of *Title VII Civil Rights Act*, under which it is necessary that the employer's harassment alters the terms and conditions of employment, see section 703 (a) (1). Immaterial prejudicing as a result of harassment, which itself has no direct relation to contractual employment obligations, only fulfils this requirement if the working environment becomes hostile. The European legislature adopted this criterion under Art. 3(3) of Directive 2000/43/EC, and Art. 2(3) of Directive 2000/78/EC.

2. Special equality protection as unjustified discrimination

After reviewing the reasons for discrimination and its possible forms, it seems 92
fitting to take a step back and have a look at the directive as a whole. **European discrimination protection** has been extended considerably, yet it **remains imperfect**. As long as discrimination is limited to a list of forbidden discrimination criteria, there will always be discrimination based on prejudicial reasons which will remain lawful. The reasons for special discrimination protection are not prescribed by nature; they are based on society's choice. The national regulations previously referred to at various points show that very different emphasis can be applied here:

Ireland, for instance, recognizes the prohibition of discrimination against mem- 93
bers of the traveller community, **France** forbids employers to discriminate against employees based on their political views, family status and customs ("*moeurs*"), the **Dutch** general equal treatment principle also forbids discrimination based on nationality. All these are arguably no less important grounds for discrimination and still, European law leaves them out. In the **USA** they are currently discussing extending *Title VII Civil Rights Act* to include discrimination based on sexual orientation. A generally accepted argument of the opposition is the idea that the various special equality propositions represent a turning away from the general equality idea and such laws could be unconstitutional (cf. particularly the debate in Romer v. Evans, 116 S. Ct. 1620: The Supreme Court ruled the amendment to the Colorado state constitution that would have prevented any city, town or county in the state from taking any action to protect homosexuals against discrimination unconstitutional). When individual groups are singled out and put under equality protection which is not granted to others, a difference in treatment is implemented for which one cannot always find a reason.

3. Discrimination by discrimination protection – Affirmative action under Art. 5 of Directive 2000/43/EC and Art. 7 of Directive 2000/78/EC

94 The difference in treatment of those left out of the special discrimination protection is enhanced by the special rule of Art. 5 of Directive 2000/43/EC and Art. 7 of Directive 2000/78/EC. According to this, the equal treatment principle does not prevent the Member States to ensure "full" equality in practice from maintaining or adopting specific measures to prevent or compensate for disadvantages linked to one of the forbidden discrimination criteria. This feels familiar at first glance considering that such provisions are also contained in Art. 157(4) TFEU and previously in Art. 2(4) of Directive 76/207/EEC (now Art. 3 of Directive 2006/54/EC). Nevertheless, one must sit up and take notice here, because the wording of the said directives once again do not reveal any doctrinal concept of promoting discriminated groups – just as the earlier completely different wording contained in the Commission's proposal (there it states in Art. 6: "This Directive shall be without prejudice to the right of the Member States to maintain measures to prevent or compensate for disadvantages suffered by person that are linked to any of the grounds referred to in Art. 1"). No account is taken of the fact that even though privileging previously disadvantaged groups can be permissible, the equality principle must be applied even to this privileging, in other words: it remains to be seen what the relationship between legal equality and substantial equality (this is most likely meant with "full equality") will be.

95 This problem is well-known by all means. A women's quota is only allowed as a soft quota, and a hard quota was ruled to be unlawful discrimination by the *ECJ* (cf. Case 450/93 – Kalanke [1995] ECR I-3051 – Frauenförderungsgesetz *(Act to Promote Women)* of Bremen, compared to Case 409/95 – Marschall [1997] ECR I-6363 – Frauenförderungsgesetz of North Rhine-Westphalia and Case 158/97 – Badeck and Others [2000] ECR I-1875 – Frauenförderungsgesetz of Hessen). The *ECJ* (Case 407/98 – Abrahamsson and Anderson [2000] ECR I-5539) declared a Swedish positive action regulation to be unlawful, *inter alia* because it also provided for women to be prioritized even when less qualified. In this case a woman was given priority for a promotion over male applicants even though she was less suitable than her competitors. This was unlawful notwithstanding the fact that the directive does not state as a requirement for positive measures that the privileged employee must be at least equally qualified as the disadvantaged colleague. But the *ECJ* was clear on this: provided that the candidates possess equivalent or "substantially equivalent" (whatever that is supposed to mean; explicitly in case 407/98 – Abrahamsson and Anderson [2000] ECR I-5539, para. 62) merits, a candidate belonging to the under-represented sex may be granted preference, as long as the candidatures are subject of an objective assessment which takes account of the specific personal situations of all candidates. This last decision especially shows that the goal that the Court wishes to achieve will most likely remain hidden in the fog of doctrinally unsubstantiable dicta: a reasonable line between substantially equivalent and not equivalent cannot be drawn.

96 Here too the law in the **United States** is some years ahead of us. *Affirmative action* according to rulings of the *U.S. Supreme Court* is only allowed if it is an appropriate means to compensate for disadvantages suffered in the past at the hands of the employers, and if it is reasonable "to remedy past discrimination". Consequently,

state laws enacted to privilege women were declared unlawful with reference to the *equal protection clause* because the advantage was not sufficiently linked to a specific disadvantage in the past (cf. particularly two decisions from the year 1977: In this case a law [Califano v. Webster, 430 U.S. 313] which provided that the *social security benefits* of widows was higher than that of widowers, was held to be effective [women in the past had fewer possibilities to support themselves by working], however, a law that required only men to prove dependency in order to be entitled to survivor's benefits, was held to be unlawful [Califano v. Goldfarb, 430 U.S. 199]). This still shows close similarities to European law. Particularly in employment law the USA is more concrete: here, it is not injustice in general that matters; rather, an employer may only give preference to an employee group if there are indications that this *minority group* has been disadvantaged in the past specifically by employers or an industry (Leading cases: Wygant v. Jackson Board of Education, 476 U.S. 267 [1986]; *Johnson v. Transportation Agency*, 480 U.S. 616 [1987]. See hereunto also *Urofsky*, Affirmative Action on Trial: Sex Discrimination in Johnson v. Santa Clara, 1997; *Leiter/Leiter*, Affirmative Action in Antidiscrimination Law and Policy: An Overview and Synthesis, 2011; *Gunther/Sullivan*, Constitutional Law, 2010, p. 810 *et seqq.*). The justification of this collective advantage by the circumstance that in the past (or even still today outside of the law) there was a collective disadvantage is made narrower by moving away from regarding employers as a group to looking at the individual employer. Yet in contrast, it is by all means possible to give preference to employees of a protected group even if they are less qualified or less suitable compared to an employee not belonging to this group. The decisive factor is the degree of the protected group's disadvantage and how far away they are from equality in terms of quota (an instructive overview is offered by *Rothstein/Craver/Schroeder*, Employment Law, 2009, § 2.16., pp. 144 *et seqq.*; see also the cautious considerations in Johnson v. Transportation Agency, 107 S. Ct. 1442 [1987]).

Case 476/99 – **Lommers** [2002] ECR I-2891

The Netherlands Ministry of Agriculture adopted a circular in 1993 advising Ministry staff that he was making available a certain number of nursery places to female staff. In 1995 128 places were available which meant a ratio of about one place for 20 female employees. Officials who obtained a nursery place from a waiting list had to make a parental contribution deducted from the official's salary with their permission.
Nursery places were exclusively available only to female employees of the Ministry, save in the case of an emergency, to be determined by the Director. An emergency for example could be the circumstance of a single father. The decision to reserve subsidised nursery places for women was taken because the number of available places was limited.
In 1995 Mr. Lommers, an official of the Ministry of Agriculture whose wife was employed in the private sector, applied for a nursery place to be reserved for his child. His request was rejected on the ground that children of male officials could only be given places in the nursery facilities in question in cases of emergency.
The making available of nursery places is to be regarded as a work condition according to the opinion of the *ECJ*. It held that there was a difference in

treatment on grounds of sex in this case. This was however justified: at the time when the Circular was adopted, the employment situation within the Ministry of Agriculture was characterised by a significant under-representation of women, both in terms of the number of women working there and their occupation of higher grades. Furthermore, a proven insufficiency of suitable and affordable nursery facilities is likely to induce female employees in particular to give up their jobs. According to the *ECJ* the measure in question grants women enjoyment of certain working conditions designed to facilitate their pursuit of, and progression in, their career. It falls in principle into the category of measures designed to improve their ability to compete in the labour market and to pursue a career on an equal footing with men. The Court ruled that regard was had to the principle of proportionality and that derogations must remain within the limits of what is appropriate and necessary.
Especially by stipulating the requirement of a proportionality test this decision represents a fundamental development of the law so far.

VIII. Parallel development: US-American Law

Parallel development: US-American Law		
Date	Legal Mechanism	Intended Effect
1940	States outside the South begin passing Fair Employment Practice laws.	Generally prohibit employment discrimination on the basis of race, color, religion, or national origin.
1964	Title VII of the Civil Rights Act of 1964	• Nation-wide prohibition against race discrimination in employment. • Anti-Discrimination law was expanded to include sex as a forbidden criterion. • Initially covered only employers with at least 100 employees.
1967	Age Discrimination Employment Act	Prohibition of age discrimination in employment.
1971	U.S. Supreme Court decision, *Griggs v. Duke Power Co.*	Unanimous court developed the disparate impact doctrine. This doctrine prohibited the application of neutral employment practices that had adverse effects on classes of workers protected under Title VII without the employer being able to demonstrate that the practices were justified by legitimate reasons.

Parallel development: US-American Law		
Date	Legal Mechanism	Intended Effect
1972	Equal Employment Opportunity Act of 1972	Lowered the number of employees necessary for an employer to be covered by Title VII to 15.
1976	U.S. Supreme Court decision, *Runyon v. McCrary*	Prohibition against racial discrimination extended to all employers. This decision expanded the century old 42 U.S.C. 1981 to provide a remedy for racial discrimination that was independent of Title VII.
1978	U.S. Supreme Court decision, *City of Los Angeles Dept. of Water & Power v. Manhart*	Prohibited actuarial based pension plans.
1978	The Pregnancy Discrimination Act of 1978	Prohibited exclusion of childbirth expenses from employer health insurance plans.
1986	U.S. Supreme Court decision, *Meritor Sav. Bank v. Vinson*	Banned sexual harassment as discriminatory.
1991	Americans with Disabilities Act	Prohibited employment discrimination based on employee disabilities.
1991	Civil Rights Act of 1991	• Permits jury trials for employment discrimination cases. • Allows plaintiff to sue employer for punitive damages.

The driving force of the progressive protection against discrimination in the international context was above all the **pioneering role of the USA**. Their discrimination prohibitions in employment law date back more than a generation earlier than the European legislation. Title VII Civil Rights Act has been a fundamental pillar of US-American employment law since 1964. It forbids discrimination based on *race, color, religion, sex or national origin* and has become a model example for numerous foreign legislative acts. Other discrimination prohibitions have followed: in 1967 the Age Discrimination in Employment Act with its differential rules to distinguish between employees by age, in 1990 the Americans with Disabilities Act, which was a milestone not only for employment law with respect to the protection and integration of handicapped people. The English versions of the anti-discrimination directives use the same wording in part with their American forerunners. And thus the almost 50 year experience of the American courts can give an indication as to what other courts could make of a comparable framework of provisions. Not in the sense that the issues we find beyond the Atlantic will arrive here too, but indeed in the sense that it could. The comparison of laws in this case offers not only a 97 supply of solutions showing how legal problems can be eliminated reasonably, but it also and above all shows which problems a new law can bring about, where conflicts will arise between employees and employers and how the courts can detect and structure categories in those cases. This approach was chosen by the *ECJ* particularly for discrimination law. In its leading case *Jenkins* (Case 96/80 – Jenkins [1981] ECR 911), in which it invented the concept of indirect discrimination for sex discrimination, even though it was not provided for by the wording of the directive, the Court referred to American experience. The opinions of the Advocate General refer specifically to the case *Griggs v. Duke-Power* (*Griggs v. Duke Power Company*, 401 U.S. 424 (1971)), where the American *Supreme Court* also invented this legal rule beyond the wording of the law (see § 1 para. 8). There are not too many limits to the possibility of a *legal transplant*, where a legal rule is moved from one legal system to another. In more recent opinions, too, the Advocate Generals draw on decisions of US courts concerning anti-discrimination law (see Advocate General *Jacobs* in his opinions of 27 October 2005 in the Case 227/04 – Lindorfer [2007] ECR I-6767 with reference to Los Angeles Department of Water and Power/ Manhart (1978) 435 US 702, 712 and 713). The most recent examples are the Advocate General *Kokott's* Opinions in the case Association Belge des Consommateurs Test-Achats (Opinions of 30 September 2010 in the Case C-236/09): This case concerned the question whether Art. 5(2) of Directive 2004/113/EC was void because primary law creates an obligation to offer unisex tariffs in the insurance sector, i. e. equal insurance premiums for men and women despite statistically differing life expectancies. The Advocate General also referred to the decision in Los Angeles Department of Water and Power/Manhart (1978) 435 US 702 in her arguments: "The Court would be keeping good company if it delivered such a judgment: more than 30 years ago the Supreme Court of the United States of America held in connection with pension insurance funds that the Civil Rights Act of 1964 prohibits different treatment of insured persons on the basis of their sex". The *ECJ* followed this in its final decision (*ECJ* of 1 March 2011, Case C-236/09 – Test-Achats). There will certainly be many more legal transplants in the future.

§ 4. Precarious Employment

Literature: *Bell*, Between flexicurity and fundamental social rights: the EU directives on atypical work, 37 European Law Journal 2012, 31–48; *Bell*, Achieving the Objectives of the Part-Time Work Directive? Revisiting the Part Time Workers Regulation, 40 Industrial Law Journal 2011, 254–279; *Buckley*, Missing the Point? The Part-time Workers (Prevention of Less favourable Treatment) Regulation 2000 (Sl. 2000, No. 1551), 29 Industrial Law Journal 2000, 260–267; *Casale*, The Employment Relationship: A Comparative Overview, 2011; *Countouris/Horton*, The Temporary Agency Work Directive: Another Broken Promise, 38 Industrial Law Journal, 329–338; *Directorate-General for Research & European Commission*, Precarious Employment in Europe: A Comparative Study of Labour Market Related Risks in Flexible Economies: ESOPE, 2011; *Fudge/Owens*, Precarious Work, Women and the New Economy: The Challenge to Legal Norms, 2006; *Heery/Salmon/Heery*, The Insecure Workforce, 2000; *Jeffrey*, The Commission Proposals on "Atypical Work": Back to the Drawing-board…Again, 24 Industrial Law Journal 1995, 296; *Koukiadaki*, Case Law Devolpments in the Area of Fixed-Term Work, 38 Industrial Law Journal 2009, 98–100; *Locke/Piore/Kochan*, Employment Relations in a Changing World Economy, 1995; *Rodgers/Rodgers*, Precarious Jobs in Labour Market Regulation: The Growth of Atypical Employment in Western Europe, 1989; *Schieck*, Agency Work – From Marginalisation towards Acceptance? Agency Work in EU Social and Employment Policy and the "implementation" of the draft Directive on Agency work into German Law 2006, 5 German Law Journal, 1233–1257; *Schomann/Rogowski/Kruppe*, Labour Market Efficiency in the European Union: Employment Protection and Fixed-Term Contracts, 1998; *Thornley/Jefferys/Appay*, Globalization and Precarious Forms of Production and Employment: Challenges for Workers and Unions, 2010; *Vosko*, Managing the Margins: Gender, Citizenship, and the International Regulation of Precarious Employment, 2011; *Vosko/MacDonald*, Gender and the Contours of Precarious Employment, 2009; *Zappala*, Abuse of Fixed-Term Employment Contracts and Sanctions in the Recent ECJ's Jurisprudence, 35 Industrial Law Journal 2006, 439–444.

I. Category

European employment law is comprised of a very diverse blend of regulations. All 1
provisions have one thing in common: the objective expressed in Art. 151 TFEU to improve and harmonize living and working conditions. Some regulations set up general standards of protection that apply to all employment relationships. These include protection against discrimination under the Directives 2002/73/EC (gender), Directive 2000/43/EC (race and ethnic origin) and 2000/78/EC (religion, disability, age and sexual identity), protection against collective redundancies under Directive 98/59/EC protection in the event of transfer of undertakings (Directive 2001/23/EC superseding Directive 77/187/EEC), the Information Directive (91/533/EEC) and the Working Time Directive (93/104/EC as amended by Directive 2000/34/EC). In addition, special standards of protection were created for specific groups of workers. These are, first and foremost, the Pregnant Workers Directive 92/85/EEC, the Protection of Young People Directive 94/33/EC, but also the Parental Leave Directive 2010/18/EU (superseding the Parental Leave Directive 96/34/EC). These focus on certain groups (pregnant workers, workers who have just given birth and those who are breastfeeding as well as "adolescents and young people" and "working parents"). Somewhere in between there are special standards of protection devised for

Precarious employment relationships

European employment law

General standards of protection for all employment relationships	Special standards of protection for atypical (precarious) employment relationships	Special standards of protection for particular groups of workers
e.g. Protection against discrimination, collective redundancies, transfer of undertakings, information about work conditions, working time	Safety at Work and Temporary Employment Directive 91/383/EEC Part-time Work Directive 97/81/EC Fixed-term Work Directive 1999/70/EC Temporary Agency Work Directive 2008/104/EC	Pregnant Workers Directive 92/85/EEC Parental Leave Directive 2010/18/EU Protection of Young People Directive 94/33/EC

"**precarious" employment** relationships, i. e. ones which are different from the standard employment relationship in terms of their contractual arrangement. The list so far is not exhaustive: No. 7 of the Community Charter of Fundamental Social Rights mentions "fixed-term contracts, part-time work, temporary work and seasonal work". But this can most certainly be extended to include further groups: home workers, teleworkers and on-call workers are equally in need of special protection.

2 This **generic term** is difficult to define. A common factor among atypical employment relationships is viewed by some to be the different contractual arrangement as regards the duration of the work contract and the working hours compared to the full-time long-term employment relationship. This however does not apply to temporary agency work because the only thing to change for the employees, who may be in a fixed-term full-time employment relationship, is the relevant place of work. It seems more accurate therefore to regard any increased vulnerability caused by the particular contractual arrangement as the relevant factor. Where there is any deviation from the standard employment relationship (consistent, full-time unlimited employment at one place of work, subject to instruction, integrated into the organizational structure), there could be a greater need for mandatory provisions to protect the worker.

3 The special standard of protection devised for precarious employment relationships has so far been achieved at European level by the Safety at Work-Temporary Work Directive 91/383/EEC, the Part-Time Work Directive 97/81/EC (extending to the UK by Directive 98/23/EC), the Fixed-Term Work Directive 99/70/EC and the Temporary Work Directive 2008/104/EC which the Member States must have implemented by the 5 of December 2011. The Green Paper "Modernising labour law to meet the challenges of the 21st century" (COM [2006] 708 final; for more on this see *Sciarra*, 36 Industrial Law Journal 2007, p. 375 *et seqq.*) tried to revitalise the issue. For one thing, the wording was changed: The term "precarious employment" borrowed from the French travail précaire was replaced by "**workers engaged on non-standard**

employment contracts". This term encompasses "fixed-term contracts, part-time contracts, on-call contracts, zero-hour contracts, contracts for workers hired through temporary employment agencies, freelance contracts, etc." Furthermore, the paper raised the question: "How might recruitment under permanent and temporary contracts be facilitated, whether by law or collective agreement, so as to allow for more flexibility within the framework of these contracts while ensuring adequate standards of employment security and social protection at the same time?" The answer to this will be crucial for the further developments of European labour law.

II. Part-time employment

**Part-time employment–
Development of legislation**

- First draft proposal of a Directive in December 1981 was not implemented

- Discrimination of part-time workers = indirect discrimination of women: ECJ 31 March 1981, ECR. 1981, 911 (Jenkins) -> diverse case-law

- 1989 no 7 Community Charter of Fundamental Social Rights; Directive Proposals for atypical employment at the beginning of the 1990s were not implemented

- Part-time Directive by virtue of framework agreement by the Social Partners 97/81/EC (initially without Great Britain who was later included by Directive 98/23/EC)

- Implementation by domestic legislation by 20 January 2000 (In Great Britain by 7 April 2000)

The road to today's European law on part-time employment was a long one. As 4
early as December 1981 the Commission submitted a first Directive proposal on part-time employment (COM [1981] 775 final of 22 December 1981) which was never passed – even in its amended version (OJ 1983, C 18/5 of 5 January 1983). This reluctance was particularly astonishing in the face of the *ECJ* addressing the issue of discrimination of part-time workers at almost the same time. It was the decision of 31 March 1981 in *Jenkins* where the Court first held that the European provisions on sex discrimination also prohibited indirect discrimination of women and therefore, in particular, the unfavourable treatment of part-time workers without objective justification (Case 96/80, [1981] ECR 911). The advancement of Community law, which the legislator had failed to contribute to, was then taken on by the judicature. In 1989 the improvement of living and working conditions in part-time employment was included in no. 7 of the Community Charter of Fundamental Social Rights which represented an important declaration of intent. However, the frequent attempts bore no fruits. Only a fraction of the Commission's Directive proposals on atypical

employment relationships of 3 August 1990 (COM [1990] 228 final; amended proposal of 9 November 1990, OJ 1990 C 305/8) were implemented by Directive 91/393/EEC; there is nothing here on part-time work. Most resistance came from Germany, but it was Great Britain that ultimately brought the proceedings to an end with their final veto (see *Jeffrey*, The Commission Proposals on "Atypical Work": Back to the Drawing-board again, ILJ 1995, pp. 296, 298). It was only when the social partners took on the issue based on the Social Treaty that it was given a fresh impetus. UNICE, CEEP and ETUC were able to agree on a framework agreement on part-time work which lead to the adoption of Directive 97/81/EC. The new law was then extended to also apply to Great Britain by Directive 98/23/EC.

5 Many European countries implemented the Directive by passing **relevant legislation**. Italy adopted the Decreto Legislativo Delegato No. 61 (25 February 2000); Germany adopted the Teilzeitbefristungsgesetz (TzBfG) which came into force on 1 January 2001; Spain implemented the Directive by the Real Decreto-Ley 19/1998 (29 November 1998); France adopted the loi no. 2000-37 (1 February 2000). For the implementation by the other member states see the implementation report (21 January 2003) by the Commissions's services available at: http://ec.europa.eu/social/main.jsp?catId=706&langId=en&intPageId=203.

1. The Part-time Work Directive 97/81/EC

6 The Part-time Work Directive stipulates only a few rules which are not contained in the Directive itself but in the framework agreement on part-time work annexed to it. The two most important provisions are the **prohibition of discrimination** in Clause 4 of the framework agreement (from now on I shall only refer to the clauses) and the employee's **right** – under certain conditions – **to switch from part-time to full-time work** and vice versa in Clause 5(3)(a) and (b). In addition, Clause 5(2) prohibits dismissals that are based on the employee's refusal to transfer from part-time to full-time. Also, employers are obligated to give information to their staff (Clause 5(3)(c)) and their representative bodies (Clause 5(3)(c)) in order to facilitate transfers from full-time to part-time work and vice versa. Furthermore, employers are encouraged to promote part-time work by facilitating access to part-time work as well as to vocational training. The guideline in Clause 5(1)(a) is directed at the Member States. They are to eliminate any obstacles to part-time work. Accordingly, governmental laws that, for instance, provide for stricter rules regarding formalities for part-time contracts compared to full-time contracts are unlawful (Case 56/07 – Michaeler and Subito GmbH [2008] ECR I–3135). There are few signs of any implementation problems; most issues appear to be straightforward and are guided by the clear provisions of the Directive.

a) Discrimination

7 The rule in Clause 4(1) has created a special case of discrimination which applies alongside the discrimination prohibitions of Directives 2002/73/EC (sex), 2000/43/EC (race and ethnic origin) and 2000/78/EC. However, there are still unresolved questions regarding the **relationship** of the prohibition of discrimination of part-time workers and **indirect sex discrimination**. It is submitted that they both exist side-by-side – the discrimination protection of part-time workers should complement and not limit the "general" discrimination protection.

8 The provisions of the Directive prohibit direct discrimination with regard to part-time work but not indirect discrimination. However, indirect discrimination can certainly be unlawful under the other discrimination laws. With regard to the standards that were developed for the other discrimination prohibitions, the same rules apply to this special discrimination provision.

b) Scope *ratione personae*

9 The scope *ratione personae* of the Directive, and thus of the prohibition of discrimination, is limited to part-time workers. A part-time worker is defined in Clause 3(1) as "an employee whose normal hours of work, calculated on a weekly basis or on average over a period of employment of up to one year, are less than the normal hours of work of a comparable full-time worker." This may sound straightforward but has occasionally raised some questions.

10 Firstly, uncertainty is caused by the **lack of any uniform definition** of employee or employment contract. As a result, one must revert to the laws of the individual Member States, pursuant to Clause 2(1). This is particularly significant for the Directive's application to civil servants – who are not "employees" e. g. under German. They are employed in public service (Art. 33(5) Grundgesetz) which is subject to the special rules of public law (see *Dütz/Thüsing*, Arbeitsrecht, 18th ed., 2013, chapter 2, para. 34). This is similar in Spanish law (Art. 8 Ley del estatuto básico del empleado público [LEBEP]). Whether the Directive still applies – which it does according to its clear wording – has remained unresolved. In *Gavieiro* (Case 444/09 and Case 456/09 [2010]) the *ECJ* seems to reject a literal application in the context of part-time work. It remains to be seen whether this rejection is desirable and will impact on all the other similar directives.

11 A case which was submitted for a preliminary ruling by the Highest Court of Austria concerned the interpretation of the Austrian Working Time Act and the question of applicability of employment and equal treatment laws on employment relationships where the working time of an employee was organised in such a way that her employer could seek her services depending on workload but she could refuse the offer of work at any time without having to justify the refusal. With respect to the latter the *ECJ* (Case 313/02 – Wippel [2004] ECR I-9483) held that this came within the scope of the framework agreement to Directive 97/81/EC.

12 The Directive also applies to so-called "vertical part-time work" (Case 395/08 and Case 396/08 – Bruno und Pettini). This is the case where part-time work consists of certain periods in which employees work full-time and other periods where the employees do not work at all. Overall this constitutes a part-time employment relationship which falls within the scope of the Directive.

c) Territorial scope

13 The Directive itself does not mention the territorial scope of the discrimination provisions. It can however be read into the definition of "comparable full-time worker": Under Clause 3(2) a **comparable full-time worker** means a full-time worker in the same establishment having the same type of employment contract or relationship, who is engaged in the same or a similar work/occupation. Due regard must also be given to other considerations which may include seniority, qualification and skills. In principle, the prohibition of discrimination therefore applies to workers within an individual company. This raises the question of what follows from there being no comparable employees within a company. There are two possibilities: For one thing,

the discrimination prohibition could be limited to the company itself in accordance with the clear wording of the Directive. Alternatively, without any comparable employees within the same company, a comparison could be drawn between part-time workers and comparable full-time employees that are employed elsewhere but on the basis of the same collective agreement or employees who would be considered comparable full-time workers in the same trade. This approach was taken by the German legislator in § 2(1) Teilzeit- und Befristungsgesetz (TzBfG). European law does not require such an application however. It is submitted that the territorial scope applies strictly within an individual company pursuant to Clause 4(1) in conjunction with Clause 3(2).

d) Comparative framework

14 Logically speaking, it is necessary to compare a part-time worker to another employee – in this case to a full-time employee – in order to determine whether discrimination is taking place (*Bell*, 40 Industrial Law Journal 2011, 254, 256 *et seq.*). This protection against discrimination does not mean that an employee is protected against unfavourable treatment, just against less favourable treatment compared to other employees. Consequently, when the comparable full-time workers carry out different work or have other qualifications or are of other seniority compared to part-time workers, it is not a question of having an objective reason (to be proven by the employer) but of there being unequal treatment (to be proven by the employee). Part-time workers and full-time workers must be engaged in **similar work**, pursuant to Clause 3(2). The term "similar work" is elaborated upon by the criteria listed in Clause 3(2) – it requires the same type of employment contract or relationship, the same or a similar work/occupation. To make the comparison, seniority, qualifications and skill level can be considered, however these criteria are not exhaustive but merely illustrative. Nevertheless, the requirement of comparability should not be interpreted too strictly, for there will be few completely identical jobs in a company. It is rather more practicable and conducive to the objective to consider the aim of the rule. Consequently, all similar, i. e. functionally interchangeable jobs, must be used to make the comparison. It is not necessary that an employee be interchangeable. The comparison must be made with respect to qualifications, work load and market value and especially with respect to the work to be performed. This application corresponds with the Directive's objective as it only requires similar but not identical work and does not apply the specifying criteria rigidly but on a case-by-case basis.

15 If comparable full-time workers or permanent workers are not treated all alike, it raises the question whom the part-time worker or fixed-term worker should be equal to. One could assume that the **comparison group** should invariably be the least favourable work conditions of full-time or permanent workers because any other difference in treatment cannot be different treatment based on part-time or fixed-term work. But this is not true in every case: Discrimination of a part-time worker can occur compared to a full-time worker who works under better conditions than his fellow full-time workers. If a worker's salary depends on the time of hire and the situation of the labour market, the part-time worker must be compared to the full-time worker hired at the same time, even if he earns more than a full-time worker who was hired at a much earlier date. If the two workers are treated differently, this indicates discrimination on grounds of part-time work. This way of application corresponds to the comparison benchmark described above, for it does not just distinguish between full-time and part-time but also applies a more detailed differentiation within these groups (such as mentioning the criterion of seniority).

Unfavourable treatment of a full-time worker switching to part-time work is also unlawful. Accumulated rights (such as paid annual leave) may not be reduced after switching to part-time work (Case 486/08 – Tirol [2010] ECR I-3527).

European labour law does not stipulate which **comparative framework** to use to detect discrimination. German law, for example, applies the group comparison method which is used in collective labour law pursuant to § 4 TzBfG (s. Annuß/ *Thüsing*, TzBfG, § 4 para. 24). In a group comparison, provisions of either the operational system or the system set up by the employer which have an inner coherence, are classified in groups (eg. provisions about basic pay and incentive pay are classified in one group). Comparability is given if a common reference point established by the above mentioned classification, refers to both groups of the employees. This is not mandatory however. English law allows an overall comparison in order to determine whether part-time workers are being discriminated against: "Where a fixed-term employee is treated by his employer less favourably than the employer treats a comparable permanent employee as regards any term of his contract, the treatment in question shall be regarded for the purposes of regulation 3(3)(b) as justified on objective grounds if the terms of the fixed-term employee's contract of employment, taken as a whole, are at least as favourable as the terms of the comparable permanent employee's contract of employment" (sec. 4(1) of The Fixed-term Employees (Prevention of Less Favourable Treatment) Regulations 2002). Hence, the English Law demands a comparison of the rules in their entirety. A poor standing in one point can be balanced by a better standing in another point. 16

The *ECJ* seems to be leaning towards the group comparison method (Case 246/09 – Bulicke [2010] ECR I-06999) – this application should normally lead to fairer results. The Directive does not however give any guidelines.

e) Specifying equal treatment – *pro-rata-temporis*-principle and complete equality

Clause 4(2) sets out the application of the *pro-rata-temporis*-principle with the provison that it should only be applied if appropriate (*Buckley*, 29 Industrial Law Journal 2000, 260, 262). The rule defines the equality principle in that the employer, as a rule, may only reduce a part-time employee's remuneration or payment in kind in proportion to the time worked (*pro-rata-temporis*). This definition is necessary as it does not follow from the equality principle itself. 17

Example 1: A collective agreement cuts all employees' – part-time as well as full-time – Christmas bonuses by 1 000 EUR. Both groups are treated equally but due to the difference in hours and salary the disadvantage is in effect more severe for one than for the other. To do this would therefore be unlawful. 18

Example 2: A collective agreement cuts all employees' – part-time as well as full-time – Christmas bonuses by 20 %. Both groups are treated equally looking at the percentage, but they are treated unequally if you look at the total sum. Even though the financial burden is in fact heavier for the part-time worker who earns a lower salary, this should not be taken to mean more favourable treatment of the full-time worker; if this means a higher deduction from the full-time worker's salary, it should not be taken to mean more favourable treatment of the part-time workers.

Example 3: A collective agreement cuts all employees' – part-time as well as full-time – Christmas bonuses; by 20 % for the full-time workers, by 10 % for the part-time workers. Both groups are treated unequally. The (lower earning) part-time workers are formally treated more favourably (i. e. treated unequally) in order to achieve an economically comparable burden (i. e. equal treatment in effect, which corresponds to the equality theory in tax law which targets a de facto equality with its progressive income tax). This more favourable treatment is unequal treatment expressly allowed by Clause 4(1) ("shall not be treated in a less favourable manner ").

19 As Clause 4(2) merely specifies the principle in Clause 4(1), the *pro-rata-temporis*-principle need not be applied if this is justified on objective grounds – though the wording of the provision has been misinterpreted in the past by not being read in conjunction with paragraph 1. The legislator actually said exactly what he wanted to say: Equality with regard to payment must be understood as proportional equality (as in example 2) and more favourable treatment of part-time workers (as in example 3) should not be prohibited.

20 The requirements of the *pro-rata-temporis*-principle are therefore the same as those of the general equality principle. Even the specifically mentioned criterion of appropriateness has little significance on its own and does not require more than the general standard for justifying discrimination (see § 3 para. 22).

21 Obviously, the *pro-rata-temporis*-principle does not apply for rights already acquired. An existing right to annual paid leave may not be reduced when an employee switches from full-time to part-time work (Case 486/08 – Tirol [2010] ECR I-3527).

f) More favourable treatment

22 If a part-time or fixed-term worker is treated more favourably than a full-time or permanent worker, this does not constitute discrimination within the meaning of Clause 4(1). This provision only forbids less favourable treatment of part-time workers and not less favourable treatment of full-time workers. An employer may therefore give part-time workers the same benefits he gives full-time workers (cf. the facts in Mt. 20, 1–16 [**workers in the vineyard**]). Though not required, it may be permissible to give part-time workers overtime payments from the first hour onwards or not have part-timers work overtime at all.

23 However, this may constitute a **violation of the equality principle** which is said to also exist in European law (Case 144/04 – Mangold [2005] ECR I-9981) which applies to both – more favourable and less favourable treatment. This principle will prevent this kind of unjustified more favourable treatment of part-time workers in future because the understanding of equality underlying the *pro-rata-temporis*-principle also applies to the general equality principle. To *generally* allow a part-time bonus (or fixed-term bonus) is therefore just as unconvincing as seeing part-time work as a reason for less favourable treatment. In such cases there could also be indirect discrimination on grounds of sex – for women account for the majority of part-time workers (*Bell*, 37 European Law Journal 2012, 31, 43). Directive 2002/73/EC does not allow more favourable treatment of a particular sex, so proof must be given that there is a concrete economic disadvantage to be offset (see § 3 para. 27 *et seqq.* and 31). However, the legal significance of this question is quite limited.

Justification of more favourable treatment – which must be determined in each individual case – may be to make up for specific disadvantages that are connected to part-time work (such as the fact that part-time workers spend more time travelling to work relative to the amount of working time).

However, these principles relating to more favourable treatment may only be applied to the prohibition of discrimination. Other requirements of the directive apply equally to both part-time and full-time workers, e.g. the provision of information (Clause 5(3)(c)) or dismissal protection (Clause 5(2)). 24

g) Justification

As known from discrimination law, less favourable treatment of part-time workers is only forbidden as far as it is not justified. Under the last part of Clause 4(1) this requirement is met when the treatment is unequal for **objective reasons** (*Bell*, 40 Industrial Law Journal 2011, 254, 263 *et seq.*). The fleshing out of these vague requirements is left to the Member States. Systematically, discrimination on grounds of part-time work must be seen as a special case of indirect discrimination on grounds of age (Case 204/04 Commission v. Germany [2006]) – for this reason the principles developed in the context of Art. 2(2) second indent of Directive 76/207/EEC as amended by Directive 2002/73/EC apply. Objective grounds exist when the discrimination is supported by a legitimate aim and is necessary and appropriate. A strict standard must be applied in this respect. Also, it follows from this application that an only putative objective reason will not suffice to constitute justification. Moreover, the employer must have specifically acted on account of the objective reason. It is not enough for the reason to exist as then the discrimination will not have been based on objective grounds. *ECJ* jurisprudence on Art. 13 EG (now Art. 19 TFEU) can be applied here: unequal treatment is justified when based on objective reasons where that "objective corresponds to a real need on the part of the undertaking and the means chosen for achieving it are appropriate and necessary" (Case 170/84 – Bilka [1986] ECR 1607; for more case law on the principle of equal-treatment see *Bell*, 37 European Law Journal, 31, 45 *et seqq.*). If an objective reason exists, the measure is justified even if the distinguishing factor is necessarily associated only with the part-time or full-time worker, for the same applies to discriminating by sex. 25

This kind of justification is possible for all types of less favourable treatment, including remuneration. Here too it is possible to depart from the *pro-rata-temporis*-principle of Clause 4(2) for objective reasons. This possibility can be derived for one thing from the fact that this principle is merely a sub-category of the general equality principle; for another, the wording "where appropriate" shows that a departure must be possible. 26

h) Legal consequences

Which consequences follow from such discrimination? Unlike the anti-discrimination directives which set out specific sanctions, Directive 97/81/EC does not provide for any express consequences. The prohibition of discrimination must however result in the discriminatory condition being void – not the part-time work as a whole, just the specific unequal treatment will be void. As a result, this condition must be replaced by the more favourable condition, i.e. the condition that applies to the comparable full-time worker who is being treated most favourably. Pursuant to the *ECJ* case-law there must be an **"upward adjustment"** (Case 33/89 – Kowalska [1990] 27

ECR I-2591). It should be noted however that only relative equality with the full-time workers along the lines of the *pro-rata-temporis*-principle is necessary, not absolute equality (i. e. if part-time workers are denied an additional benefit given to full-time workers, this benefit must be granted to the part-time workers proportionately). The described principles would at any rate have an *ex nunc* effect.

28 The directive gives no indication however whether these principles can be applied with respect to the past (*ex tunc*). The language of the directive is surprisingly vague on this point. Whereas the wording of the prohibition of discrimination in conjunction with the objective of the law clearly means that part-time workers must be treated equally in future, this does not necessarily apply to the past. It may be one of the directive's aims to promote and protect the equality of full-time and part-time workers, but to derive a past effect from this is debatable. Moreover, the provisions do not stipulate sanctions (such as a duty to pay for damages). Such a provision would be a strong indication that equality should be established retroactively – the causal damage then being lack of or insufficient granting of benefits. It should be noted that discrimination on grounds of part-time work was developed as a special case of indirect discrimination on grounds of age. Directive 2002/73/EC provides for an express duty to impose sanctions in Art. 8 d in order to secure an efficient application of the Directive. These could include compensation for damages and must be "effective, proportionate and dissuasive". This effect combined with the principle of *effet utile* means that any benefit must be granted retroactively, as far as this is actually possible. In this respect, the discrimination law principles apply here too (cf. § 3 paras. 18 *et seqq.*). Consequently, a retroactive adjustment seems to be obligatory. It is therefore imperative to grant benefits retroactively until the statute of limitations expires.

2. Extension and reduction of working time

29 Under Clause 5(3)(a) and (b) the employer is obligated to consider "requests by workers to transfer from full-time to part-time work that becomes available in the establishment" and "requests by workers to transfer from part-time to full-time work or to increase their working time should the opportunity arise" as far as possible. This phrasing indicates voluntary cooperation on the employer's part. It is certainly not a **mandatory provision**. Nevertheless, although the provision does not stipulate a mandatory requirement, it is not completely non-binding either. Instead, the provision expresses that the transfer from full-time to part-time should be facilitated. The Directive is addressed to the Member States and not the employers as such. They are required to make the transfer between these work forms flexible. The Member States can, but do not have to, introduce an obligation to transfer. Furthermore, the fact that, generally, employers need not promote transfers between full-time and part-time work, is shown by the fact that transfer requests are only to be considered "as far as possible". In turn, it can be concluded from this phrasing that the Directive only wishes to promote transfers if they can be implemented by the employer without difficulty, not however if operational circumstances do not allow it.

3. Obligations to provide information

30 Clause 5(3)(c) establishes a specific obligation to provide information. Employers should provide "timely information on the availability of part-time and full-

time positions in the establishment [...]". The wording of the Directive suggests that this does not mean a duty on the employer's part in the strict sense of the word – he should merely make an effort to provide the information. The requirement to make an effort alone does not constitute an obligation, the phrasing is even less committal than the corresponding provisions in Clause 5(3)(a) and (b). The same applies to the obligation to provide information to representative bodies under Clause 5(3)(e). This provision also merely serves to encourage the Member States to implement suitable measures and similar provisions to facilitate transfers.

4. Promotional measures

The requirements in Clause 5(3)(d) regarding positive measures to promote 31 access to part-time work or access by part-time workers to vocational training does not need much elaboration (for more on this see *Bell*, 40 Industrial Law Journal 2011, 254, 265). Employers are only required to "give consideration" to measures but are not obligated to do so. Nevertheless, under particular circumstances it could constitute discrimination within the meaning of Clause 4(1) if different levels of access to vocational training are granted to full-time and part-time workers. The principles described above then apply.

5. Dismissal protection

Aside from the equality provisions already described, the protection of part-time 32 workers should also include specific dismissal protection laws, Clause 5(2). This clarifies that the refusal to transfer from full-time to part-time or vice versa does not constitute a valid reason for dismissal, irrespective whether this behaviour could constitute a valid reason under general principles. Despite this fact, dismissal for other reasons – such as operational grounds – is still possible. The worker is only meant to be protected against a dismissal based on the reasons illustrated (*Bell*, 40 Industrial Law Journal 2011, 254, 276).

III. Fixed-term work

1. Genesis and content

For the most part, the development of European law with respect to fixed-term 33 employment ran more or less parallel to the legislation of part-time work; legislation of the two forms of work could usually be found in the same directives. It is only recently that they have evolved independently of each other. Provisions regulating fixed-term employment were included in the Directive 91/383/EEC, and therefore preceded part-time work legislation, whereas the framework agreement between EGB, UNICE and CEEP on fixed-term employment contracts was not adopted till 18 March 1999. This became Directive 1999/70/EC which included the framework agreement in its annex. The Directive's most important provision is probably Clause 5(1) of the framework agreement on fixed-term employment contracts (henceforth only the Clause will be named) regarding measures to prevent abuse arising from the use of successive fixed-term employment contracts (*Koukiadaki*, 38 Industrial Law Journal 2009, 89 *et seq.*). Pursuant to this, the Member State can introduce the following measures to prevent abuse: "(a) [by defining] objective reasons justifying

Fixed-term work – Development of legislation

- First Directive proposal of 1982 not implemented
- Number 7 of Charter of Fundamental Social Rights of 1989
- Directive Proposals regarding atypical employment relationships at beginning of 1990s; Directive 91/383/EC
- Directive 1999/70/EC based on Regulation of 18 June 1999
- Implementation by domestic laws until 10 July 2001

the renewal of such contracts or relationships; (b) [by limiting] the maximum total duration of successive fixed-term employment contracts or relationships; (c) [by limiting] the number of renewals of such contracts or relationships."

34 In addition to these measures to prevent abuse, Clause 4 prohibits discrimination against fixed-term workers which is virtually identical to the ban on discrimination against part-time workers. Furthermore, Clause 6 affords workers certain information rights in order to facilitate the transfer from fixed-term employment to permanent employment and in paragraph 2 requires workers to be given access to training opportunities.

Case C-290/12 – **Oreste Della Rocca** v. **Poste Italiane SpA**

Who is covered by the provisions? The case concerned a temporary agency worker who had been supplied on a series of fixed-term contracts to an end user (i. e. the Italian postal service). When his assignment came to an end, he argued that the EU Fixed-term Work Directive (No. 99/70) applied to him, with the result that he was now in an open-ended employment relationship with the end user. The ECJ ruled that Council Directive 1999/70 does not apply either to the fixed-term employment relationship between a temporary worker and a temporary employment business or to the employment relationship between such a worker and a user undertaking. The court reasoned its decision mainly with the wording of the Fixed-term Work Directive, explicitly saying, that its scope does not extend to fixed-term workers placed by temporary employment agencies at the disposal of end users. In addition to that the court argued, that such workers are separately protected by the specific provisions of the EU Temporary Agency Workers Directive 2008/104/EC.

The decision was unexpected by most jurists. The court mainly relied on the wording of the preamble – though, according to the Court's case-law, the preamble to a European Union act has no binding legal force and cannot be relied on either as a ground for derogating from the actual provisions of the act in question or for interpreting them in a manner clearly contrary to their wording (Case C-308/97 *Manfredi* [1998] ECR I-7685). And: The protection, Directive 2008/104/EC provides, is different than the protection against chain contracts provided for in Directive 1999/70/EC. One cannot be used for substitution of the other.

2. Regulatory content

The aim of the Directive is to afford the greatest possible protection to fixed-term workers. They should not be treated any less favourably than permanently employed workers on account of the fixed-term nature of the employment. Moreover, the permanent employment contract is still considered to be the standard form of employment (preamble, second paragraph) – consequently fixed-term contracts are only to be permitted under special circumstances. Workers should be protected against instability of employment (*Zappala*, 35 Industrial Law Journal 2006, 439, 440). 35

a) Measures to prevent the use of successive fixed-term contracts

The key provision regarding the protection of fixed-term workers is Clause 5. It affords protection to employees in as much as the use of fixed-term contracts must not lead to the abuse of existing laws, i. e. there must be no circumvention of key protection standards. The issue here is that it is possible to bypass certain protective laws such as dismissal protection because the permanent employment contract is the general form of employment and the fixed-term contract is therefore a deviation from this standard (cf. the preamble of the framework agreement). However, it is recognized that "fixed-term employment contracts respond, in certain circumstances, to the needs of both employers and workers." It is therefore necessary to find a "balance between flexibility in working time and security for workers" (cf. the preamble of the framework agreement). In short, fixed-term employment should only be permitted where it is necessary (e. g. for flexibility reasons) but not where its application merely serves to avoid the standard employment relationship. It is for this reason that Clause 5(1) provides for three measures which can be introduced in order to prevent this abuse. The Member States are the ones to implement these measures. 36

The Directive is imprecisely phrased on this point. Nevertheless, it is undisputed that 'measures to prevent abuse' means legislation in particular, the content of which must be based on the Directive's guidelines. Accordingly, the Member States are required to prevent abuse by adopting legal provisions that restrict the use of fixed-term contracts. 37

Clause 5(2) leaves it up to the Member States to decide when employment relationships are successive. This leeway should not be unlimited; employee protection must be taken into account at all times. Consequently, it is not in conformity with the Directive's aim if the national law stipulates that contracts are only successive if they are separated by less than 20 days (Case 212/04 – Adeneler [2006] ECR I-6057; see also *Zappala*, 35 Industrial Law Journal 2006, 439 ff). 38

39 The Member States are required to implement the Directive and create specific rules regarding fixed-term contracts. However, significant problems arise in this context:

aa) Statement of reasons

40 The Directive gives no indication as to the way the Member States should implement its guidelines. It is conceivable therefore that the Member States use the same wording as the Directive, i. e. that they require an "**objective reason**" to justify a fixed-term contract. A definition of objective reasons is given in the decision *Del Cerro Alonso* (Case 307/05 [2007] ECR I-7109; see also *Koukiadaki*, 38 Industrial Law Journal 2009, 89, 98 *et seq.*; *Bell*, 37 European Law Journal, 31, 39). According to this, unequal treatment is "to be justified by the existence of precise and concrete factors, characterising the employment condition to which it relates, in the specific context in which it occurs and on the basis of objective and transparent criteria in order to ensure that that unequal treatment in fact responds to a genuine need, is appropriate for achieving the objective pursued and is necessary for that purpose". The Directive was implemented in this way e. g. in Germany (§ 14(1) TzBfG, § 14(2a) and § 14(3) TzBfG). Several German scholars (*Rolfs*, EAS B 3200 para. 37; KR-*Lipke*, Annex II of § 620 BGB, § 14 TzBfG paras. 28 *et seqq.*) submit that this kind of general reference to objective reasons that can justify fixed-term contracts does not meet the standards of European law. They refer to the case-law of the *ECJ* which stipulates that in order to implement a directive, it is essential for national law to guarantee "that individuals are made fully aware of their rights and, where appropriate, may rely on them before the national courts" (Case 144/99 – Commission v. Netherlands [2001] ECR I-3541, para. 17). They claim that a general implementation would require extensive study of case-law in order to obtain legal certainty. However, reviewing *ECJ* case-law more closely, doubts arise as to whether the conclusions drawn are as far-reaching as argued. The claim that a general reference with no independent substance of its own is not in conformity with European law is seemingly based on singular statements made by the *ECJ* taken out of the context of their respective decisions and made into general principles. It is settled *ECJ* case-law that legislative action on the part of each Member State is not necessarily required in order to implement a directive (Case 144/99 – Commission v. Netherlands [2001] ECR I-3541, para. 17; Case 365/93 – Commission v. Greece [1995] ECR I-499, para. 9; Case 29/84 – Commission v. Germany [1985] ECR I-1661, para. 23). It must only be guaranteed that the legal position under national law is sufficiently precise and clear (Case 144/99 – Commission v. Netherlands [2001] ECR I-3541, para. 17; Case 236/95 – Commission v. Greece [1996] ECR I-4467, para. 13; Case 59/89 – Commission v. Germany [1991] ECR I-2607, para. 18; Case 363/85 – Commission v. Germany [1987] ECR I-1733, para. 7; Case 29/84 – Commission v. Germany [1985] ECR I-1667, para. 23). The cases where the *ECJ* held that implementation was insufficient were all cases where there were much greater uncertainties. To use the reference to objective reasons does not therefore violate European law *per se*. It is merely necessary that there be specific case-law on this matter, i. e. that objective reasons have been defined by the courts and the criteria are therefore uniformly applied and straightforward (for more about the concept of "objective reason" see *Zappala*, 35 Industrial Law Journal 2006, 439, 441).

It is however not permitted to create objective reasons that justify the renewal of fixed-term contracts when these reasons are merely based on legal provisions allowing the renewal (Case 378/07 – Angelidaki [2009] ECR I-3071). This clarifies that the objective reasons for a renewal and a genuine need must actually exist; a fiction of objective reasons will not suffice but instead must be justified by concrete reasons that are connected to the work and the relevant conditions (Case 212/04 – Adeneler [2006] ECR I-6057). 41

The question whether it is lawful, in cases where there is a permanent need for replacement, to hire a person on successive short-term contracts based on the (generally valid) reason of replacing another employee temporarily, has been part of a reference for a preliminary ruling before the *ECJ* (*Bundesarbeitsgericht* (*BAG*), reference of 17 November 2010 – 7 AZR 443/09 (A)). In answer to this question referred for a preliminary ruling the ECJ has decided that in these cases the closing of several consecutive fixed-term contracts is allowed. However, it is incumbent on the member states, to see to it that clause 5(1)(a) of the FTW Framework Agreement is enforced. For this they have to examine if the prolongation of short-term contracts actually serves to cover a temporary need for replacement (Case 586/10 – **Kücük** [2012]). 42

bb) Implementation obligation of the Member States

The considerations illustrated above provide the answer to the second problematic issue, which is the question whether the Member States may introduce measures or whether there is an obligation to do so. The Directive states that the Member States "shall [...] introduce [...] one or more of the following measures [...]". This suggests an obligation to take action. The wording of the provision is a strong indication of this: Reference is made specifically to at least one or more of the described measures – a complete failure to implement would therefore constitute a violation of the Directive. This argument is further supported by the Directive's objective. This can only be achieved effectively if the Member States actually take measures. A non-binding order would not accomplish this. It will however suffice to introduce at least one of the three measures. Pursuant to the clear wording of the Directive, this would do justice to the protective purpose and implies a prevention of abuse. The only thing subject to review is whether the measure that is introduced actually meets the Directive's requirements, but not whether the level of protection is achieved – this is irrefutably presumed. 43

Consequently, however, this interpretation does not mean that the Member States must limit their measures to those provided in the Directive. Any regulations that are not included in the Directive remain permissible, but it may not be enough to realise a lower limit with respect to achieving prevention of abuse. 44

It is for this reason that the *ECJ* held (Case 144/04 – **Mangold** [2005] ECR I-9981) that a Member State may not adopt a national rule that allows fixed-term contracts to be concluded for no objective reason in cases where the employee has reached a certain age. The provision in question was the German § 14(3) Teilzeitbefristungsgesetz which was in force until 1 June 2007. Not one of the three measures set out in the Directive to prevent abuse in fixed-term employment was implemented; but to completely refrain from using these instruments constitutes a violation and thus there was no effective restriction of the use of consecutive fixed-term contracts. It will therefore not meet the Directive's requirements for the Member States to create their own reasons for allowing fixed-term contracts. 45

46 The crucial aspect in the *ECJ* decision in Mangold was the **absence of proportionality**: "In so far as such legislation takes the age of the worker concerned as the only criterion for the application of a fixed-term contract of employment, when it has not been shown that fixing an age threshold, as such, regardless of any other consideration linked to the structure of the labour market in question or the personal situation of the person concerned, is objectively necessary to the attainment of the objective which is the vocational integration of unemployed older workers, it must be considered to go beyond what is appropriate and necessary in order to attain the objective pursued" (para. 65). The aim of § 14(3) Teilzeitbefristungsgesetz was accepted by the Court but the means to achieve it were considered too harsh. This is why it was not possible to interpret the provision as meeting the requirements of an "objective reason" within the meaning of Clause 5(1)(a).

47 However, in normal cases it will not be necessary for Member States to create their own reasons for allowing fixed-term employment, as the Directive is worded very openly and therefore covers most cases. Requiring an objective reason leaves a wide margin which allows the construction of an unlimited number of cases. The restriction of duration and number of renewals also has far-reaching effects. Other measures suitable for preventing repeated fixed-term employment do not exist, so the enumeration of measures must be seen as exhaustive and not illustrative.

48 Should a Member State not implement the Directive, individuals can rely on the Directive on the **principle of non-discrimination** under Clause 4(1) as against the state (Case 152/84 – Marshall [1986] ECR 723; Case 187/00 – Kutz-Bauer [2003] ECR I-2741; Case 268/06 – Impact [2008] ECR I-2483) – according to the *ECJ* the Directive is unconditional and sufficiently precise for individuals to rely on it before a national court (Case 444/09 and 456/09 – Gavieiro [2010]; Case 268/06 – Impact [2008] ECR I-2483). This application is only possible in a vertical relationship, i. e. if the state or a state agency is the employer. The state is denied the possibility to plead non-implementation or non-sufficient implementation of a directive into national law, as it is its own responsibility to ensure, that the directive is implemented. In contrast, neither Clause 5(1) nor Clause 8(3) is sufficiently clear and precise; an individual cannot rely on these if the Member State failed to implement (Case 378/07 – Angelidaki [2009] ECR I-3071). A direct effect of a directive in a horizontal relationship between individuals is ruled out. Consequently, an employee cannot rely on the directive being enforced against the private employer.

cc) Legal consequences in the event of unlawful fixed-term contracts

49 The Directive does not stipulate any specific consequences in the event of unlawful fixed-term contracts (*Zappala*, 35 Industrial Law Journal 2006, 439, 443). The most effective consequence would be to turn the unlawful fixed-term contract into a permanent employment contract. This kind of consequence is actually set out in Clause 5(2)(b) – but this is not mandatory for all cases of unlawful fixed-term contracts. Therefore, deeming an unlawful fixed-term contract to be a permanent contract cannot be the mandatory consequence. This has been confirmed by the *ECJ* (Case 53/04 – Marrosu and Sardino [2006] ECR I-7213; Case 180/04 – Vasallo [2006] ECR I-7251). Nevertheless, the Member States must provide for a legal consequence that has a comparable effect; this is the only way to prevent abuse arising from the use of fixed-term contracts (*Zappala*, 35 Industrial Law Journal 2006, 439, 443).

b) Discrimination prohibition

The prohibition of discrimination of fixed-term workers is based on the implementation of Clause 4 of the framework agreement on fixed-term employment as part of the Directive 1999/70/EC. This was the first of its kind at the European level, though national legislation existed before then. French law, in particular, gave significant impetus to the European legislation. Since July 1990 Art. L. 122-3-3 *Code du travail* (now Art. L 5132-11-1) has stipulated that the remuneration that a fixed-term worker receives must be at least as high as that of a permanent worker in proportion to the period of employment (*Verkindt*, Droit social, 1995, pp. 870 *et seq.*). 50

Aside from these national rules, it was mainly the improved enforcement of the prohibition of discrimination against women and the prohibition of indirect sex discrimination that contributed to the adoption of European legislation. No. 9 of the general considerations to the framework agreement on fixed-term work specifically states that more than half of fixed-term workers in the European Union are women and that this agreement can contribute to improving equality of opportunities between women and men. There is however no case-law where the *ECJ* has considered discrimination against fixed-term workers to be unlawful indirect sex discrimination and the national courts offer far less case-law on this matter than on discrimination against part-time workers. There, it was usually the legality of a fixed-term contract that was at issue, not the contractual conditions as such; but it is only the latter that is covered by the discrimination prohibition. Nevertheless, there seems to be a clear motivation on the part of the European legislator to view the discrimination protection of fixed-term workers as a form of indirect discrimination protection of female workers. This interpretation cannot be disputed considering the almost identical wording in the part-time work legislation which also constitutes indirect discrimination protection. Although this is not mentioned explicitly in directive (see para. 8). Consequently, it is necessary to view these discrimination prohibitions side-by-side – what applies to the law regarding part-time work equally applies to the law regarding fixed-term work. 51

aa) Content

With regard to the **scope of the prohibition of discrimination** against fixed-term workers, the principles relevant to part-time work can be applied for the most part because of the identical wording. The statements made with respect to the scope *ratione personae*, territorial scope as well as to comparison groups can be adopted accordingly (cf. paras. 9 *et seqq.*, 13, 14). Especially as regards the scope *ratione personae* possible changes must be taken into consideration in light of recent *ECJ* case-law (Case 444/09 and Case 456/09 – Gavieiro Gavieiro [2010]). According to the *ECJ*, a civil servant (under Spanish law) falls within the scope of the Directive, which is a departure from the previous law on Clause 2(1) where employees in the public sector fell within the scope, but not civil servants (Case 212/04 – Adeneler [2006] ECR I-6057; Case 53/04 – Marrosu and Sardino [2006] ECR I-7213; Case 180/04 – Vasallo [2006] ECR I-7251). The changes are far-reaching and are reasonable in order to prevent circumvention of the protection afforded by the Directive (Case 307/05 – Del Cerro Alonso [2007] ECR I-7109). Whether this line will be followed consistently remains to be seen – the currently pending reference for a preliminary 52 ruling from the *Tribunal Superior de Justicia de Canarias* (Spain) may give some guidance (reference for a preliminary ruling of 2 November 2010 – C-517/10). A similar case was settled by order of the court of 1 October 2010 (reference for a preliminary ruling from the *Tribunale di Rossano* – Italy – C-3/10). Following this, it is certainly impermissible to take fixed-term workers who are employed for less than 6 months out of the scope (Case 486/08 – Tirol [2010] ECR I-3527).

53 The *pro-rata-temporis*-principle is set out expressly as a specific form of equal treatment with regard to fixed-term work, too – there is less significance here however than in the context of part-time work. Remuneration in particular is paid according to the daily or monthly working time – which is identical in the case of a fixed-term and a permanent employee – equal treatment is therefore imperative. Exceptions arise only where the benefit paid depends on a certain period of time, such as annual bonuses. If the fixed-term worker only worked from January to June, then he will be entitled to such a bonus if the permanent worker is entitled, but he may be entitled to 50 % of the full bonus.

54 The wording of the Directive does however allow for unequal treatment if it can be justified on objective grounds. This applies equally to a departure from the *pro-rata-temporis*-principle.

bb) Legal consequences

55 Like the Part-Time Work Directive, the Fixed-Term Work Directive contains no express provisions with regard to the legal consequences of discrimination. But the wording and the purpose of the principle of non-discrimination demands that on finding discrimination, the consequence must be **equal treatment** (prospectively). The question remains whether the employer – just like in the context of part-time workers – must equalize the work conditions retroactively in cases of fixed-term employment. The language of the Directive certainly does not require this. The argument that this is a form of indirect sex discrimination – as is the case for part-time work – for which sanctions must be imposed, does not have no more weight here. A connection between non-discrimination of fixed-term workers and non-discrimination of part-time workers may have been intended by the Directive, but this does not constitute solid evidence to that effect. It must be noted however that the anti-discrimination provisions of the two directives contain the same phrasing. This calls for an identical application – the legal consequences of discrimination against part-time and fixed-term workers must be the same. The creators of the directives could have not had any other intention. Therefore, it is submitted that equal treatment must be implemented retroactively (within the national statutes of limitations). There is another argument in favour of this application: discrimination protection would be ineffective if it were not implemented retroactively. An employer could discriminate with impunity. His only risk would be future equal treatment but the discrimination in the past would be essentially validated. This cannot be correct. An effective prevention of discrimination can only be achieved by eliminating this unequal treatment.

c) Duties to inform; access to training possibilities

56 In addition to the central provision regarding discrimination protection, Clause 6(1) sets out the employer's duty to inform fixed-term workers about vacancies in the undertaking. Unlike the Part-Time Work Directive this is a real duty, not just a

mission statement. The motive behind this is the possible transfer from a fixed-term to a permanent employment relationship which is seen as the norm. Beyond the wording of the Directive, the duty to inform about vacancies applies not only to those becoming available but especially to already existing vacancies.

Clause 6(2) imposes an additional duty onto the employer to facilitate access to 57 appropriate training opportunities in order to enhance their skills and career development. Fixed-term workers should not be considered "second-class workers". This duty is also more pronounced than the corresponding duty in the Part-Time Work Directive. However, it must be noted that the employer must only carry out this duty "as far as possible". Although the wording does not prescribe this expressly, this exception must be interpreted broadly. The duty to train can only go as far as such training can objectively be considered appropriate and will actually have an improving effect on the worker. The employer is not generally forced to offer training programmes to all fixed-term workers.

IV. Temporary agency work

1. Origins and starting point in European law

As early as the beginning of the 1980s the Council and Parliament adopted 58 **Resolutions** emphasizing the common position with a view to regulating temporary agency work and protecting the workers concerned (OJ C-002, 4 January 1980, p. 1 and OJ C-260, 24 October 1981, p. 54). Following this, the Commission submitted a **Directive Proposal** in 1982 which was amended in 1984 but was never adopted (see Directive Proposal, 6 April 1984, OJ C-33, p. 1; Directive Proposal, 7 May 1982, OJ C-128, p. 2). In a second attempt in 1990, the Commission chose a different path and no longer focussed on the different types of contracts but instead proposed an array of fundamental provisions that aimed to generally provide a minimum amount of protection for those working in atypical employment relationships (COM [1990] 228 final, OJ C-224, 8 September 1990, p. 8). This initiative was rewarded with success; it lead to the adoption of **Council Directive 91/383/EEC** of 25 June 1991 supplementing the measures to encourage improvements in the safety and health at work of workers with a fixed-duration employment relationship or a temporary employment relationship. The Commission and the Council then let the social partners take over who – as of 1996 – negotiated framework agreements regarding, first part-time workers and then fixed-term contracts. Whereas agreements were reached in these two areas, which were subsequently implemented in Directives 97/81/EC and 1999/70/EC, the social partners realized in May 2001 that they would not see eye to eye on the matter of temporary agency work (see already in No. 13 of Directive 1999/70/EC where the social partners declared that they would consider the need for a similar Directive relating to temporary work). The Commission subsequently resumed their activities which lead to another **Directive Proposal** (COM [2002] 149 final; amended version COM [2002] 701 final; see also the Opinion of the Economic and Social Committee, OJ C-061, 14 March 2003, p. 124). Although this proposal was accepted by the Commission in an amended version on 28 November 2002, it too failed in the end, particularly because of resistance in Great Britain and Germany. The most contentious issue was the principle of equal treatment (Art. 5 of the Directive Proposal). The debate finally came to an end in 2008 when the **Directive 2008/104/EC** on temporary agency work was adopted. It was to be implemented by the Member States by the 5 December 2011 and was based on the 2002 proposal. The Council was able to agree politically on a common position, so now the temporary agency work is also regulated by a Directive (for more about the regulatory history see *Schiek*, 10 German Law Journal 2004, 1233, 1240).

2. Substantive regulations in the Temporary Agency Work Directive 2008/104/EC

59 At the beginning of the explanatory memorandum of the Directive Proposal, on which the Directive is directly based, there is an overview which tries to summarize the different national rules relating to temporary agency work. The aim was to use these as a basis for a European consensus. All of the amendments proposed have role models in the laws of the Member States, albeit in different States. This method is reflected in the Directive itself too – none of the provisions are European in origin but were compiled from the Member States' legal systems.

60 Looking at the provisions in the Directive one finds that the European legislator has been quite restrained – not all national rules have been adopted. Some provisions, such as the prohibition of using agency workers in industrial disputes, are certainly wide-spread in the EU (see e. g. in French law Art. L. 1251-10 Code du travail; in Spanish law Art. 8(b) of Act 14/1994 of 1 July 1994; in Austrian law § 9 Arbeitskräfteüberlassungsgesetz) but were still not included in the draft proposal – most likely because of Art. 153(5) TFEU. There are no proposals for a maximum quota of temporary agency workers within a company (unlike the Italian social partners agreement [8 %]). There are more generous national rules but also stricter ones.

61 The main provisions of the Directive are the **equality principle** in Art. 5 and the **specific information** and **access provisions** in Art. 6. In addition, Art. 7 contains provisions relating to workers' representatives. According to Art. 2 of the Directive, the aim of the Directive is "to improve the quality of temporary agency work" and to "ensure that the principle of equal treatment is applied to temporary agency workers". Clearly, it does not wish to prevent or restrict temporary agency work but acknowledges it as a legal form of employment – a result which cannot be taken for granted considering the fact that some Member States used to forbid or severely restrict temporary agency work. Following the Directive's aim, temporary agency work should not be banned but the (temporary agency) workers should be protected inasmuch as the equal pay principle should apply (Art. 5(1)) subject to the exceptions allowed under Art. 5(2)-(4) which must provide an adequate level of protection.

a) Scope of application

62 According to Art. 1(1) the Directive applies to "workers with a contract of employment or employment relationship with a temporary work agency who are assigned to user undertakings to work temporarily under their supervision and direction". This section therefore provides a definition of temporary agency work (see also *Countouris/Horton*, 38 Industrial Law Journal 2009, 329, 330; for the distinction to other triangular relationships see *Schiek*, 10 German Law Journal

2004, 1233, 1234). Paragraph 2 stipulates that public as well as private undertakings fall within the scope as long as they are engaged in economic activities. The term '**economic activities**' must, however, be interpreted very broadly, as the term also includes activities not operating for gain – as the second part of paragraph 2 points out. To differentiate between gainful and non-profit temporary agency work is therefore not permitted under European law.

In spite of this, it is possible for the Member States to make stricter rules relating to gainful temporary agency work than to non-profit temporary agency work; the Directive specifically does not wish to protect the institution of temporary agency work as such but just wants to keep the consequences it entails to a minimum. It would be very difficult to ban temporary agency work altogether; this can only be done in compliance with Art. 4 of the Directive. 63

b) Equal treatment principle – Prohibition of discrimination

The **explanatory memorandum** sets out that ten States have either legislation, contractual agreements or codes of conduct that apply the principle that temporary agency workers shall receive pay at least equal to that which a permanent worker in the undertaking carrying out identical or similar tasks would receive (see COM [2002] 149 final, p. 5: Austria, Denmark, Netherlands, Belgium, France, Italy, Portugal, Spain, Luxembourg and Greece are mentioned). There are however significant differences among these States (cf. also Recital 10 of the Directive) seeing that the principle allows exceptions to a great extent. 64

See e. g. the very soft wording of **§ 10(1) Arbeitskräfteüberlassungsgesetz (Austria)**: "The worker is entitled to an appropriate, usual wage that must be paid at least once a month and must be accounted for in writing. Collective rules that apply to the agency shall remain unaffected. In assessing the appropriateness of wages the collectively agreed wages which are paid to comparable workers in the undertaking for carrying out comparable work shall be taken into consideration." 65

Other countries (such as Germany) used to apply and still apply the "**agency model**" where the worker was considered an employee of the agency. This meant that the agency was able to pay lower wages than the user undertaking. This disadvantage was offset by the fact that the agency worker was able to receive payments even during times he/she was not working. This was not possible in countries that already had the equal pay principle but those workers in return had the advantage of receiving the same wages as the other workers in the user undertaking ("**user model**"). The countries which applied the "agency model" did not have an equal treatment principle (*Schiek*, 10 German Law Journal 2004, 1233, 1244). 66

Nevertheless, it makes sense that the European legislator pursued the idea of equal treatment. It had already successfully used the prohibition of discrimination as a method of worker protection in a number of Directives pertaining to a number of characteristics: At the beginning there was gender in Directive 75/117/EEC and it continued with race and ethnicity in Directive 2000/43/EC and religion, belief, disability, age and sexual orientation in Directive 2000/78/EC. The prohibitions of discrimination against part-time and fixed-term workers in Directives 87/81/EC and 1999/70/EC were a significant step. This was the first time that certain forms of employment were the subject of discrimination legislation instead of a particular characteristic of the specific worker. The focus is on the contract, not the worker. The purpose is not to prevent discrimination against certain groups but to imple- 67 ment **distributive justice**. The rule adopted in Art. 5 of the Directive is a consistent development of this idea, on its way to an all-encompassing equality principle in employment law which does not yet exist in European law and probably will not exist in the near future. In addition, the Directive contains a special equalisation mandate relating to "access to the amenities or collective facilities in the user undertaking, in particular any canteen, child-care facilities and transport services" in **Art. 6(4)**. Therefore, equal treatment is not just limited to the employment and working conditions within the meaning of Art. 5(1), Art. 3(1)(f).

aa) The principle

68 Art. 5(1) of the Directive stipulates that temporary agency workers must be, for the duration of their assignment, treated at least as favourably in terms of basic conditions as comparable workers recruited directly by the user undertaking. Art. 3(1)(f) defines basic working and employment conditions as those relating to working time, overtime, breaks, rest periods, night work, holidays and public holidays in its subparagraph (i) and as those relating to pay in subparagraph (ii).

69 In principle therefore, the temporary agency worker (cf. the definition in Art. 3(1)(c)) may not be treated less favourably than other (permanent) workers in the user undertaking (Art. 3(1)(d)). Significantly, this equal treatment principle is limited to the "**duration of the assignment**" (Art. 3(1)(e)); the temporary agency worker remains an agency worker when he is not assigned to a user undertaking but there are no European rules that apply to the pay and other working conditions which he receives during this time (*Countouris/Horton*, 38 Industrial Law Journal 2006, 329, 332). An equality principle to that extent would not be in conformity with the legal theory of the Directive – the Directive always refers to the permanent workers in the user undertaking as the comparison group. It prohibits less favourable treatment compared to this group in order to take away any appeal of temporary work in terms of costs. This danger does not exist where a temporary agency worker has not been assigned.

70 Aside from this, the discrimination protection afforded to temporary agency workers resembles that of the Directives on part-time and fixed-term workers. For example, temporary agency workers may be treated more favourably than the permanent work force in the user undertaking. The Directive sets out minimum standards but does not attempt to create total equality.

bb) The exceptions

71 However, the possible **exceptions to the prohibition of discrimination** are extensive. Under **Art. 5(2)** the Member States may provide an exemption to the equality principle "where temporary agency workers who have a permanent contract of employment with a temporary-work agency continue to be paid in the time between assignments" (so-called user model). This is not the case in a lot of European countries – the agency model is much more common. In France, for example, the agency work contract only lasts for the duration of the assignment (see Art. L. 1251-6 Code du travail). In other legal systems – in Germany for example – the agencies are obligated to pay their temporary agency workers even during periods when they are not assigned to a user undertaking. This system is not mandatory as paragraph 2 demonstrates. There is no – European – principle that wages must be paid even when a worker is not working. The Directive recognizes

the danger that temporary agency contracts are synchronized with the duration of the assignment (which, as shown, is possible in some European countries) and attempts to prevent this by introducing the equality principle. When a worker is paid in between assignments (which is not compatible with the synchronization model) there is no comparable situation – the worker receives his wages even though he is not working during this time. As a result, the less favourable treatment during the assignment is balanced out by this advantage – the temporary agency workers are not treated less favourably if you look at the whole time-frame (cf. Recital 15 of the Directive).

Art. 5(3) of the Directive provides that the Member States may give the social 72
partners at the appropriate level the option of concluding collective agreements that derogate from the principle in paragraph 1 if they ensure an appropriate level of overall protection of temporary agency workers (this is the same in Spanish law, cf. Art. 1(1)(a) of Act 14/1994 of 1 July 1994). Due to the general principle that collective agreements represent a fair balance of the parties' rights (which is at least partly recognized by European law, see Case 45/09 – **Gisela Rosenbladt** [2010], where the social partners were specifically given extensive discretion in negotiating collective agreements), one might assume that any collective agreement relating to temporary work would offer such an appropriate level of protection. Consequently, there would be no danger for the temporary agency worker in these circumstances. It remains uncertain however, whether the Directive puts up any additional protective barriers – in light of the general principle of fairly balanced collective agreements – considering the fact that it only allows derogations from the equality principle while "respecting the overall protection". The Directive seems quite unclear in this respect – but it must be assumed that the guarantee of overall protection is implied in collective agreements at least in countries where collective agreements are recognized as generally being a fair balance of rights, as in Germany, where a so called "Angemessenheitsvermutung" is recognized by the courts.

Finally, **Art. 5(4)** gives the Member States themselves the right to derogate from 73
the equality principle – but only when there is no system in law for declaring collective agreements universally applicable. The Member States can therefore take the place of the parties to the collective agreements. This can only be done on the condition that "an adequate level of protection" is provided. There is no implied assumption that a piece of legislation upholds the adequate level of protection for temporary workers. The Directive gives no other guidelines on this matter. Only paragraph 4 offers the example of a "qualifying period for equal treatment". This implies that such a rule would provide adequate protection. Nevertheless, even in this context an assessment must be made as to the adequacy – there must be an objective reason for introducing such a qualifying period. In addition, the term "**qualifying period**" shows that equality can be achieved and that it must be feasible to do so – otherwise the equality principle could be completely circumvented by national laws. The Directive cannot have intended this as it would contradict the protective function. The example of a qualifying period should therefore be interpreted strictly.

c) Access to employment

A major objective of the Directive is to facilitate access to permanent employ- 74
ment for temporary agency workers. It recognizes that temporary agency work can

be a stepping stone to a "normal" employment relationship and permanent job in the user undertaking and facilitates the transfer. **Art. 6(1)** of the Directive states: "Temporary agency workers shall be informed of any vacant posts in the user undertaking to give them the same opportunity as other workers in that undertaking to find permanent employment." This provision considers the idea of an in-house employment market. It aims to activate the existing hiring opportunities and to avoid frustration within the workforce that could arise when outsiders are hired despite there being qualified workers in the company. The goal is to achieve a transfer from temporary agency work to permanent employment – temporary agency work should be a stepping stone and not a permanent institution (cf. also Recital 11 of the Directive).

75 This goal is promoted further by the provisions in **Art. 6(2) and (3)**. Pursuant to these, no clauses, such as requiring payment of commission fees, shall be allowed if they prohibit or have the effect of preventing the conclusion of a contract of employment or an employment relationship between the user undertaking and the temporary agency worker after his assignment. In addition, temporary-work agencies may not charge workers any fees in exchange for arranging for them to be recruited by a user undertaking, or for concluding a contract of employment or an employment relationship with a user undertaking after carrying out an assignment in that undertaking (Art. 6(3)).

d) Employee representation

76 Art. 8 of the Directive provides the **employee representative's right** to receive "**suitable information"** on the use of temporary agency workers. The Directive is therefore stricter than Clause 7(3) of the framework agreement on fixed-term work that is the basis of Directive 1999/70/EC. There, the employer need only give consideration – and only as far as possible – to the provision of appropriate information to existing workers' representative bodies about fixed-term work in the undertaking. The usefulness of this provision is debatable. Its role models were laws in other Member States, such as in French law where there is the obligation to provide information on the number of temporary agency workers, Art. L. 2323-10 (and 2323-9 and 2323-17) Code du travail. Additionally, there is an obligation to show contracts with temporary-work agencies to the *comité d'entreprise*. In Spain the employer must provide information on every use of temporary agency workers and the reason for it within ten days of assignment, according to Art. 9 of the Act 14/1994 of 1 July 1994.

77 **Art. 7** contains further provisions concerning employee representation. Paragraph 1 sets out that temporary agency workers shall count for the purposes of calculating thresholds in the temporary-work agency – an important rule seeing as they are in fact (albeit special) employees of the temporary-work agency. This provision is not surprising. Paragraph 2 on the other hand reveals a more peculiar rule in that it sets out that temporary agency workers may count for the purposes of calculating thresholds in the user undertaking. This is peculiar because they may not be – as in German law – employees of the user undertaking; however, their similarity to employees does mean that it must at least be possible to count them. The fact that they would then be counted twice – in the temporary-work agency as well as in the user undertaking – is rather odd. This can be avoided by the option provided in Art. 7(3) which does not require counting temporary agency workers in the tempor-

ary-work agency if they are counted in the user undertaking. The Directive does not however give the temporary workers the right to choose which undertaking they are counted in.

e) Consequences of non-compliance

Unlike the Directive on part-time and fixed-term work, the Temporary Agency Work Directive sets out specific legal consequences in the event of non-compliance with the Directive's provisions. The Member States shall provide, under Art. 10, for "appropriate measures" that shall apply in the event of an infringement. The Member States must ensure that the rights given by the Directive can be enforced. Also, they are to provide **"effective, proportionate and dissuasive" penalties** that apply in the event of an infringement. The wording is the same in the Discrimination Directives (cf. Art. 15 Direction 2000/43/EC; Art. 17 Direction 2000/78/EC; Art. 8(d) Direction 2002/73/EC, see also § 3 at 12 *et seqq.*). Examples of penalties are fines in the event of infringements of information obligations. 78

Violations of the equality principle result in an **upward adjustment** which means that the temporary agency worker must be treated in the same way as the comparable employee in the user undertaking that receives the highest benefits. This effect not only applies *ex nunc* but also retroactively. This is the only way to ensure effective punishment and equal treatment at the same time. 79

§ 5. Transfer of undertakings

Literature: *Collins*, Transfer of Undertakings and Insolvency, 18 Industrial Law Journal 1989, 144–158; *Collins*, Employment Rights in Connection with Transfers of Parts of Groups of Companies, 25 Industrial Law Journal, 1996, 59; *Davies*, Transfers – The UK Will have To Make Up Its Own Mind, 30 Industrial Law Journal 2001, 231–235; *Great Britain Department of Trade and Industry*, Employment rights on the transfer of an undertaking, 2002; *Hall*, Beyond Recognition? Employee Representation and EU law, 25 International Law Journal 1996, 15–27; *Körner*, The Impact of Community Law on German Labour Law: The Example of Transfer of Undertakings, European University Institute Working Papers, Law No. 96/8, 12; *Laulom*, The European Court of Justice in the Dialogue on Transfers of Undertakings: A Fallible Interlocutor in Labour Law in the Courts, in: Sciarra (ed.), Labour Law in the Courts – National Judges and the Court of Justice, 2001, pp. 145–178; *Leccese*, Italian Courts, the *ECJ* and Transfers of Undertakings: A Multi-Speed Dialogue?, 5 European Law Journal 1999, No. 3, 311–330; *McMullen*, Business Transfers and Employee Rights, 1998; *McMullen*, TUPE Transfers: The Cracks Still Show, 30 Industrial Law Journal 2001, 396–400; *McMullen*, An Analysis of the Transfer of Undertakings (Protection of Employment) Regulations 2006, 35 Industrial Law Journal 2006, 113–139; *McMullen*, The 'Right' to Object to Transfers of Employment under TUPE, 37 Industrial Law Journal 2008, 169–177; *Novella/Vallauri*, Employee Rights on Transfer of Undertakings: Italian Legislation and EC Law, 14 European Law Journal 2008, No.1, 62; *Selwyn*, Law of Employment, 17th ed., 2012; *Valdés Dal-Ré*, Transfers of Undertakings: An Experience of Clashes and Harmonies between Community Law and National Legal Systems, in: Sciarra (ed.), Labour Law in the Courts – National Judges and the Court of Justice, 2001, pp. 179–197.

I. Objectives and development

1. Objectives

The idea behind the regulations concerning the transfer of undertakings is a simple one: Mere **change of ownership of a business should have no consequences for the employee.** Without adequate regulations protection against dismissal would be severely reduced. The seller, who then no longer has a business, could dismiss all employees on operational grounds, and those employees could not demand of the buyer, with whom the employees have no contractual relationship, to be hired. At collective level such statutory regulations also ensure the continuity of the observance of collective agreements. Moreover, liability risks between the former employer and the new employer must be distributed reasonably. As evidenced by the third recital, Directive 2001/23/EC is primarily concerned with employee protection. This is also made clear by Art. 8 which allows existing regulations more favourable to employees to remain in place. 1

2. Development

At the beginning of the 1970s, before the first Transfer of Undertakings Directive 77/187/EEC of 14 December 1977 was created, there was an increase of mergers and acquisitions at European level. To counteract the resulting risks for employees the Council adopted a socio-political action programme on 21 January 1974 including, *inter alia*, a directive concerning the preservation of claims and benefits in cases of mergers and rationalization measures (Council Resolution concerning a social action programme OJ 1974 C-13/1). The Commission submitted a proposal for a 2 directive to the Council on 31 May 1974 based on Ex-Art. 100 EC-Treaty (now Art. 115 TFEU). After going through the legislative procedure the Directive 77/187/EEC on the approximation of the laws of the Member States relating to the safeguarding of employees' rights in the event of transfers of undertakings, businesses or parts of businesses was adopted on 14 December 1977. The directive was amended by Directive 98/50/EC of 29 June 1998. Essentially, comments made by the *ECJ* on the interpretation of the original directive were incorporated into the legal text. In addition, the legal position of employee representatives was strengthened and stricter notification duties were put in place. The original Directive 77/187/EEC and the amending Directive 98/50/EC were promulgated on 12 March 2001 as the new **Directive 2001/23/EC.**

3 The introduction of the Transfer of Undertakings Directive to protect workers in the event of a transfer of undertakings at European level was preceded in some Member States by a **national debate** as to its necessity. It was recognized early on that the purchase of an undertaking threatens the employees' claims and that it was necessary to create laws that regulate the relationship between employees and the take-over undertaking, i. e. that ensure that the employees' legal position which they had before the transfer is maintained.

4 **German law** already had a law, § 613 a Bürgerliches Gesetzbuch, as early as 1972 which protected workers in the event of a transfer of undertakings. It was considered necessary to introduce § 613 a BGB after the courts were repeatedly forced to reject – for lack of a legal basis to do otherwise – any transfer of the employment relationships to the buyer (*BAG* of 18 February 1960 – 5 AZR 472/57; *BAG* of 29 November 1962 – 2 AZR 176/62). After the Transfer of Undertakings Directive came into force, § 613 a BGB had to be amended to accommodate the European requirements.

5 In **French law**, regulations concerning the transfer of undertakings were created as early as 1928 (Art. L 1224-1 previously Art. L 122-12, al 2 Code du Travail, previously Art. 23, al 7 then 8 Livre 1), cf. *Couturier*, Droit du Travail, I/Les Relations Individuelles du Travail, 1998, p. 373).

6 **Italian** pre-directive law also recognised the principle of an automatic transfer of employment relationships when a business is transferred (see *Leccese*, Italian Courts, the ECJ and Transfers of Undertakings: A Multi-Speed Dialogue?, 5 European Law Journal 1999, No. 3, 311–330).

7 In the **United Kingdom**, however, the legal relationships were not transferred before the directive was implemented by the Transfer of Undertakings (Protection of Employment) Regulations 1981 (TUPE) (see *Barnard*, EC Employment Law, 2000, p. 446; *Selwyn*, Law of Employment, 2004, pp. 229 *et seqq.*). At common law the transfer of any business resulted in the termination of any existing contract of employment because the employee's contract could not be transferred without his consent (see *Bolwell v Redcliffe Homes Ltd* and *Nokes v Doncaster Amalgamated Collieries Ltd* [1940] AC 1014).

8 Still today the ***ECJ*** is instrumental in advancing the development of the law of transfer of undertakings. Just as in the early years, the Court adjudicates upon important questions of interpretation (see e. g. the judgments Case 466/07 – Klarenberg [2009] ECR I-803; Case 242/09 – Albron Catering; Case 463/09 – CLECE).

II. Existence of a transfer of undertaking

9 The sole condition for the application of the directive is that there be a transfer of undertaking. In Art. 1(1) of Directive 2001/23/EC this is defined as **any transfer of an undertaking, business, or part of an undertaking or business to another employer as a result of a legal transfer or merger**. This definition requires further elaboration. In practice it is often a matter of dispute.

1. The terms "undertaking" and "business"

Whereas in the original Directive 77/187/EEC the scope of application was limited to the transfer of undertakings, businesses or parts of a business, it was extended to include parts of an undertaking by the amending Directive 98/50/EC. The *ECJ* does not distinguish between these terms however, but groups them all under the definition of **'economic entity' meaning an organised grouping of resources which has the objective of pursuing an economic activity, whether or not that activity is central or ancillary** (consistent practice of the Court since Case 24/85 – Spijkers [1986] ECR 1119). To distinguish between them would not make much sense anyway, as the smallest entity of part of an undertaking is always contained in the terms 'undertaking', 'business' and 'part of a business'; therefore only the definition of part of an undertaking is significant. The transfer of a business or of part of a business are considered transfers of undertakings based on the *ECJ*'s definition. 10

In **Italian Law** the transfer of an undertaking has been defined in Art. 32 of Decree No. 276/2003, which implements Directive 2001/23/EC (Decreto Legislativo 10 settembre 2003, n. 276 *Gazzetta Ufficiale* n. 235 del 9 ottobre 2003 – Supplemento Ordinario n. 159). The Art. sets out that a transfer of an undertaking is "any operation that results in a change of ownership of the organised economic entity, as a result of a legal transfer or merger, ... regardless of the contractual agreement or measure forming the basis of the transfer, including usufruct and leasing of an undertaking." (*Novella/Vallauri*, Employee Rights on Transfer of Undertakings: Italian Legislation and EC Law, 14 European Law Journal 2008, No. 1, 62). 11

The **Spanish Supreme Court** of Justice of the province of Extremadura found in one of it's decisions with reference to *ECJ* case law, that the decisive criterion for the existence of a transfer of undertaking to the effects of Directive 2001/23/EG and Art. 44 EC is that the economic entity preserves its identity, which in particular results from the effective continuation of its exploitation or its reinstatement, however, such an entity may also result from other elements, such as the personnel which it integrates, the organization of its work, its methods of exploitation or if applicable the means of exploitation of which it disposes (STSJ Extremadura de 10 de enero de 2006, Recurso n.°713/2005). 12

It must be an organisationally independent entity that pursues as a minimum a **partial objective** of its own within the main objective of the business. It is not required that the partial objective differs from the main business objective but it must have an identity of its own. An ancillary function will suffice according to the *ECJ* judgment in *Watson Rask*. In that case a company canteen was taken over by the company Philips A/S. Even though the canteen is merely an ancillary activity for the transferor without a necessary connection with its company objects, it is considered a distinguishable part of a business (Case 209/91 – Watson Rask [1992] ECR I-5755, para. 17). The *ECJ* ruled similarly with respect to cleaning operations in a bank (Case 392/92 – Christel Schmidt [1994] ECR I-1311). In **German law**, for instance, it is not considered a distinguishable part of a business by virtue of the judgments of the *Bundesarbeitsgericht* when an IT-service provider merely transfers singular programmes and data to a succeeding contractor (*BAG* of 24 April 1997 – 8 AZR 848/94) or a transport company transfers one lorry (*BAG* of 26 August 1999 – 8 AZR 718/98). 13

14 According to the *ECJ* in *Rygaard* the economic activity must be carried out in a **stable** way and must not be limited to performing one specific works contract. In the underlying facts of the case the awarder of a building contract cancelled the contract with the plaintiff's employer and hired a different firm of carpenters. This new contractor took over the plaintiff only until completion of work started by the plaintiff's former employer. The *ECJ* rejected a transfer of undertaking because the original employer merely made available to the new contractor certain workers and material for carrying out the works in question (Case 48/94 – Rygaard [1995] ECR I-2745, para. 20 *et seqq.*).

15 Under Art. 1(1)(c) the entity is not only **economic** when it is operating with a view to profit (before its codification this was already settled case-law of the *ECJ* in Case 382/92 – Commission v. United Kingdom [1994] ECR I-2435, para. 44 *et seqq.* and Case 343/98 – Collino [2000] ECR I-6659, para. 30 *et seqq.*; Case 463/09 – CLECE [2011], para. 26). The economic nature is only precluded when it exclusively involves the exercise of public authority. The reorganization of structures of a public administration or the transfer of administrative functions from one public administration to another are therefore not transfers of undertakings within the meaning of the Directive (Case 298/94 – Henke [1996] ECR I-4989, para. 14 *et seqq.*). If it is not exercising public authority, then it is an economic entity even when the transferred service was contracted out by a public body, such as a municipality, or, as is the case with public transport, the service is strongly regulated. The *ECJ* held that the Directive is applicable to the transfer of an activity which involves the assistance of addicts and is carried out by a foundation, a legal person with no view to profit (Case 29/91 – Redmond Stichting [1992] ECR I-3189). In English law the Transfer of Undertakings (Protection of Employment) Regulations 1981 (TUPE 1981) did not apply to non-commercial undertakings such as charities but this exception was removed following this *ECJ* decision. The TUPE 1981 have since been amended to specifically include non-profit undertakings, see Regulation 3 of TUPE 2006. The Directive also applies to the transfer of an activity involving domestic help for persons in need, from a public body to a private law company (Joined Cases 173/96 & 247/96 – Hidalgo and others [1998] ECR I-8237), to the transfer of the operation of a telecommunications service from a public body within the state administration to a private law company established by a public body which holds its entire capital (Case 343/98 – Collino [2000] ECR I-6659), to the transfer of activities relating to publicity for a municipality from a non-profit-making association to the municipality (Case 175/99 – Mayeur [2000] ECR I-7755) and to the transfer of the operation of bus routes (Case 172/99 – Liikenne [2001] ECR I-745).

16 **Special rules** apply where the undertaking is a temporary work agency, i. e. an undertaking that hires employees but has them work for another company under its direction and receives remuneration from this company. The Court ruled in the Jouini case that agency workers formed part of the temporary work agency and could be transferred along with it (Case 458/05 – Jouini [2007] ECR I-7301).

2. Retaining its identity

17 The question of whether identity has been retained is central. To assess this – as the *ECJ* pointed out in *Spijkers* – all notable circumstances characterizing the

transaction must be taken into account. The *ECJ* mentioned **seven criteria** specifically, namely:

- The type of undertaking or business,
- the transfer of tangible assets,
- the transfer of intangible assets,
- whether the majority of its employees are taken over,
- the transfer of customers,
- the degree of similarity between the activities and
- the period for which those activities were suspended.

These criteria are not to be considered in isolation but are merely single factors in 18
an **overall assessment** (settled case-law of the *ECJ* since Case 24/85 – Spijkers [1986] ECR 1119). The term retention of identity is therefore a typological term: none of the aforementioned criteria are necessary and none are sufficient criteria on their own for the term 'transfer of undertaking'. The decisive element is whether a functional organisation is taken over, i. e. whether the transferee profits from an existing organisation or, figuratively speaking, walks into a ready-made business. If, however, a new work structure is established, then the identity is not retained, even if the business activity is continued unchanged. For mere succession in respect of function does not constitute a transfer of a business (settled case law of the *ECJ* since Case 13/95 – Ayse Süzen [1997] ECR I-1259, para. 15 *et seq.*). In the following, the *ECJ*'s seven criteria will be examined in detail. This can be summarized in a **rule of thumb**: an undertaking is transferred if it doesn't close down. The **test** is: Following a typological assessment, is the organization in the hands of the transferee identical to the organization in the hands of the transferor?

A rather recent judgment of the *ECJ* in the **case Klarenberg** has given rise to 19
uncertainty.

Case 466/07 – **Klarenberg** [2009] ECR I-803

From 1 January 1989 Mr Klarenberg was employed by ET Electrotechnology GmbH ('ET'), a company specialising in the development and manufacture of products in the field of industrial automation, and measurement and control technology, for the steel industry. From 1 May 1992, Mr Klarenberg headed the "R&D/ET-Systems/Network/Interface technology and bus systems" unit of ET. That unit was itself subdivided into three teams, namely R&D/ET Systems, headed by Mr Klarenberg, Data Processing/Network/Server Systems/Data protection, and Production/Control Cabinets/Circuit Boards, headed by Mr Neumann, who was also deputy head of the whole unit. Ferrotron specialises in the design and manufacture of products in the field of measurement and control techniques for the steel industry. On 22 November 2005, ET entered into an 'asset and business sale and purchase agreement' with Ferrotron and its parent company in respect of the following products, developed by the "R&D/ET-Systems/Network/Interface technology and bus systems" unit of ET, and called 'ET'DecNT', 'Et-DecNT light', 'ET-DecNT Power Melt', 'ET'TempNet', 'ET' OxyNet' and 'FT7000'. Pursuant to that agreement, Ferrotron's parent company acquired all the rights over the software, patents, patent applications and inventions relating to the abovementioned products, as well as all the rights over the product names and technical know-how. Ferrotron acquired the development hardware and the inventory of product materials belonging to ET, as well as a related list of suppliers and of customers. Ferrotron also re-engaged a certain number of ET employees, namely Mr Neumann and three engineers from the R&D/ET-Systems team. In addition, those employees also carry out duties in relation to products other than those acquired by Ferrotron from ET. On 17 July 2006, insolvency proceedings were initiated against ET, upon which Mr. Klarenberg brought an action before the German Labour Court in Wesel to declare his employment relationship transferred to Ferrotron. His case was dismissed. Mr. Klarenberg brought proceedings against Ferrotron Technologies GmbH before the *ECJ*. The *ECJ* held that the Directive applies even where the part of the undertaking transferred does not retain its organisational autonomy, provided that the functional link between the various elements of production transferred is preserved, and that that link enables the transferee to use those elements to pursue an identical or analogous economic activity.

20 For many commentators this does not make much sense. The identity of a business is the identity of its organization. Where the organization is a different one, so is the business. Suffice it to point to the critical response to this judgment in academic literature (s. *Beltzer*, Transfers of Undertaking – recent developments at the European Level, European Employment Law Cases, No. 44, 2009, available at: http://dare.uva.nl/document/182513, p. 10).

a) Type of undertaking or business

21 In considering the type of undertaking or business a distinction is made primarily between **asset reliant** undertakings (i. e. those with significant tangible and intangible assets) and **labour intensive** undertakings (i. e. those without significant tangible and intangible assets). This assessment, to be made beforehand, is then used to determine the degree of importance to be attached to the other criteria (settled case law of the *ECJ* since Case 13/95 – Ayse Süzen [1997] ECR I-1259, para. 18; Case 463/09 – CLECE [2011]). The transfer of tangible assets such as premises or furnishings is less relevant for a labour-intensive but non-asset reliant service undertaking, whereas intangible assets such as know-how or the taking over of the workforce may be of great importance in such undertakings. In asset reliant undertakings, such as those where expensive machinery is used, e. g. in the automobile industry, the tangible assets must be considered a key factor. There, the taking over of the workforce is of less importance.

b) Transfer of tangible assets

22 Tangible assets include all physical assets such as the buildings, the machines, the furnishings or the fleet of vehicles. It was a contentious issue till the *ECJ* decision in *Güney-Görres* (Case 232/04 – Güney-Görres [2005] ECR I-11237) whether tangible assets should be taken into account if they are not transferred for independent commercial use.

Case 232/04 – **Güney-Görres** [2005] ECR I-11237

The security checks on passengers and their baggage at the Düsseldorf airport were originally carried out by the private undertaking Securicor. To carry out the security checks on passengers a large amount of expensive aviation equipment was used which was the property of the State of Germany and made available to Securicor. The maintenance of the equipment was the responsibility of the German State. Securicor could not obtain any additional benefit from it. Having been awarded the new contract, the security company Kötter continued to use this equipment, but dismissed many of the employees. The fact that few of the employees were taken over raised the question as to which extent the continued use of this equipment could be taken into account in determining whether there was a transfer of undertaking.

Under the previous case-law of the ***Bundesarbeitsgericht***, a transfer of assets existed only under the condition that the assets were used on an independent commercial basis (*BAG* of 11 December 1997 – 8 AZR 426/94, AP No. 171 to § 613 a Bürgerliches Gesetzbuch (BGB); *BAG* of 22 January 1998 – 8 AZR 775/96, AP No. 174 to § 613 a BGB; *BAG* of 22 July 2004 – 8 AZR 350/03, AP No. 274 to § 613 a BGB). According to the BAG, this is the only way to distinguish between working with assets and working on assets. This is based on concerns that otherwise in cases of providing services such as cleaning buildings, the buildings could be regarded as tangible assets. As Securicor could not obtain an additional benefit from the equipment, then, according to the criteria developed by the *Bundesarbeitsgericht*, this was not an independent commercial use of the equipment. Therefore, such equipment could not be taken into consideration when determining whether there was a transfer of business.

The *ECJ* ruled against the BAG in *Güney-Görres* in that even assets not transferred for independent commercial use are to be considered. The Court stated in its short reasons that the criterion of independent commercial use can neither be derived from the wording of Directive 2001/23/EC nor from its objectives, which are to ensure the protection of workers where there is a change of undertaking or business and to allow the completion of the internal market (para. 40).

Even assets which are not used in an independent commercial manner, like the security equipment used at Düsseldorf airport, must therefore be taken into account in the overall assessment. Then again, it was not decided whether they can make an undertaking without significant tangible assets into an undertaking with significant tangible assets. If this were not the case and if, in a first step, the airport security company were to have been categorized as an undertaking without significant tangible assets, then the existing tangible assets would have had little importance, even if they were to be considered. As a reaction to the judgment in *Güney-Görres*, the BAG has given up the criterion of independent commercial use and now takes assets not for independent commercial use into consideration without restriction when determining the identity of an undertaking (*BAG* of 6 April 2006 – 8 AZR 222/04, BAGE 117, 349–360).

c) Transfer of intangible assets

23 Intangible assets include, for example, **licensing rights, know-how, distribution rights or goodwill**. For instance, with undertakings in the music industry or in pharmaceutical development, these will usually be the decisive assets as they are significant for the activity.

d) Taking over the workforce

24 In assessing whether an entity has retained its identity, the question as to the relevance of taking over the workforce was answered by the *ECJ* notably in the decisions *Christel Schmidt* and *Ayse Süzen*. These principles were recently confirmed again in the CLECE case (Case 463/09 [2011]).

Case 392/92 – **Christel Schmidt** [1994] ECR I-1311

A savings bank with several branch offices decided to have its premises cleaned by a cleaning company. The savings bank dismissed Christel Schmidt who had been hired by the savings bank itself to clean that branch office. The cleaning company offered to employ Schmidt on less favourable terms which she declined. Instead, she brought an action against the cleaning company challenging her dismissal. No tangible or intangible assets were transferred, only Christel Schmidt was to be taken over to perform the same task.

Under the case law of the ***Bundesarbeitsgericht*** prior to the judgment in *Christel Schmidt* the transfer of staff was merely a legal consequence of a transfer of undertakings and could therefore not be decisive in determining the existence of a transfer. The transfer of possessors of know-how could only be an additional indication when tangible or intangible assets were transferred (*BAG* of 22 May 1985 – 5 AZR 30/84, AP No. 42 to § 613 a BGB; *BAG* of 9 February 1994 – 2 AZR 781/93, AP No. 104 to § 613 a BGB; *BAG* of 14 July 1994 – 2 AZR 55/94). This case-law does not represent a German particularity: the British Employment Appeal Tribunal ruled no differently in related cases (*Dines v. Initial Health Care Services Ltd and Pall Mall Services Group Ltd* [1993] IRLR 521, see on this *Bercusson*, European Labour Law, 1996, p. 239 *et seq.*; *Selwyn*, Law of Employment, 13th ed., 2004, p. 234.). However, this decision was reversed by the Court of Appeal.

The *ECJ* abandoned this restrictive jurisprudence with its decision of 14 April 1994. According to the *ECJ*, the taking over of the workforce can suffice, even if no assets whatsoever are transferred. The safeguarding of employee's rights which, as stated in its title, constitutes the subject-matter of the directive, cannot depend on the consideration of one factor. The argument that only one employee is affected by the transfer was not accepted by the Court because the directive protects employees of all undertakings and parts thereof, regardless of number.

25 As a result it was feared that every mere **succession as to function**, i. e. every transfer of responsibilities such as awarding a new contract, could be considered a transfer of undertaking. The decision in *Merckx* seemed to support this supposition. In that case a car dealership in the greater area of Brussels was taken over by a

company which continued to employ 20 % of the previous company's workforce. According to the *ECJ* the fact that no tangible or intangible assets were transferred was not conclusive to preclude the existence of a transfer of undertaking because it was an activity that did not require any significant tangible assets (Joined Cases 171/94 & 172/94 – Merckx [1996] ECR I-1253, para. 21).

It was not until *Ayse Süzen* that the *ECJ* made it clear that not every succession as 26
to function represents a transfer of undertaking.

Case 13/95 – **Ayse Süzen** [1997] ECR I-1259

Like in the judgment of Christel Schmidt this case was about a cleaning company. A school awarded the contract to clean its premises to a different cleaning company and the previous contractor and employer of the plaintiff Ayse Süzen dismissed the employees working as cleaners at the school. Staff or assets were not taken over by the new contractor.

The *ECJ* ruled that the mere fact that the activity was continued was not enough to support the conclusion that a transfer of undertaking had occurred. The identity of non-asset reliant undertakings emerges from other factors, such as its workforce, its management staff, the way in which its work is organized, its operating methods. The deciding factor is whether a significant part of the workforce, in number and skill, is taken over. This did not happen here, therefore there was no transfer of undertaking. "The mere loss of a service contract to a competitor cannot therefore by itself indicate the existence of a transfer within the meaning of the directive. In those circumstances, the service undertaking previously entrusted with the contract does not, on losing a customer, thereby cease fully to exist, and a business or part of a business belonging to it cannot be considered to have been transferred to the new awardee of the contract." (para. 16).

The *Süzen* test has been criticized as being circular: Whether the employees have a right to be transferred depends on whether they have been transferred (see *McMullen*, TUPE Transfers: The Cracks Still Show, 30 Industrial Law Journal 2001, 396–400). To counteract this, the English Employment Appeal Tribunal (EAT) and the Court of Appeal (CA) adopted a purposive approach to the application of TUPE: if the motive of the new employer in not hiring the employees is to avoid application of TUPE then the employees would be deemed transferred (see ECM (Vehicle Delivery) Service Ltd v Cox [1998] IRLR 416 (EAT); [1999] IRLR 559 (CA)). In 2006, the TUPE was amended to include a specific provision (Regulation 3 of TUPE 2006) that qualifies service provision changeovers as transfers of undertakings. This provision makes it no longer necessary to resort to the *Süzen* test and is permissible under Art. 8 of the Directive because it is more favourable to employees (for more details see *McMullen*, An Analysis of the Transfer of Undertakings (Protection of Employment) Regulations 2006, 35 Industrial Law Journal 2006, 113–139).

As the *ECJ* confirmed in *Friedrich Santner et. al.*, mere succession as to function 27
will not suffice (Joined Cases 127/96, 229/96 & 74/97 – Friedrich Santner and others [1998] ECR I-8179). The **definitive percentage** that would represent a significant part of the workforce was explored by the **German** *Bundesarbeitsgericht* in the

following years. To begin with, it must be taken into consideration how qualified the employees are that are taken over. If the employees have little qualifications and are easily replaceable, then a large part of the workforce would need to be transferred in order to conclude that there is a continued existence of the previous work organisation. 75 % is not enough in the case of bringing meals to hospital beds in a hospital (*BAG* of 10 December 1998 – 8 AZR 676/97), in the case of cleaning operations, however, the taking over of 85 % of the workforce will suffice (*BAG* of 11 December 1997 – 8 AZR 729/96). If an undertaking is characterized by the expert knowledge and the qualifications of its employees, then it may be enough, in addition to other criteria, because of their know-how, to conclude that a significant part of the workforce was taken over. For instance, in the case of guarding a nuclear plant the taking over of 22 of its 36 employees, including four shift foremen and the rest of the management staff, can be considered a significant part of the workforce because in this qualified activity they represent the significant know-how (*BAG* of 14 May 1998 – 8 AZR 418/96). The Labour Chamber of the **Spanish Supreme Court** held in its decision from 29 May 2008 (STS – Sala de lo Social – de Madrid de 29 de mayo 2009, Recurso n° 3617/2006), that for the existence of a transfer of undertaking under Art. 44 of the Employee Statute (Real Decreto Legislativo 1/1995, de 24 de marzo, por el que se aprueba el texto refundido de la Ley del Estatuto de los Trabajadores), which regulates the transfer of undertaking, it would not be sufficient to allocate employees from one business organisation to a different company, here the assignment of cleaning services to another company. In order for a transfer of undertaking to exist, there also has to be a transfer of assets, including the infrastructure and business organisation of the previous business (Ibid., Fundamentos de Derecho, Segundo 1.). More importantly the court established that "the decision of a company to transfer its workforce to another is not equivalent to taking over the workforce, which the Community doctrine considers to be a transfer of undertaking, provided that such transfer is peaceful, effective and real. This is not the case, where the unilateral decision of one party was impugned upon a large number of employees" (Ibid., Fundamentos de Derecho, Segundo 3). Hence, if there is no transfer of a material element and there is no taking over of the workforce it cannot be considered a transfer of undertaking within the scope of Art. 44 of the Employee Statute.

28 The *ECJ* found in the *Hidalgo* case (joined Cases 173/96 & 247/96 – Hidalgo and others [1998] ECR I-8237) case that in certain sectors an economic entity may be able to function without possessing a considerable amount of tangible or intangible assets wherefore the retention of its identity may not depend on the transfer of such assets. Therefore, it found that in certain labour-intensive sectors, "a group of workers engaged in a joint activity on a permanent basis may constitue an economic entity." (para. 32) This entity may continue to be recognized as such after its transfer "where the new employer does not merely pursue the activity in question but also takes over a major part, in terms of their number and skills, of the employees specially assigned by his predecessor to that task. In those circumstances the new employer takes over a body of assets enabling him to carry on the activities or certain activities of the transferor undertaking on a regular basis." (para. 32)

29 As much sense as it may make to ensure a certain amount of protection for those activities with no significant assets by regarding the taking over of staff as a factor in determining whether identity

has been retained, this jurisprudence presents a policy problem. If an employer continuing an activity wishes to avoid the consequences of a transfer of undertaking, he will strive to take over only a small part of the previous workforce. **As a result, this wide interpretation of a transfer of undertaking in order to achieve protection of the previous employer's workforce could backfire** (see also *Davies*, Transfers – The UK Will have To Make Up Its Own Mind, 30 Industrial Law Journal 2001, 231–235).

Closely related to this issue is the question whether the transfer of executive employees can constitute a transfer of undertakings. According to the *ECJ* in UGT-FSP an economic entity preserves its autonomy if, after the transfer, the organisational powers of those in charge of the entity transferred remain, within the organisational structures of the transferee, essentially unchanged as compared with the situation pertaining before the transfer(Case 151/09 – UGT-FSP).

e) Transfer of customer base

The transfer of the customer base can also be a factor in retaining the identity of 30 an undertaking. The conventional way of transferring the customer base is to take over the **customer file** or a **dealership**. (see Joined Cases 171/94 & 172/94 – Merckx [1996] ECR I-1253). In the case of a canteen which is not run on an independent commercial basis, the ***Bundesarbeitsgericht*** does not regard the customers of the canteen as being the canteen director's client base but as being that of the party tendering the contract (*BAG* of 11 December 1997 – 8 AZR 426/94). After the *ECJ* judgment in *Güney-Görres*, according to which the question of whether tangible assets were transferred does not depend on their independent commercial use, it is questionable whether this jurisprudence can be upheld. As the BAG does not take independent commercial use into consideration anymore when determining the type of business (*BAG* of 6 April 2006 – 8 AZR 222/04), there is a great deal to support the assertion to not consider this criterion in determining the transfer of a customer base either.

The **Spanish Supreme Court of Justice of Catalonia** decided in its judgment 31 from 8 November 2007 that there was no transfer of an undertaking and hence no right of the employees to be taken over by the new undertaking renting the premises in question, where the previous lessee ceases his activity due to his retirement. The personnel, among others, based their claim to be taken over by the new lessee, on the fact that, "apart from the price which has been paid for the taking over of the premises, it is not the material elements which are relevant, but the inmaterial elements such as the client base, since the old and new undertaking are dedicated to the same activity". The Court decided in the light of European case-law that the transfer of the client base in the present case is not significant, since the restaurant in question is located in the city center of Figuras, where one can assume that there are a lot of walk-in customers, which in turn means that the customers are not necessarily the same as the previous owner's customers (STSJ de Cataluña de 10 de Marzo de 2008, Recurso n.° 2170).

f) Degree of similarity between the activities

Similarity between the activities is not sufficient in itself to preserve the identity. 32 Otherwise any succession as to function would constitute a transfer of undertaking. As a rule, the **transfer of the customer base coincides** with the similarity of the activity because the customer base usually remains the same when the purpose of the undertaking remains the same. According to the *ECJ* in *Redmond Stichting*, it is sufficient if only a **part of the activities** is transferred to another undertaking.

There, a foundation, which provided assistance and social and recreational activities to drug addicts, was closed down. A newly established foundation continued this support to drug addicts in form of providing only assistance. The *ECJ* held that the directive covers the transfer of undertakings and businesses and parts of businesses and that this can be equated with independent activities of a special nature (Case 29/91 – Redmond Stichting [1992] ECR I-3189).

g) The period for which those activities were suspended

33 The last criterion according to the *ECJ* is, finally, the period for which an activity is suspended. This way, the continuation of a business is distinguished from the closure of a business, i. e. the final decision to close down the business for an indefinite, considerable period. A general period cannot be determined as it depends on the activity in question whether the new proprietor can **still profit from the previous business** or whether it has already been liquidated. According to the *ECJ*, in the case of seasonal businesses, customary closing and continuation in the next season does not in itself lead to the loss of the identity of the economic entity (Case 287/86 – Ny Mølle Kro [1987] ECR 5467). In the case of retail stores the key element is whether the customer ties remain despite the discontinuation.

3. Transfer to the new employer

34 The transfer to a new employer of a business presupposes a change of the legal entity. The employer is the person who henceforth is **"responsible" for carrying on the business and who incurs the obligations of an employer** towards employees of the undertaking (Joined Cases 173/96 & 247/96 – Hidalgo and others [1998] ECR I-8237). The person responsible is the person carrying on the business in their own name, regardless of the question of ownership; even in the case of a new lease there could be a transfer of undertaking (Case 287/86 – Ny Mølle Kro [1987] ECR 5467; see in English law also *Young v Daniel Thwaites & Co Ltd*). It is not necessary for the new employer to carry on the business for his own account. It is of no consequence if the profits are transferred to someone else (*BAG* of 20 November 1984 – 3 AZR 584/83) or if the previous employer continues to conduct himself as employer towards the employees and the customers (*BAG* of 12 November 1998 – 8 AZR 282/97). A chattel mortgage does not in itself effectuate a transfer of undertaking, because it usually does not change the usufruct of the previous owner (*BAG* of 20 March 2003 – 8 AZR 312/02). In the case of a company it is not enough for the partners to change or the legal structure to be changed (*BAG* of 20 March 2003 – 8 AZR 312/02). A transfer of undertaking can also occur when the purchaser is a public body (such as a municipality) as long as the seller is a private company (cf. Case 151/09 – UGT-FSP [2010]; Case 463/09 – CLECE [2011]).

4. Legal transfer or merger

35 The *ECJ* adopts a very wide interpretation of the term **legal transfer**. **Direct legal relations** are **not** required. For instance, a transfer of undertaking was confirmed in the case of a new lease of a discotheque even though there were no contractual relations between the old and the new lessee (Case 324/86 – Danny's Dance Hall [1988] ECR 739). The same was held with regard to the termination of a lease of a beechwood veneer factory which the owner first retook into his possession before

selling it shortly afterwards (Case 101/87 – Bork International [1988] ECR 3057) and with regard to the awarding of a contract to a bus company by a public authority to operate bus routes which were previously operated by a different company (Case 172/99 – *Oy Liikenne* [2001] ECR I-00745).

The *ECJ* has affirmed a legal transfer even when it was based on a **unilateral decision by a public authority**. For example, in the decision in *Redmond Stichting* it was considered to be a transfer of undertaking when a public authority terminated the subsidy paid to one foundation and instead granted subsidies to another foundation with a similar aim (Case 29/91 – Redmond Stichting [1992] ECR I-3189). In *Collino*, the *ECJ* accepted a transfer of undertaking with regard to the decision by a public authority to grant a private-law company an administrative concession for activities which had been carried out previously by a public body within the state administration. (Case 343/98 – *Collino* [2000] ECR I-6659). It seems questionable as to what extent this interpretation can be reconciled with the wording of Art. 1(1)(a) with respect to several language versions of Directive 2001/23/EC. A comparison of the different language versions shows that there are terminological differences. Whereas the German, French, Italian and Dutch versions refer only to transfers resulting from a contract (*"vertragliche Übertragung"*, *"cession conventionnelle"*, *"cessione contrattuale"* and *"overdracht krachtens overeenkomst"*), which, in turn, would mean that those resulting from an administrative measure or judicial decision are excluded, the English and Danish versions ("legal transfer" and *"overdragelse"*) indicate a much wider scope (Case 135/83 – Abels [1985] ECR 469). This is why the *ECJ* interprets its meaning in light of the **protective purpose of the directive**. From the employee's point of view, it makes no difference for what reason the undertaking has changed hands. Consequently, the wide interpretation adopted by the *ECJ* is in conformity with the directive. 36

Aside from the legal transfer of undertakings, the Directive mentions in its Art. 1(1)(a) the **merger** of undertakings. A merger is defined in Art. 3(1) of Directive 78/855/EEC (amendments have been proposed by COM [2010] 391) as the operation whereby one or more companies are wound up without going into liquidation and transfer to another all their assets and liabilities in exchange for the issue to the shareholders of the company or companies being acquired of shares in the acquiring company and a cash payment, if any, not exceeding 10 % of the nominal value of the shares so issued or, where they have no nominal value, of their accounting par value. This definition is significant for the Directive on the Transfer of Undertakings, too. As a result of the merger, the newly-formed company takes over the legal position of the transferring company or the merging companies by virtue of universal succession – and thereby the successor succeeds to the rights and obligations arising from the employment relationships. 37

5. Transfer of undertakings in insolvency

Art. 5(1) of Directive 2001/23/EC specifically states that the Member States need not lay down provisions, where the transferor is the subject of bankruptcy proceedings or "any analogous insolvency proceedings which have been instituted with a view to the liquidation of the assets of the transferor". This provision was not included in the original Directive 77/187/EEC. Despite this, the *ECJ* had previously decided in an unbroken line of authority that the directive should not apply in cases 38 of bankruptcy of the transferor but that the Member States could order the same legal consequences for these cases (Case 135/83 – Abels [1985] ECR 469; Case 179/83 – Industriebond FNV [1985] ECR 511; Case 19/83 – Wendelboe [1985] ECR 457; Case 362/89 – d'Úrso [1991] ECR I-4105). According to the *ECJ*, the directive was not created to protect employees in the event of insolvency (this is the objective of Directive 2008/94/EC). It is doubtful whether the legal consequences stipulated in the directive in fact protect the employees in this situation or whether in effect they harm them by frightening off prospective purchasers.

39 Considering this aim, the Court, or rather Art. 5(1), is very restrictive. The exception applies only when the aim is, first and foremost, the liquidation of the assets of the transferor and not when the aim is to secure the estate and, if possible, carry on the undertaking. Therefore, the directive applies especially in the event of establishing hive-off companies, which is common in order to temporarily continue the undertaking. (*McMullen*, 35 Industrial Law Journal 2006, 131 *et seq.*; *Oetker*, EAS, B 7200 para. 91). Pursuant to Art. 5(2) to (4), the Member States may lay down exceptions for this case that accommodate a restructurer's interests (below para. 77).

40 However, in accordance with the jurisprudence of the *ECJ* (consistent practice of the *ECJ* since Case 135/83 – Abels [1985] ECR 469, para. 24) Art. 5(1) expressly allows the Member States to extend the scope of the provisions on transfers of undertakings to cases of insolvency. In **German law**, by virtue of an *argumentum e contrario* from § 128(2) Insolvenzordnung (InsO), it follows that § 613 a BGB is applicable to insolvency of the transferor without restriction. There, the assumption that a dismissal is socially justified is extended to include (the condition) that it does not conflict with § 613a(4) BGB. This presupposes the applicability of § 613 a BGB in cases of insolvency. According to the case-law of the **German** *Bundesarbeitsgericht*, certain modifications apply merely with regard to the continued liability of the transferor (settled case-law since *BAG* of 17 January 1980 – 3 AZR 160/79). In English law, the old Regulation 4 of TUPE 1981 purported to enable avoidance of the TUPE 1981 on insolvency disposals by the methodology of "hiving down" (see on this *McMullen*, 35 Industrial Law Journal 2006, 131 *et seq.*; *Collins*, Transfer of Undertakings and Insolvency, 18 Industrial Law Journal 1989, 144–158). The effects of this provision were rendered nugatory by the House of Lords decision in *Litster v Forth Dry Dock and Engineering Co Ltd [1989] IRLR 161* and the High Court decision in *Maxwell Fleet and Facilities Management Ltd [2000] ICR 717*, and have since been removed from the TUPE. Now, the application of TUPE 2006 is only excluded in cases of insolvency when insolvency proceedings have not been instituted with a view to liquidation of the assets of the transferor, see Regulation 8(6) of TUPE 2006.

III. Legal consequences of a transfer of undertaking

41 A transfer of undertaking produces legal consequences on many levels. The most important effects for employee protection are those concerning individual rights. The directive also stipulates consequences for the employee representatives. Aside from this it is imperative to illustrate the changes for works agreements and collective agreements. Finally, there are special provisions concerning the liability between the transferor and the transferee as well as for the event of insolvency or bankruptcy of the transferor. There is not really a copious amount of *ECJ* case law on this matter; but judgments of the *BAG* can be found in abundance.

1. The individual employment relationship

a) Succession to the rights and obligations

Pursuant to Art. 3(1) first sentence of the directive, the transferor's rights and obligations arising from an **employment relationship** existing on the date of a transfer shall be transferred to the transferee. Pursuant to the express stipulation in Art. 2(1)(d) of the directive, the term "employment relationship" is based on the national definition of employee. The aim of the directive is not complete approximation, but merely partial harmonization. Art. 2(2) prevents circumvention of the directive by adopting a narrow definition of employment relationship. Under this, part-time workers, fixed-term workers and temporary workers may not be excluded. Under **German law**, applying the decisive German definition of employee has the result that members of a company body and free-lance workers are not protected by § 613 a BGB. Under the laws of other Member States this can differ. 42

In the event of part of an undertaking being transferred, the relevant employee must **belong** to the transferred part (Case 287/86 – Ny Mølle Kro [1987] ECR 5467). It is not sufficient that a person employed in the department not transferred carries out work for the transferred part of the business. In the event of overlap, this is decided by the core of the activities. In *Botzen/Rotterdamsche Droogdok Maatschappij* (Case 186/83 – [1985] ECR 519) the *ECJ* determined the issue of employment by referring to whether or not the department of the organization to which they were assigned and in which the employment relation took effect was the one which had been transferred (this approach has been considered unhelpful, see *Selwyn*, Law of Employment, 2004, p. 232. Following this approach, see in English case-law *Sunley Turriff Holdings Ltd v Thomson*, where the plaintiff's claim of unfair dismissal was upheld. The plaintiff, who formally had an employment contract with the holding company also carried out considerable work for the subsidiary company. The subsidiary company was sold and he was not transferred. He was later made redundant. According to the Scottish EAT, the plaintiff must be regarded as an employee of the part of the undertaking transferred. This approach was applauded by **UK commentators**, see e. g. *Collins*, Employment Rights in Connection with Transfers of Parts of Groups of Companies, 25 Industrial Law Journal, 1996, 59). An employment relationship that has been terminated exists until the end of the notice period. 43

In principle, the transfer **does not change** the rights and obligations that arise from the employment contract. However, one must take note of two special cases. Firstly, company-related obligations such as restraints of trade now continue to be effective with modifications as regards the transferee. Secondly, contracts with third parties are not transferred even if they were only entered into on account of the employment contract. For instance, the share option plan of the parent company does not have to be guaranteed by the transferee, because the employment contract and the guarantee contract are two separate contracts with different legal subjects. 44

Finally, Art. 3(4) contains an exception with respect to **benefits under supplementary company or intercompany pension schemes**. The Member States need not stipulate the transfer of these benefits but must adopt other measures necessary to protect the interests of employees. 45

b) Prohibition of dismissal

46 Dismissal on grounds of the transfer of undertaking is prohibited for the transferor as well as for the transferee (Case 319/94 – Dassy [1998] ECR I-1061, para. 34) by Art. 4(1) of the directive. It is however permitted to dismiss employees for economic, technical or organisational reasons, even if these result from the transfer. Whether the transfer was the prevailing reason for the dismissal is ascertained by considering the objective circumstances. There is typically an infringement if the dismissal takes effect around the time of the transfer and the employees are taken on again by the transferee (Case 101/87 – Bork International [1988] ECR 3057; Case 319/94 – Dassy [1998] ECR I-1061, para. 39). Restructuring the undertaking before the transfer should nevertheless be possible. The *ECJ* found that a previous employee did not come within the scope of Directive 2001/23/EC (Case 386/09 – Briot [2010]).

c) The employee's right to object and to be informed

47 The directive has no provision stipulating that the employee may object to the transfer of the employment relationship and, as a result, remain with the previous employer retroactively. Art. 3(1) of the directive stipulates a transfer without the need for the employee's consent. Nevertheless German law allows an employee to object to a transfer of his employment relationship (§ 613a(6) BGB).

48 Doubts arose concerning the **conformity** of the right to object **with European Law** in 1988 after the *ECJ* decision in Berg and Busschers (joined Cases 144/87 & 145/87 – [1988] ECR 2559). In this Dutch case the employee had not consented to discharge the transferor from the obligations arising from the employment relationship. Under the national law there was neither a right to object nor any requirement of consent. The *ECJ* ruled that, subject to their being no such national law, the transferor is discharged from the obligations arising from the employment relationship irrespective of the employee's consent. The reason is that Art. 3(1) second sentence of the directive gives the Member States the power to provide for joint liability of the transferor and the transferee but does not require it. According to the *ECJ*, this neither conflicts with the aim pursued by the directive to safeguard workers' rights nor with the recognized principle in domestic law according to which no one may assume the debt of a third party without the creditor's consent. The directive pursues its own concept of protection by making it possible for the employees to continue their employment relationships under the same conditions.

49 Following this decision, several German Labour Courts referred the question to the *ECJ* for preliminary ruling, whether the right to object, which was consistent case-law of German courts, was in conformity with European Law. In *Katsikas et. al.* in 1992 the Court held that the directive did not preclude such a right (Case 132/91 – [1992] ECR I-6577). The *ECJ* did not base this decision on the 'most favourable provision' principle of Art. 8 of the directive but on the **fundamental rights of the employee**. Whilst the directive allows the employee to continue his employment relationship with the transferee, it does not oblige him to do so because the employee has a fundamental right to choose his employer. In the event of the employee not continuing the employment relationship with the transferee, it is for the Member States to decide whether the employment relationship is continued with the transferor or whether it is terminated (as the national laws of

dismissal vary widely among member states, the *ECJ*'s abstention from adjudicating on the effect of the objection was unfortunate, see on this *McMullen*, The 'Right' to Object to Transfers of Employment under TUPE, 37 Industrial Law Journal 2008, 169–177; *Laulom*, The European Court of Justice in the Dialogue on Transfers of Undertakings: A Fallible Interlocutor in Labour Law in the Courts, in: Sciarra (ed.), Labour Law in the Courts – National Judges and the Court of Justice, 2001, p. 145–178; critical also *Valdés Dal-Ré*, Transfers of Undertakings: An Experience of Clashes and Harmonies between Community Law and National Legal Systems, in: Sciarra (ed.), Labour Law in the Courts – National Judges and the Court of Justice, 2001, p. 179–197).

Katsikas, confirmed in the decision *Temco Service Industries SA* (Case 51/00 – [2002] ECR I-969), **does not lead to the conclusion that a right to object must be provided for under European law.** Otherwise the *ECJ* would have had to have ruled differently in *Berg and Busschers*, where such a right was not provided for. In fact, one must assume that in view of the fundamental right, which has not been well-defined by the *ECJ*, it is sufficient that the employee has a right to terminate the employment relationship. 50

Lodging an objection poses **risks** for the employee. He remains in the employ of the transferor as a result of the objection but the transferor can dismiss him for operational reasons if he is unable to keep him on. Consequently, lodging an objection only makes sense from the employee's point of view if only part of an undertaking has been transferred and there is a possibility of being able to work in the remaining part of the undertaking. As a constitutive right the objection cannot be rescinded or revoked. Only a termination agreement between the three parties – employee, new and previous owner – can then be concluded. 51

In the UK, the High Court considered whether an employee could object to a transfer after it had taken place (*New ISG Ltd v Vernon and Others* [2008] IRLR 115). In this case, the identity of the buyer was not made known to the employees until the day of the sale, making it impossible to exercise an objection beforehand. The High Court construed TUPE 2006 purposively in light of the directive's objectives and held that in these circumstances, where the identity of a purchaser is not learned by the employees until the day of sale, then the employees have validly objected to the transfer even though the objections were made after the sale was completed (see for more detail *McMullen*, The 'Right' to Object to Transfer of Employment under TUPE, 37 Industrial Law Journal 2008, 173 *et seqq.*). Under **German law** the right to object is linked to the employer's obligation of disclosure of the information surrounding the transfer. The employee can raise an objection within one month of being **notified** pursuant to § 613a(5) BGB (see also *McMullen*, The Right to Object to the Transfer of Employment under TUPE, 37 Industrial Law Journal 2008, 169–177; *McMullen*, Business Transfers and Employee Rights, 1998, Ch. 16, para. 16 [204]; *Körner*, The Impact of Community Law on German Labour Law: The Example of Transfer of Undertakings, European University Institute Working Papers, Law No. 96/8, p. 12). The notification is a legal obligation which can be enforced. This obligation which was not set out in Art. 7(6) of the directive until 2001 applies to certain cases and must therefore be transposed as a legal obligation pursuant to Art. 9 of the directive. Art. 7(6) stipulates a duty to inform the employees only in the event that the undertaking has no employee representatives (see below at para. 69). 52

53 **British legislators** have set out a duty to inform in Reg. 13 and 14 of the *Transfer of Undertakings (Protection of Employment) Regulations 2006*, whereby the employee representatives are to be informed in a timely manner (Reg. 13(2)). Representatives are usually trade union representatives (Reg. 13(3)(a)), failing that, employee representatives appointed or elected by the affected employees (Reg. 13(3)(b)(i)) or, failing that also, employee representatives elected by any affected employees, for the purposes of this regulation, in an election satisfying the requirements of Reg. 14(1) (Reg. 13(3)(b)(ii)). In **France** the *comité d'entreprise* is to be informed of any changes in the organisation of the undertaking pursuant to Art. L. 2323-19 *Code du travail.* This includes the transfer of undertakings.

54 The **aim** of the obligation to notify is to give the employee a basis for weighing his other options. Therefore, the employee must be informed of the date of the transfer, the reason for the transfer, the legal, economic and social implications of the transfer for the employees and any measures envisaged in relation to the employees.

2. Collective agreements/Worker representation

a) Continuance in force of the collective agreements

55 Concerning the continuance in force of the agreements made in work council agreements and collective labour agreements the directive attempts to strike a balance between the employee's interest in survival and the redemption interest of the new employer. Art. 3(3) of the directive stipulates that the transferee shall continue to observe working conditions agreed in any collective agreement for at least one year. The *ECJ* as well as Art. 3(1) only award protection to **employees who were employed at the time of the transfer**. Thus, the employer need not extend the collectively agreed working conditions to employees recruited after the transfer (Case 287/86 – Ny Mølle Kro [1987] ECR 5467, para. 26; Case 101/87 – Bork International [1988] ECR 3057, para. 17).

56 **German law** knows **two mechanisms** which lead to a continuance in force. Prior-ranking is a continuing normative effect, which results from common rules. On a subsidiary level collective arrangements are transformed into the contract of employment pursuant to § 613 a para. 1 sentence 2 to 4 BGB, and therefore do not continue to be an independent source of employee rights.

57 **Spanish Law** does not only stipulate for the continuance of the contract of employment after a transfer of undertaking, but Art. 44(1) of the Employee Statute (Real Decreto Legislativo 1/1995, de 24 de marzo, por el que se aprueba el texto refundido de la Ley del Estatuto de los Trabajadores, Art. 44) does also forsee the continuance in force of the respective collective agreements. Art. 44(1) Employee Statute sets out that "A change in the title of an undertaking, of a workplace or of an autonomous production entity does not in itself extinguish the employment relationship. The new employer has to assume the labour rights and duties as well as the social security of the previous undertaking, including the pension compromises, according to the terms as set out in their specific regulations and in general all social protection obligations, which the transferor had acquired". So, not only the acquired rights are guaranteed but also more generally the maintenance of the professional status of the employee by conserving the legal regime applicable in the previous undertaking, such as the collective agreements (*A. Desdentado Bonete*, La

sucesión de empresa: una lectura del nuevo artículo 44 del Estatuto de los Trabajadores desde la jurisprudencia, Revista del Ministerio de Trabajo y Asuntos Sociales, No. 38, 2009, pp. 241–266). Nevertheless, two problems were encountered in the Spanish legal system with respect to collective agreements. Firstly, the scope of the guarantee to maintain the collective agreement of the previous undertaking, where there is a new collective agreement within the ambit of the new undertaking available and secondly, the ways in which a certain degree of homogeneity between the employee regime of the transferring and the new undertaking may be achieved, where the application of the previous collective agreement would disrupt the labour regime of the new undertaking (*A. Desdentado Bonete* ibid.).

The problem of the concurrence of collective agreements has been solved by the Spanish Supreme Court, which established that simply the most favourable norm is applicable. Furthermore, it also said that the guarantee of Art. 44 Employee Statute is of a non-permanent character, in order to avoid the failure of a homogeneous regulation (*A. Desdentado Bonete* ibid.). Additionally, it may also be possible and not contrary to Art. 44 Employee Statute to reach a unifying agreement between the undertakings concerning the different wage structures. 58

The view of the Spanish Supreme Court is reflected in Art. 44(4) Employee Statute which explicitly establishes that the problem of concurrence is resolved by preference for the collective agreement of the transferring undertaking. Also, the temporal character of the guarantee may be deduced from this provision, which maintains that the previous collective agreement is applicable only until the date of it's expiry or the entry into force of a new collective agreement for the transferred undertaking. 59

Nevertheless, and more in line with European Law, the **Italian Supreme Court** came to the conclusion in a recent decision that the previous collective agreement will continue to apply with respect to intangible rights, such as e. g. supplementary pension schemes and health insurance (Sentenza della Suprema Corte n° 10614 del 13 maggio 2011). 60

Case C-108/10 – **Ivana Scattolon** v. **Ministero dell'Istruzione, dell'Università e della Ricerca**

Ms Scattolon, employed by the municipality of Scorzè (Italy) as a cleaner in State schools, carried out that task as a member of the administrative, technical and auxiliary (ATA) staff of the local authority. As from 2000, she was transferred onto the list of State ATA employees and placed on a salary scale corresponding, on that list, to nine years of service. Having failed to obtain from the Ministero dell'Istruzione, dell'Università e della Ricerca recognition of her service of about 20 years with the municipality of Scorzè and considering that she had thus suffered a considerable reduction in her remuneration, Ms Scattolon brought an action before the Tribunale di Venezia (Italy) seeking recognition of the whole of that length of service.

The Tribunale di Venezia asks the Court of Justice whether EU legislation on the maintenance of workers' rights in the event of the transfer of an undertaking applies to the takeover, by a public authority of a Member State, of staff employed by another public authority. Should that question be answered in the

affirmative, the Italian court also asks whether, in order to calculate the remuneration of transferred workers, the transferee must take those workers' length of service with the transferor into account.
The Court of Justice finds first, that the takeover by a public authority of a Member State of staff employed by another public authority and entrusted with the supply to schools of auxiliary services such as maintenance and administrative assistance constitutes a transfer of an undertaking where that staff consists in a structured group of employees who are protected as workers by virtue of the domestic law of that Member State. More important was the answer to the second question. The Court considers that, whilst it is permissible for the transferee to apply, from the date of transfer, the working conditions laid down by the collective agreement in force with the transferee, the arrangements chosen for salary integration of the transferred workers must be in conformity with the aim of EU legislation on protection of the rights of transferred workers. The court stated: "Implementation of the option to replace, with immediate effect, the conditions which the transferred workers enjoy under the collective agreement with the transferor with those laid down by the collective agreement in force with the transferee cannot therefore have the aim or effect of imposing on those workers conditions which are, overall, less favourable than those applicable before the transfer". It is unclear, how wide this statement has to be interpreted, especially, considering following decisions like the **Alemo-Herron Case** (C-426/11 of 18 July 2013), where the court stated, that employees who transfer to a new organisation are not entitled to the benefit of collectively agreed terms where those terms are agreed to after the date of the transfer and the new organisation was not a party to the negotiation of those terms.

b) Preservation of the legal status and function of the employee's representation

61 Pursuant to Art. 6(1) sentence 1 the legal status and function of the employee's representation must be preserved on the same terms, when the undertaking continues to be autonomous and the necessary conditions for the constitution of the employee's representation are fulfilled. The "representatives of employees" are defined as representatives of the employees according to the laws or common practices of the Member States in Art. 2(1) (c). Unlike before Directive 98/50/EC employee representatives in the administrative, directory and supervisory organs of corporations are no longer explicitly excluded.

62 The undertaking's administrative structure also continues to exist assuming the identity of the undertaking is retained, which according to the wording of Art. 6(1) sentence 1 is authoritative at company level. In Art. 6(1) sentence 3 it is suggested to the Member States to provide for an employee's representation in the case where bankruptcy or insolvency proceedings with the aim of the liquidation of assets have been instituted against the transferor. In this situation the transfers of undertakings according to Art. 5(1) are exempted from the application of the directive. The suggestion in Art. 6(1) sentence 3 is of pure declaratory nature, because the Member States could provide for such a settlement anyway pursuant to the 'most favourable

provision' principle in Art. 8. By means of Art. 6(1) sentence 3, the European legislator merely shows how important an employee's representation is to him.

By preserving the employee's representation the **reconstitution or reappointment** thereof is not prevented according to the statutory exemption in Art. 6(1) sentence 2. According to this the winding up of the previous employee's representation is possible if it has been provided for by national laws and administrative provisions or practices or if it has been agreed upon with the employee's representation. 63

In case the undertaking loses its identity and it completely merges into another undertaking or part thereof, there is no protection by Art. 6(1) sentence 1. In that case sentence 4 of the respective article applies. Then the Member States have to provide for an employee's representation during the transition period until a new one has been formed. 64

In the *UGT* judgment, the *ECJ* was concerned with a preliminary question which arose in a Spanish dispute regarding the in-house take over of the Ayuntamiento de La Línea de la Concepción (the local government of the town La Línea de la Concepción) of public services which had been outsourced into four private undertakings. The services to be taken over involved caretaking and cleaning in public schools, street cleaning and maintenance of parks and gardens (Case 151/09 – Federación de Servicios Públicos de la UGT (UGT-FSP) v. Ayuntamiento de La Línea de la Concepción, María del Rosario Vecino Uribe & Ministerio Fiscal [2010] para. 12). The employees who had been exercising these tasks had been taken on by the local government and integrated into its staff. "Those same employees all remain in the same posts and carry out the same duties as before the takeover, in the same places of work and under the orders of the same immediate managers, without any significant changes in their working conditions, the sole difference being that those ultimately in charge, above those immediate managers, are now competent elected officials, namely, the municipal councilors or the mayor." (Ibid., para. 13.) The real problem concerned the lawfully appointed representatives of the employees of the four private undertakings, which after the take-over submitted to the local government of La Línea a request for some time off in order to fulfill their duties as representative. These requests were, however, rejected since their integration into the municipal workforce meant that they were no longer the lawfully appointed representatives (ibid., para. 14). The Federación de Servicios Públicos de la UGT, a trade union and the concerned representatives, brought an action against the local government. The Spanish Court decided to stay proceedings and essentially asked the *ECJ* whether a transferred economic entity would preserve its autonomy within the meaning of Art. 6(1) Directive 2001/23/EC under the given circumstances in the present case. The *ECJ* ruled that the entity would indeed preserve its autonomy where the powers of those entrusted with the entity remain the same within the organizational structure of the acquirer. It further said that the mere change of the persons in charge would not result in the loss of autonomy, except where such change results in powers "which enable them to organize directly the activities of the employees of that entity and therefore to substitute their decision-making within that entity for that of those immediately in charge of the employees." (para. 57). 65

c) Information and Consultation of the Workers' Representation

66 Art. 7 of the Transfer of Undertakings Directive provides for the information and consultation of the employee representatives. Section 1 deals with the information, section 2 with the consultation. Sections 3 to 6 provide for exceptional and supplementary arrangements.

67 According to a judgment of the *ECJ* in 1994 the information and consultation duties result in **a duty to designate the employee's representation**. Otherwise, the duties of the Transfer of Undertakings Directive would have no impact (Case 382/92 – Commission v. United Kingdom and Northern Ireland [1994] ECR I-2435, para. 18).

68 On account of this judgment the **British legislator** was forced to constrain its "single channel" model of employee representation. Until then, employee representation was restricted to representation by the trade unions which were not recognized by all employers (see *Davies*, A Challenge to Single Channel?, 23 International Law Journal 1994, 272–285; *Davies/Kilpatrick*, UK Worker Representation After Single Channel, 33 International Law Journal 2004, 121–151; *Hall*, Beyond Recognition? Employee Representation and EU law, 25 International Law Journal 1996, 15–27). Sec. 13(3) TUPE now provides that either a trade union recognised by the employer or other representatives elected by the employees have to be consulted. Thus, aside from the trade unions other forms of employee representation are now provided for, see *Barnard*, EC Employment Law, 2000, p. 451 *et seq.* on the previous law.

69 However, the **European legislator** has provided for a special arrangement in its Art. 7(6) in case an undertaking does not have an employee's representation. This, however, is merely a catch-all provision which shall at least guarantee a minimum protection, where a Member State has not met its obligations or the small business exception is applicable. According to Art. 7(5) Member States are allowed to exempt undertakings or businesses from the information and consultation duty if the election or nomination of a collegiate body representing the employees is not provided for. This way, a certain degree of flexibility is maintained for small businesses with no or only one employee representative (Commission proposal, COM(94) 300 final, para. 41). Considering, on the other hand, that the information and consultation duty should not lose all impact, the Member States must lay down such thresholds quite low that solely exempt small businesses. In **Germany**, employees can usually elect a works council at the establishment size of at least 5 employees, that consists of three members (§ 9 S. 1 Betriebsverfassungsgesetz (BetrVG)) and possesses information and consultation rights pursuant to § 111 BetrVG, if the company has more than 20 employees. The German thresholds are in conformity with the directive by solely exempting small businesses. The alternative information of the individual employees as envisaged in Art. 7(6) of the directive is implemented by § 613 a Abs. 5 BGB and exceeds the requirements of the directive (see above para. 52).

70 In **Spanish law**, the situation is very similar to German law. Art. 44(6) of the Employee Statute (Real Decreto Legislativo 1/1995, de 24 de marzo, por el que se aprueba el texto refundido de la Ley del Estatuto de los Trabajadores, Art. 44(6)) contains the information duty. Specifically, it sets out that the transferor as well as the transferee will have to inform the employee representatives of the employees affected by the transfer, of the date of transfer, the motives for the transfer, the legal, economic and social consequences for the employees and measures forseen concerning the employees (Real Decreto [...] Art. 44(6), ibid.). Additionally, like in

German Law, it has also been set out that where an undertaking does not have legal representatives, the transferor and transferee shall facilitate the abovementioned information to the affected employees. So, also Spanish law exceeds the requirements of the Directive.

The transferor as well as the transferee are obliged **to inform the employee's representation**; the transferor before the execution of the transfer, the transferee before the employees are directly affected. By this differentiated arrangement of the times, it is guaranteed that the employers can foresee the changes, so as to actually be able to inform the employees. The information has to include the time of the transfer, the reasons for the transfer, the consequences of the transfer for the employee and the measures intended for the employees. 71

A **consultation** as regards measures in relation to the employees is necessary pursuant to Art. 7(2) of the directive. The duty concerns the person who wants to take such measures. The concept of measure has to be interpreted broadly in order to protect the employees and therefore encompasses every change of the economical, legal and social position of the employee which has been effectuated in the course of the transfer, which has a material detrimental impact on the employees. The consultations must be conducted with the aim to reach an agreement, but a duty to agree does not exist unlike the commission proposal of 1974 (Proposal of the Commission of 31 May 1974, COM (74) 351/2 final, Art. 8(2)). 72

The **arbitration board model** in Art. 7(3) replaces the information and consultation set out in section 1 and 2. This was inserted at the **insistence of Germany** which made its consent to the text of the directive dependant upon the retention of the German provisions on the change in conduct of the business (§§ 111 *et seq.* Betriebsverfassungsgesetz (BetrVG)). For this reason Art. 7(3) is largely similar to §§ 111 *et seq.* BetrVG. Information and consultation are not required in all mentioned cases in sections 1 and 2, but only if the executed transfer provokes a change in the conduct of the business, which may have material disadvantages for the employees as a consequence. In return for this relaxation an enforceable arbitration procedure has to be provided for. 73

3. Further liability of the transferor

Albeit not imperative under Union law but expressly allowed in Art. 3(1) sentence two of the directive, some Member States made provisions for joint liability. 74

In **German law** § 613 a paras. 2 and 3 BGB set out the joint and several further liability of the transferor for obligations passed on to the transferee to the extent they arose before the transfer and become due within a year. The idea underlying this liability is that the transferor has received returns for the undertaking, which were also generated by the workforce. As a result the employee receives an additional debtor.

In **Luxembourg**, when an insolvent business is transferred, there will be joint liability of the transferor and transferee for those employment obligations which arose before the transfer. These are deduced from the employment contract or relationship which existed at the date of the transfer. In cases where the transfer is within three months after the insolvency of the business, the contracts which have 75 been terminated due to the insolvency will be automatically renewed (*Schintgen/ Faber*, Le Contrat de Travail, 2010, p. 254).

76 Pursuant to Art. 44(3) of the Statute of Employees **Spanish Law** sets out that the transferor and transferee are jointly liable for obligations arising out of the employment relationship which have been incurred before the transfer and which could not be satisfied. Furthermore, they will also be jointly liable for the debts which have been made after the transfer, when the transfer has been declared as delinquent.

4. Particularities in insolvency proceedings

77 To the extent that the transfer of the undertaking is captured by the directive notwithstanding the insolvency of the transferor, i. e. when the liquidation of the assets is not the sole aim of the proceedings (Art. 5(1) of the directive), the Member States may provide for certain **exceptional provisions** according to Art. 5(2) to (4). First of all, they may prescribe that debts which were payable before the institution of the insolvency proceedings shall not be transferred to the transferee pursuant to Art. 5(2)(a), if the claims of the employees have been safeguarded otherwise. According to Art. 5(2)(b) Member States may allow for alterations to the working conditions, if they serve the restructuring, and hence the preservation of jobs. Such provisions can be maintained by the Member States for such undertakings which are in a situation of serious economic crisis and are subject to judicial supervisions pursuant to Art. 5(3). However, no exceptional provisions can be newly introduced for those undertakings. Furthermore, according to Art. 5(4) Member States must ensure that the insolvency proceedings are not abused to circumvent the transfer of undertaking regulations.

78 The **German legislator** did not make use of the possibilities to create exemptions. According to the case-law of the *Bundesarbeitsgericht (BAG)* § 613 a BGB is applicable in insolvency to the extent that it deals with the protection of the employees and their representation. § 613 a BGB is teleologically reduced in so far as it stipulates the liability of the transferee for previously accrued debts. The allocation principles of the insolvency proceedings are prior-ranking for those debts (settled case law since *BAG* of 17 January 1980 – 3 AZR 160/79; *BAG* of 20 June 2002 – 8 AZR 459/01). Otherwise, the employee would be preferred before the other creditors contrary to the principle of equitable satisfaction, as they would receive a new debtor. The remaining creditors would be disadvantaged this way because the purchase price for the undertaking would be reduced accordingly (settled case law since *BAG* of 17 January 1980 – 3 AZR 160/79; *BAG* of 4 July 1989 – 3 AZR 756/87, AP No. 10 to § 1 BetrAVG Betriebsveräußerung). Therewith, the BAG in its case-law makes use of the exception of Art. 5(2)(a) of the Directive in conformity with European law.

79 Art. 44 of the **Spanish statute** for employees (Real Decreto Legislativo 1/1995, de 24 de marzo, por el que se aprueba el texto refundido de la Ley del Estatuto de los Trabajadores) which is applicable to transfer of undertakings, does not foresee any exception to the safeguarding of terms and conditions of employment where a transfer is effectuated in the event of bankruptcies or any analogous insolvency proceedings, if there is a continuation of the economic entity. It is the public authority who is responsible for the supervision of such insolvency proceedings which may decide to reduce the debts owed to the employees when they are

transferred to the transferee. Furthermore, the Spanish Insolvency Law (Ley 22/2003, de 9 de julio, Concursal) sets out that the transferee and the representatives of the employees may agree to change the collective work conditions with the aim of safeguarding the undertaking (*Sargeant*, Implementation Report Directive 2001/23/EC, Human European Consultancy, June 2007, Official Website of the European Commission – Directorate-General for Employment, Social Affairs and Equal Opportunities).

In the UK, on the other hand, the legislator has made use of Art. 5 of the Directive **80**
as can be seen in the already mentioned TUPE Regulations. It has been among others set out that at least some of the debts the employer owes to the employees will not be transferred to the new employer. These debts concern obligations such as statutory redundancy payments as well as sums of payments, such as arrears of payment, payments in lieu of notice, holiday pay or a basic award of compensation of unfair dismissal. Pursuant to Art. 5(2) of the Directive the TUPE Regulations also allow the transferee to make changes to the terms and conditions of employment where there is a situation of insolvency, subject to approval by the employee representatives.

§ 6. Protection against collective redundancies

Literature: *Craig*, "Establishment" and redundancy consultation, 14 Employment Law Bulletin 1996, 9; *Dine*, Why not employee participation in the European Community context?, 16 (2) Company Lawyer 1995, 44; *Neilson*, The extent of the obligation to consult about the reason for redundancies, 82 Employment Law Bulletin, 2007, 7; *Warren*, Employee involvement and staff consultation in Europe, 13 European Lawyer 2001, 34.

I. Collective redundancies as an issue of employment law

A dismissal, that is, the termination of an employment relationship at the employer's initiative, has a severe impact on an employee's life. His long-term plans for the future are called into question, and he is often forced to leave his roots behind in order to find work in another area. Consequently, one of the main objectives of employment law has always been to protect employees against random or unfair dismissals (sec. 94 and sec. 98 of the British Employment Rights Act 1996, § 1 of the German Kündigungsschutzgesetz). Consequently, in most European states some form of dismissal protection limits an employer's ability to hire and fire at will. This is especially true in cases where, following economic restructurings, a great number of employment relationships are terminated simultaneously. Not only is the need for protection multiplied by the plethora of dismissals in the event of collective redundancies. The employer's actions take on a new dimension: Particularly, but not only, in markets that are restricted to a certain region, laying off a large number of employees leads to a backlog of manpower supply. This makes it even more difficult for the laid-off worker to return to employment. The individual worker requires even more protection in this case. 1

The European Union first dealt with this phenomenon in the **Directive 75/129/ EEC** of 17 February 1975 on the approximation of the laws of the Member States relating to collective redundancies. Amendments and clarifications followed in **Directives 92/56/EEC** of 24 June 1992 and **98/59/EC** of 20 July 1998. The Directorate-General for Employment and Social Affairs announced in 2010 that it would review Directive 98/59/EC and possibly propose amendments. 2

This Directive obligates the employer to consult the employees' representatives in the event of collective redundancies. It stipulates which issues must be dealt with in these consultations and which information the employer must provide. Furthermore, the Directive sets out the procedure to be followed in these cases. 3

At the heart of Directive 98/59/EC is the awareness that "greater protection should be afforded to workers in the event of collective redundancies while taking into account the need for balanced economic and social development within the Community" (Recital 2 of Directive 98/59/EC). Under Art. 1(1) of Directive 98/59/EC "collective redundancies" means dismissals effected by an employer for one or more reasons not related to the individual workers concerned where, according to the choice of the Member States, the number of redundancies is either, over a period of 30 days, at least 10 per cent of the number of workers in establishments normally employing more than 20 and less than 100 workers, at least 10 per cent in establish- 4 ments normally employing at least 100 but less than 300 workers, at least 30 per cent in establishments normally employing 300 workers or more, or, over a period of 90 days, at least 20 per cent, whatever the number of workers normally employed in the establishments in question. The Directive does not apply to dismissals of workers in establishments governed by public law or of the crews of seagoing vessels or dismissals effected under contracts of employment concluded for limited periods of time or for specific tasks. **Germany** transposed these instructions in its §§ 17(1), 22, 23(2) Kündigungsschutzgesetz; in part going beyond the level of protection afforded by the Directive. The **United Kingdom** preferred a 'copy-out' transposition in sec. 188 of the Trade Union and Labour Relations (Consolidation) Act 1992.

5 Pursuant to Arts. 2 and 3, if the threshold numbers are reached, the employer must inform and consult the workers' representatives in good time and inform the competent public authority of the intended redundancies. The consultations with the workers' representatives shall cover ways and means to avoid or limit the intended collective redundancies as well as to mitigate the consequences by recourse to accompanying social measures aimed, *inter alia*, at aid for redeploying or retraining workers made redundant. Art. 2(3) presents a list of elements to be supplied to the workers' representatives by the employer. This list was adopted in § 17(2) Kündigungsschutzgesetz, Art. L-1233-10 *Code du travail* and sec. 188(4), Trade Union and Labour Relations (Consolidation) Act 1992. The notification of the public authority shall contain any comments made by the workers' representatives (Art. 3(1) of Directive 98/59/EC).

6 'Workers' representatives' means the workers' representatives provided for by the laws or practices of the Member States. Under sec. 188 of the Trade Union and Labour Relations (Consolidation) Act 1992 the trade union representatives must be consulted. Art. L-1233-8 *Code du travail* stipulates the notification of the *comité d'entreprise* or the *délégués du personnel*. In **Germany**, the works council must be consulted; the competent public authority is the *Bundesagentur für Arbeit*.

7 A further consequence of collective redundancies next to the notification duties is, pursuant to Art. 4 of the Directive, that the redundancies do not take effect earlier than 30 days after the notification of the public authority. The public authority can extend this period of time to 60 days under certain circumstances. Under Art. 5, the Member States may apply or introduce laws, regulations or administrative provisions which are more favourable to workers or promote or allow the application of collective agreements more favourable to workers. Art. 6 sets out that Member States shall ensure that judicial and/or administrative procedures for the enforcement of obligations are available to the workers' representatives and/or the workers.

II. Definitions employed by the *ECJ*

8 The interpretation of the terms used in the directive has, as is so often the case, presented certain difficulties. Court cases regarding Directive 98/59/EC are rare. The *ECJ* has recently however had the opportunity to clarify some important terms of the Directive.

1. The term "establishment"

9 In Case 270/05 – Athinaïki Chartopoiía [2007] ECR I-1499 the *ECJ* ruled that Art. 1(1)(a) is to be interpreted to mean that a production unit comes within the

concept of 'establishment' for the purposes of the application of Directive 98/59/EC. According to this, an 'establishment' is the unit to which the workers made redundant are assigned to carry out their duties. The entity in question need not have any legal, economic, financial, administrative or technological autonomy. The case concerned a Greek company that had decided to shut down one of its three separate production units and to dismiss the employees who worked in that unit. The employees successfully challenged the dismissals in court. The Court of Appeal dismissed the company's appeal on the ground that the production unit in question did not constitute an establishment and did not therefore fall under the Greek exception rule which implemented the derogation contained in Art. 4(4) of Directive 98/59/EC. Under this rule, the competent authority need not be notified about the collective redundancies if the termination of the establishment's activities is the result of a judicial decision (see also Case 235/10 – Claes [2011]). That provision had been interpreted by the Greek national courts as also applying where the termination is the result of a unilateral decision by the employer. Although the production unit was considered to be an establishment within the meaning of the Directive, the *ECJ* held that the plaintiff could not rely on the exception rule because the derogation in Art. 4(4) is limited to terminations as a result of judicial decisions.

Particular aspects need to be considered in the event of **collective redundancies in a group of undertakings**. Pursuant to Art. 2(4) of the Directive the notification obligations apply irrespective of whether the decision regarding collective redundancies is being taken by the employer or by an undertaking controlling the employer. In considering alleged breaches of the information, consultation and notification requirements laid down by this Directive, account shall not be taken of any defence on the part of the employer on the ground that the necessary information has not been provided to the employer by the undertaking which took the decision leading to collective redundancies. In the **Case 44/08 – AEK [2009] ECR I-8163** the *ECJ* held that Art. 2(1) and (4) of the Directive are to be interpreted to mean that in the case of a group of undertakings consisting of a parent company and one or more subsidiaries, the obligation for the subsidiary which has the capacity of employer to consult workers' representatives arises only where that subsidiary, within which collective redundancies may be made, has been identified. Consultations with the workers' representatives can be started only if it is known in which undertaking collective redundancies may be made. Where the parent company of a group of undertakings adopts decisions likely to have repercussions on the jobs of workers within that group, it is for the subsidiary whose employees may be affected by the redundancies, in its capacity as their employer, to start consultations with the workers' representatives. It is therefore not possible to start such consultations until such time as that subsidiary has been identified. On the other hand, the adoption, within a group of undertakings, of strategic decisions or of changes in activities which compel the employer to contemplate or to plan for collective redundancies gives rise to an obligation on that employer to consult workers' representatives. The creation of the obligation on the employer to start consultations on contemplated collective redundancies cannot depend on whether the employer is already able to supply to the workers' representatives all the information required by Art. 2(3)(b) of the Directive (Case 44/08 – AEK [2009] ECR I-8163). This decision is consistent with the previous case-law on the interpretation of the Directive which has always focussed on the 10 practical efficacy of the consultation procedure. It is only right that the dependent company as the employer is the one that is obligated to conduct the consultation procedure. But there are difficulties pinpointing the exact time when this obligation arises. The *ECJ*'s decision seems to be a little contradictory on this point. It is submitted that the consultation obligations arise once the relevant bodies of the parent company take a decision that will probably result in collective redundancies and – in addition – when the subsidiary, within which the collective redundancies may be made, has been identified.

2. The term "redundancy"

11 Of greater significance was the decision in *Junk* (Case 188/03 – [2005] ECR I-885) regarding the term "redundancy". Did this mean the termination of the employment relationship upon expiry of the period of notice or did it mean the declaration of the notice of dismissal? Referring to the purpose of the Directive 98/59/EC, the *ECJ* ruled that 'redundancy' is to be interpreted to mean the declaration to terminate the contract of employment and that this may not be carried out before the end of the consultation and notification procedure. The purpose of the directive, as set out in Art. 2(2), is to avoid terminations of contracts of employment or to reduce the number of such terminations. The achievement of that purpose would be jeopardized if the consultation of workers' representatives were to be subsequent to the employer's decision. It follows that an employer cannot terminate contracts of employment before he has engaged in the consultation procedure, i. e. before the employer has fulfilled his obligations under Art. 2. Accordingly, Art. 3(1) refers to 'projected' redundancies having to be notified to the public authorities.

12 The *ECJ* has decided that cases where the termination of employment contracts of an entire staff occurs as a result of the death of the employer do not constitute collective redundancies (Case 323/08 – Rodríguez Mayor [2009] ECR I-11621).

13 The law regarding collective redundancies applies in addition to national laws protecting against unfair dismissals. How these concepts interact can be illustrated by the **Mono Car Styling** case before the *ECJ* (Case 12/08 – [2009] ECR I-6653). The Belgian case dealt with the question whether the Directive precluded a national law which introduced procedures intended to permit both workers' representatives and the workers themselves as individuals to ensure compliance with the obligations laid down in that Directive, but which limited the individual right of action of workers in regard to the complaints which may be raised and made that right subject to the requirement that workers' representatives should first have raised objections with the employer and that the worker concerned has informed the employer in advance of his intention to query whether the information and consultation procedure has been complied with. The issue was therefore, whether the dismissal protection afforded to the individual employee can be made subject to the consultation of the workers' representatives. The *ECJ* held that the right to information and consultation provided for in Directive 98/59/EC is intended to benefit workers as a collective group, not the individual worker. This right is collective in nature and afforded to the workers' representatives. A national rule limiting the individual worker's right to make a claim before a court is therefore permissible.

3. Penalties in the event of non-compliance

Art. 6 sets out that Member States 'shall ensure that judicial and/or administrative procedures for the enforcement of obligations under this Directive are available to the workers' representatives and/or workers'. This is a clear instruction for the Member States to provide either the employee or the workers' representatives, or both, with a judicial remedy in order to enforce the information, consultation and notification duties. According to the jurisprudence of the *ECJ*, penalties imposed to ensure compliance with directives must be effective, proportionate and dissuasive. 14

In the **United Kingdom**, redress to the courts is only available to the trade unions, under sec. 189 of the Trade Union and Labour Relations (Consolidation) Act 1992. In **Belgian law**, the workers' representatives have a right to challenge non-observance of consultation and notification obligations before a court. Art. 67 of *la loi du 13 février 1998* gives workers an individual right of challenge, although it is limited in regard to the complaints which may be raised and subject to the conditions that workers' representatives should first have raised objections and that the worker concerned has informed the employer in advance of his intention to challenge compliance with the information and consultation procedure. These conditions placed on the exercise of challenge were found to be in conformity with the Directive in the *ECJ* case *Mono Car Styling* (see above, Case 12/08 – Mono Car Styling [2009] ECR I-6653). In Denmark an employer risks a criminal fine and may have to pay compensation to each employee in the event of violating the consultation and notification procedures, but the dismissals remain effective, § 11 *et seqq.* of Act no. 414, *Lov om Kollektive Afskedigelser*. There are similar sanctions in **French law**, which include the dismissals being declared void (Art. L-1233-1 *et seqq. Code du travail*). The **German** *Kündigungsschutzgesetz* has no express penalty provisions in the event of non-compliance with the notification and consultation duties. However, the absence of penalty provisions for non-compliance with the notification obligations does not present a problem: the notification to the public authority must contain comments made by the works council (§ 17 Kündigungsschutzgesetz). Consequently, in the absence of a notification of the works council and, with that, any comments to be forwarded to the public authority, any redundancies declared are ineffective under § 18(1) Kündigungsschutzgesetz. In turn, the employee can make a claim before the Labour Court. This meets the requirements set out in Art. 6 of Directive 98/59/EC. Non-compliance with the consultation obligations, however, does not render the redundancy ineffective under German law. Consequently, German law allows for collective redundancies to be effective without prior consultations. This seems to be not consistent with the requirements set out in Art. 6 of the Directive. The German legislators have the option of declaring such redundancies ineffective or of giving the works council a judicial remedy to enforce the consultation obligation. A cumulation of both instruments would be permissible under European law, as they would be measures that are effective, proportionate and dissuasive. 15

§ 7. Working Time

Literature: *Adnett/Hardy*, Reviewing the Working Time Directive: rationale, implementation and case law, 32 Industrial Relations Journal 2001, 114–125; *Blanpain*, European Labour Law, 13th ed., 2012; *Ewing*, Swimming with the Tide: Employment Protection and the Implementation of European Labour Law, 22 Industrial Law Journal 1993, No. 3, 165–180; *Hardy*, Harmonising European Working Time in an Enlarged EU: A Case of Failed 'Humanisation'?, 22 International Journal of Comparative Labour Law and Industrial Relations 2006, 563–601; *Mair*, Maternity Leave: Improved and Simplified?, 63 Modern Law Review 2000, No. 6, 877–886; *v. Prondzynski*, Council Directive 93/104/EC Concerning Certain Aspects of the Organization of Working Time, 23 Industrial Law Journal 1994, No. 1, 92–95.

I. General

Regulating working time has always been a core issue of employment law. The 1 first employment laws dealt with precisely this matter (see for the USA the famous legislation on working time for bakers in the case *Lochner v. State of New York*, 198 U.S. 45 (1905)). For a long time the rules of working time were a *domain reservé* of the Member States. Slowly but surely European labour law has evolved in this area, too. **Directive 2003/88/EC** in particular deals with certain aspects of the **organization of working time** as well as **night and shift work**. It was adopted on the basis of Art. 137(2) first sentence (b) EC [now Art. 153(2) first sentence (b) TFEU] in conjunction with Art. 137(1)(a) EC [now Art. 153(1)(a) TFEU] and represents a re-codification of its predecessor Directive 93/104/EC, which was amended considerably by Directive 2000/34/EC. Both predecessor directives were consolidated and repealed by Directive 2003/88/EC. This re-codification was meant to create more transparency and clarity in the law of European working hours (Recital 1 of Directive 2003/88/EC). The first EC set of laws concerning the organization of working hours are however far older than the first directive on this subject. As early as in the 1970 s one came across the first endeavours to harmonize the Community in this area. The Recommendation 75/457/EEC (Council Recommendation of 22 July 1975 regarding the principle of a 40-hour week and four weeks' annual paid holidays, OJ 1975 L-199/32) stipulated the first obligations regarding weekly maximum working hours and the minimum annual holiday. As a recommendation though, this measure was not binding. It was not until Directive 93/104/EC that the first binding obligations were imposed on national laws concerning working hours. Its adoption was highly controversial. It took three years of negotiations before it was enacted. The **United Kingdom** continued to resist the directive even after its adoption (for further details on the background of the directive see *Prondzynski*, 23 Industrial Law Journal 1994, 92 et seq.; *Hardy*, 22 International Journal of Comparative Labour Law and Industrial Relations 2006, pp. 563 *et seqq.*; for details on the British government's opposition see *Adnett* and *Hardy*, 32 Industrial Relations Journal, 2001, pp. 114 *et seqq.*).

2

Case 84/94 – **United Kingdom ./. Council** [1996] ECR I-5755

After the Working Time Directive was adopted the United Kingdom brought an action under Art. 173 EC-Treaty (today's Art. 263 TFEU) before the *ECJ* for the annulment of the Directive. It applied for the annulment of Directive 93/104/EC in its entirety, and in the alternative, Arts. 4, 5(1) and (2), 6(2) and (7). The United Kingdom pleaded that Art. 118 a EEC, as it then was, was not a legal basis for the directive because there were no scientific indications to attest that the Working Time Directive is a measure with a genuine and objective link to the health and safety of workers within the meaning of Art. 118 a EC-Treaty. Furthermore, it claimed a breach of the principle of proportionality and infringement of essential procedural requirements. Finally, the applicant pleaded that the Council had misused its powers as the directive contained measures which, in the opinion of the United Kingdom, had no objective connection with the purported aim. The *ECJ* did not uphold this view for the most part. Rather, it supported a broad interpretation of the scope of application of Art. 118 a EEC. Art. 118 a confers upon the Community internal legislative competence in the area of social policy. On this basis, minimum requirements can be adopted to improve the protection of the safety and health of workers. Only Art. 5(2) of Directive 93/104/EC was annulled by the *ECJ*. This Art. stipulated that the minimum weekly rest period under Art. 5(1) must, in principle, include Sundays. In the *ECJ*'s opinion there is no sufficient reason why Sunday is more closely connected with the health and safety of workers than any other day of the week. Therefore, a prohibition of work on Sundays could not be based on Art. 118 a EC Treaty.

3 The Directive 2003/88/EC represents the centrepiece of the European law of working hours. In addition there is a number of other special rules for certain areas of activity (see para. 7). The Directive only sets out the **minimum requirements** for the protection of safety and health with respect to the organization of working time, under Art. 1(1). Therefore, the Member States and the Social Partners may apply provisions which are more favourable than those contained in the Directive to protect workers' safety and health, Art. 15. Conversely, the Directive does not justify a reduction of the level of existing worker protection in the Member States, Art. 23. Aim of the Working Time Directive is an **improvement of workers' safety and health** at work (Recitals 2 and 4 of Directive 2003/88/EC). To this end it compiles rules concerning daily and weekly minimum rest periods, minimum annual leave, breaks and maximum weekly working hours, as well as certain aspects of night and shift work and patterns of work, Art. 1(2).

4 **The European provisions only apply to the amount of work to be performed by a worker but do not regulate the obligation to pay remuneration.** So if the European provision for example includes standby service in the calculation of working hours and thus restricts the maximum length, then this does not say anything about how this is to be remunerated.

II. Scope of application

5 The **scope** of the Directive 2003/88/EC covers, **in principle, all sectors of activity, both public and private**, Art. 1(3) first sentence. This includes, e. g.: industrial,

agricultural, commercial, administrative, service or vocational, cultural and leisure activities, Art. 1(4) of Directive 2003/88/EC in conjunction with Art. 2(1) of Directive 89/391/EEC (Framework Directive on Protection at Work). Seafarers as defined in Directive 1999/63/EC are excluded under Art. 1(3) second sentence of Directive 2003/88/EC. Furthermore, under Art. 1(4) of Directive 2003/88/EC in conjunction with Art. 2(2) first sentence of Directive 89/391/EEC the rules do not apply to certain specific public service activities, e. g. the armed forces, the police, and the civil protection services where their characteristics inevitably conflict with the application. Nevertheless, the Member States have a duty under Art. 1(4) of Directive 2003/88/EC in conjunction with Art. 2(2) second sentence of Directive 89/391/EEC to ensure as far as possible that the safety and health of workers is protected in light of the objectives of the Framework Directive on Protection at Work as well as the Working Time Directive.

Case 303/98 – **Sindicato de Medicos de Asistencia Publica (Simap)** 6
[2000] ECR I-7505

In the Simap case the Tribunal Superior de Justicia de la Comunidad Valenciana submitted the question to the *ECJ*, inter alia, whether doctors who work for the public health service fall within the scope of application of the Working Time Directive or if they are excluded from the scope of application by Art. 1(4) of Directive 93/104/EC in conjunction with Art. 2(2) second sentence of Directive 89/391/EEC. The *ECJ* supported a broad interpretation of the scope of the Directive 89/391/EEC. It noted that this can be derived from the objective to improve workers' safety and health protection as well as from the wording of its Art. 2(1). By implication, the exclusions from the scope of Directive 89/391/EEC and therefore also its Art. 2(2) must be interpreted narrowly. Moreover, Art. 2(2) of Directive 89/391/EEC excludes only certain specific activities in the public service which are meant to secure public safety and order and are indispensible to the common good. As a rule such activities cannot be equated with the activities of doctors. Doctors who work in the public health service therefore do not fall under the exception of Art. 2(2) of Directive 89/391/EEC. They are not excluded from the scope of this Directive nor the scope of the Working Time Directive under Art. 1(4) of Directive 93/104/EC in conjunction with Art. 2(2) second sentence of Directive 89/391/EEC.

Case 397/01 to 403/01 – **Pfeiffer**
[2004] ECR I-8835

The restrictive interpretation of the exception provision in Art. 2(2) of Directive 89/391/EEC was confirmed by the *ECJ* in the Pfeiffer case. That matter concerned the question whether emergency workers are covered by the directive. The Court held once again that the scope of Directive 89/391/EEC is to be construed broadly and the exception provision therefore restrictively. Under this assumption the *ECJ* explained that Art. 2(2) of Directive 89/391/EEC does not exclude civil protection services as such from the scope of the directive, only "certain specific activities" of these services the characteristics of which inevitably conflict with the rules laid down by the directive. This exclusion must therefore be interpreted in such a way that its scope is restricted to what is strictly necessary in order to safeguard the interests which it allows the Member States to protect. The exclusion was adopted purely for the purpose of ensuring the proper operation of services essential for the protection of public health, safety and order in cases, such as a catastrophe, the gravity and scale of which are exceptional and a characteristic of which is the fact that, by their nature, they do not lend themselves to planning as regards the working time of teams of emergency workers. The civil protection service in the strict sense can be clearly distinguished from the activities of emergency workers. Even if a service such as the one with which the national court was concerned must deal with events which, by definition, are unforeseeable, the activities which it entails in normal conditions and which correspond moreover to the duties specifically assigned to a service of that kind are nonetheless capable of being organised in advance, including the working hours of its staff. The service thus exhibits no characteristic which inevitably conflicts with the application of the Directive 89/391/EEC and/or the Working Time Directive. Emergency services therefore do not fall within the exception by virtue of Art. 1(4) of Directive 93/104/EC in conjunction with Art. 2(2) second sentence of Directive 89/391/EEC. Whether an emergency worker is regarded as a mobile worker to which the Working Time Directive only has limited application (discussed forthwith), the *ECJ* did not have to decide because the provision, which was only introduced by the Amendment Directive 2000/34/EC, was not yet applicable to the case. On the other hand, the *ECJ* rejected applying the exception for road transport in Art. 1(3) of Directive 93/104/EC to the activities of an emergency worker.

7 Moreover, by virtue of Art. 14, the Working Time Directive does not apply where other Community instruments contain more specific requirements concerning certain occupations or occupational activities. Such provisions exist, inter alia, for **pregnant women and women who have recently given birth** (Directive 92/85/EEC; for an outline *Ewing*, 22 Industrial Law Journal 1993, No. 3, pp. 165 *et seqq.*; for details on implementation in the UK see *Mair*, 63 Modern Law Review 2000, pp. 877 *et seqq.*), for **children and young people** (Directive 94/33/EC), for seafarers on ships (Directive 1999/63/EC), for flying workers in civic aviation (Directive 2000/79/EC) and for persons performing mobile road transport activities (Regulation (EC) No. 561/2006; Directive 2002/15/EC; for an outline on all these directives see *Blanpain*, European Labour Law, 2006, pp. 368 *et seqq.*, 465 *et seqq.* and 471 *et seqq.*). One must take into account here that the exclusion applies only where special rules exist. Where there are no special rules the Working Time Directive still applies.

8 In addition, the Working Time Directive's application is limited regarding **mobile workers**, workers on off-shore installations as well as workers on board seagoing fishing vessels, Art. 20 and 21 of Directive 2003/88/EC. Mobile worker means any worker employed as a member of travelling or flying personnel by an undertaking which operates transport services for passengers or goods by road, air or inland waterway, Art. 2 No. 7 of Directive 2003/88/EC. A legal definition of activities on off-shore installations is contained in Art. 2 No. 8 of the Directive. The exceptions from

the scope of the Working Time Directive must be distinguished from the derogation possibilities that are provided for by virtue of Arts. 17–19 of the directive for a great number of areas of activity. Whereas in the case of exceptions the directive does not apply or only in part, where national law does not provide otherwise, the Working Time Directive in principle applies fully to areas of activity for which derogations are possible, however derogating regulations by virtue of the aforementioned provisions may be adopted by means of national law.

Which **persons are covered** by the Directive 2003/88/EC is determined by the terms "worker" and "employer". These terms have a specific meaning in European law that do not necessarily correspond with the existing definitions in the individual Member States (Case 428/09 – Union syndicale Solidaires Isère, para. 28). "Worker" within the meaning of Art. 1(4) of Directive 2003/88/EC in conjunction with Art. 3(a) of Directive 89/391/EEC means any person employed by an employer, including trainees and apprentices but excluding domestic servants. "Employer" within the meaning of Art. 1(4) of Directive 2003/88/EC in conjunction with Art. 3(b) of Directive 89/391/EEC means any natural or legal person who has an employment relationship with the worker and has responsibility for the undertaking and/or establishment. 9

III. Working time

"Working time" under Art. 2 No. 1 of Directive 2003/88/EC means any period during which the worker is working, is at the employer's disposal and carrying out his activity or duties, in accordance with national laws and/or practice. The antonym to this is the **rest period**. This means any period which is not working time, Art. 2 No. 2 of Directive 2003/88/EC. 10

11

Case 151/02 – **Jaeger** [2003] ECR I-8389

In the Simap case the *ECJ* had to consider the question whether stand-by service or on-call duty is considered working time in terms of Art. 2 No. 1 or a rest period in terms of Art. 2 No. 2 of Directive 93/194/EC. In the Jaeger case this question was submitted to it again for a preliminary ruling with reference to the German law of working time. The German law of working time distinguishes between readiness for work, on-call service and stand-by service. Readiness for work means the employee must make himself available to his employer at the place of employment and is obliged to remain continuously attentive in order to be able to take action on his own initiative in case of need. A characteristic of on-call service is that the employee must be present at a particular place determined by the employer either on or outside the premises and must keep himself available to provide services on demand of the employer. As long as his services are not needed he may rest or keep himself occupied with something else. Finally, the stand-by service is characterized by an employee who does not have to be present at a particular place determined by the employer but must merely be reachable at all times in order to perform his professional tasks at short notice and without delay. Whereas readiness for work has been considered full working time under German law, stand-by service and on-call service has in principle been regarded as a rest period. Only the times the employee actually performs his professional tasks during his stand-by or on-call service was recognized as working time. The *ECJ* rejected this view. According to its opinion, on-call service is working time in its entirety for the purposes of Art. 2 No. 1 of Directive 93/104/EC. Conversely, stand-by service as a rule is not considered working time within this meaning. Under Art. 2 No. 1 of the Working Time Directive, working time is any period during which the worker is working, is at the employer's disposal and carrying out his activity or duties, in accordance with national laws and/or practice. On-call service unquestionably fulfils the first two conditions of this definition. In addition, the employee's duty to be present at the work place in order to provide his professional services and to be available must be seen as coming within the ambit of the performance of his duties, even if the activity actually performed varies according to the circumstances. The situation is different with stand-by service. Even though they are at the disposal of their employer, in that it must be possible to contact them, the fact remains that in that situation employees may manage their time with fewer constraints and pursue their own interests. In this case only time linked to the actual performance of services must be regarded as 'working time' within the meaning of the Working Time Directive. This view was confirmed by the *ECJ* in subsequent judgments in other contexts (cf. for example Case 397/01 through 403/01 – Pfeiffer [2004] ECR I-8835; Case 12/04 – Abdelkader Dellas i.a./Premier ministre and Ministre des Affaires sociales, du Travail et de la Solidarité [2005] ECR I-10253; Case C-258/10 – Grigore).

IV. Organization of working time

1. Maximum weekly working hours

12 Art. 6 of Directive 2003/88/EC provides for a **maximum weekly working time** of **48 hours**. Overtime is included in this. The Member States may lay down a reference period of up to four months for this maximum weekly working time pursuant to Art. 16(b). Higher weekly working times may be offset within this period of time as long as the weekly working time within the reference period does not exceed 48 hours on average. In the calculation of this average, the periods of paid annual leave and sick leave shall not be included. The instructions of the Directive concerning maximum weekly working time can be implemented by national legal and administrative provisions, collective agreements or agreements between the social partners. A **maximum daily working time** is **not** provided for by the Directive **expressly**. However, Art. 3 of Directive 2003/88/EC stipulates a daily minimum rest period of 11 hours (discussed forthwith). By implication, the maximum daily working time therefore may not exceed 13 hours.

13 A national rule that allows an employee to be transferred to another job against his will because he demanded the weekly working time limit be complied with, is a violation of Art. 6(b) of Directive 2003/88/EC. It undermines the employee's right to work within the maximum weekly working time and the practical effect of the provision (*effet utile*). The fact that the employee does not suffer a specific (financial) detriment by the transfer is immaterial (cf. Case 243/09 – Fuß [2010], this case involved a fireman who – after requesting compliance with the working time limits – was transferred from on-call duty to a post involving office duties at

the same salary). A detriment within the meaning of Art. 22(1) of Directive 2003/88/EC is only significant where national measures implement the provision, which was not the case here. Art. 22(1) of Directive 2003/88/EC gives the Member States the option of not applying Art. 6 under certain circumstances. Above all, it is necessary for the employee to agree to work in excess of the weekly working limit (Art. 22(1)(a)). No employee may suffer any detriment because of his refusal to perform such work (Art. 22(1)(b)).

2. Rest periods

The antonym to working time – as mentioned earlier – is the rest period. 14
Pursuant to Art. 2(b) of Directive 2003/88/EC this means any period which is not working time. The Working Time Directive for one thing stipulates in its Art. 3 a **minimum daily rest period**. Pursuant to this, every worker is entitled to a minimum rest period of eleven consecutive hours per 24-hour period. Additionally, Art. 5 of Directive 2003/88/EC lays down a **minimum weekly rest period**. According to Art. 5(1) of the directive this shall be a minimum uninterrupted rest period of 24 hours per each seven-day period plus the 11 hours' daily rest. The resulting minimum rest period of 35 hours may be reduced to 24 hours pursuant to Art. 5(2) if objective, technical or work organisation conditions justify this. The Member States may lay down a reference period of up to 14 days for the minimum weekly rest period under Art. 16(a) of the Working Time Directive. Within this period it is possible to offset a reduced weekly rest period if the weekly rest period within the period does not exceed 35 or 24 hours on average.

3. Breaks

Rest periods must be distinguished from breaks. Under Art. 4 of Directive 2003/ 15
88/EC every worker is entitled to a break where the working day is longer than six hours. The details, particularly the length and the conditions under which these breaks are granted, are to be laid down primarily by collective agreements or agreements between the social partners and only subsidiarily by national laws. Whether breaks constitute working time as set out in Art. 2 No. 1 or rest periods as set out in Art. 2 No. 2 of Directive 2003/88/EC is unclear.

4. Annual leave

According to Art. 7(1) of the Working Time Directive every worker is entitled to 16
a **minimum period of paid annual leave** of **four weeks**. The details are determined by the conditions for the entitlement to, and granting of, leave laid down by national legislation and/or practice. Except where the employment relationship is terminated, the minimum period of paid annual leave may not be replaced by an allowance in lieu thereof, Art. 7(2) of Directive 2003/88/EC. This is because the purpose of the right to paid annual leave is to enable the worker to rest and to enjoy a period of relaxation and leisure (Case 486/08 – Tirol [2010], para. 30). As such the *ECJ* considers the right to annual leave to be a particularly significant principle of social law in the Community (now the Union) (consistent case-law, see e. g. Case 173/99 – BECTU [2001] ECR I-04881, para. 43; Case 342/01 – Merino Gómez [2004] ECR I-2605, para. 29; Case 486/08 – Tirol decision [2010], para. 28).

17 In **German law**, § 3(1) BUrlG (Bundesurlaubsgesetz) ensures a statutory minimum period of paid annual leave of 24 working days and is in compliance in this respect with the Working Time Directive. However, § 4 BUrlG (Bundesurlaubsgesetz) lays down that this entitlement to leave is acquired by the worker only after the employment relationship has been in existence for six months. Whether this restriction is permissible under European law is in dispute. The *ECJ* held that a British regulation under which a worker's entitlement to paid annual leave did not arise until a worker had been continuously employed for 13 weeks with the same employer was incompatible with the Working Time Directive (Case 173/99 – BECTU [2001] ECR 2001 I-4881; see also Cases 131/04 and 257/04 – Robinson-Steele and others [2006] ECR I-2531 regarding "rolled up" payment and case comment by *Bogg*, European Law Review 2006, 892–905). In that case a worker lost all entitlement to annual leave at the end of his employment relationship without having achieved the minimum work period of 13 weeks. German law is different here. In case of termination of the employment relationship before expiration of the waiting period under § 4 BUrlG (Bundesurlaubsgesetz), the worker is entitled to partial leave under § 5(1) BUrlG. Whether the German law meets the requirements of the Directive 2003/88/EC with this regulation is in dispute.

18

Case 486/08 – **Zentralbetriebsrat der Landeskrankenhäuser Tirol**
[2010] ECR I-3527

A right to paid annual leave that has already been accumulated remains with no restrictions until it expires. It may not be reduced or be granted only with a reduced level of holiday pay. The *ECJ* had to decide a case where an employee transferred from a fulltime position to part-time employment. He was not able to take the leave he had accumulated while working fulltime within the reference period, so he took it at a time when he was already working part-time. The national law (which was § 55(5) of the L-VBG) provided that in the event of a change in employment the annual leave which has not yet been taken would be adjusted proportionally to the new contract – in this case this meant a reduction of leave or pay. This was considered to be incompatible with the Part-time Work Directive (cf. also § 4, para. 14). The worker must be entitled to actual rest for relaxation and leisure. The taking of annual leave in a period after the reference period has no connection to the hours worked by the worker during that later period. Consequently, a change, and in particular a reduction, of working hours when moving from full-time to part-time employment cannot reduce the right to annual leave that the worker has accumulated during the period of full-time employment.

19 Criticized by many German commentators was the *ECJ* decision concerning a question **submitted for preliminary ruling by the *Landesarbeitsgericht Düsseldorf*** (Case 350/06 – Schultz-Hoff [2006] ECR I-179). Persons who are incapacitated due to illness for a long period of time and whose employment relationship ends because of termination or retirement, often lose their entitlement to annual leave because they cannot take leave due to their continuous incapacity. Pursuant to the

consistent practice of the *Bundesarbeitsgericht* (e. g. recently *BAG* of 11 April 2006 – 9 AZR 523/05) this entitlement to annual leave lapsed due to the statutory limitation (§ 7(3) BUrlG) at the latest by the end of the carry-over period, i. e. by the 31 March of the following year. If leave cannot be taken in a continued employment relationship, e. g. because of incapacity to work until the end of the carry-over period without the employer being at fault, then the entitlement is extinguished at this point in time due to the limitation, without entitlement to compensation in lieu thereof or entitlement to substitute leave arising. The *ECJ* has found this to be incompatible with European law: Art. 7(1) of Directive 2003/88/EC must be interpreted to mean that workers must certainly receive a minimum paid annual leave of four weeks, and so specifically in the case where leave is not taken because the worker has been on sick leave for the whole leave year, it must be granted at a later time. This is surprising given that even Art. 9 of Convention No. 132 of the ILO contains the rule that leave must be granted and taken no later than one year or 18 months after expiration of the leave year. Considering this, one would have expected an unlimited entitlement to annual leave to be expressed more clearly if this had been intended by the EC-Directive. By its ruling in the case KHS presenting a convincing teleological approach the *ECJ* has also deduced a time limit to the claim to holiday or payment (**Case 214/10 – KHS [2011]**): The recreational function of leave could only take effect, if the granting of the leave in the carry-over period is still related to the reference period. Yet, any carry-over period must be substantially longer than the reference period in respect of which it is granted. The *ECJ* did not define an exact time limit, but in the case KHS it ruled that a time limit of 15 months is appropriate. It was however decided differently and therefore the **French law** is probably also incompatible with European law (see *Cass.* soc. of 28 January 2004 – RJS 4/04, no. 423). In another ruling concerning Art. 7(1) of Directive 2003/88/EC, the *ECJ* has decided that this provision precludes national provisions or practices which make entitlement to paid annual leave conditional on a minimum period of ten days' or one month's actual work during the reference period (Case 282/10 – Dominguez [2012]). Such a restriction was laid down in Art. L. 223-2 (1) of the *Code du travail*, which has been declared contrary to European law by the *ECJ*.

V. Night and shift work

In its third chapter the Directive 2003/88/EC contains special rules for night and shift workers. **Night worker** under Art. 2 No. 4(a) of Directive 2003/88/EC means any worker who, during night time, works at least three hours of his daily working time as a normal course. Additionally, any worker is considered a night worker under Art. 2 No. 4(b) of the Working Time Directive who is likely, during night time, to work a certain proportion of his annual working time, as defined at the choice of the Member State concerned either by national legislation following consultation with the social partners or by collective agreements or agreements between the social partners conducted at national or regional level. **Night time** according to the Directive 2003/88/EC means, under Art. 2 No. 3, any period of not less than seven hours, as defined by national law, and which must include, in any case, the period between midnight and 5.00 o'clock. The term '**shift work**' is legally defined in Art. 2 No. 5. It means any method of organising work in shifts whereby 20 workers succeed each other at the same work stations according to a certain pattern, including a rotating pattern, and which may be continuous or discontinuous, entailing the need for workers to work at different times over a given period of days or weeks. Therefore, a shift worker is any worker whose work schedule is part of shift work, under Art. 2 No. 6 of Directive 2003/88/EC.

21 Art. 12 of Directive 2003/88/EC obligates the Member States, expressed as a general clause, to take the measures necessary to provide, on the one hand, night workers and shift workers with safety and health protection appropriate to the nature of their work, and on the other hand to ensure appropriate protection and prevention services or facilities with regard to the safety and health of night workers and shift workers which are equivalent to those applicable to other workers and are available at all times.

22 Special rules, exclusively applicable to night workers, are included in Arts. 8–11 of Directive 2003/88/EC. First of all, its Art. 8 determines the **length of night work**. According to Art. 8(1)(a) of Directive 2003/88/EC normal hours of work for night workers may not exceed an average of eight hours in any 24-hour period. The reference period, within which a longer period of night work may be made up for, is to be defined after consultation of the social partners or by collective agreements or agreements concluded between the social partners at national or regional level as laid down by Art. 16(c) of Directive 2003/88/EC. In calculating the average working time within the reference period, the minimum weekly rest period, which must be granted pursuant to Art. 5 of the Working Time Directive, is not taken into account. Where night work involves special hazards or heavy physical or mental strain, a worker may not work more than eight hours in a 24-hour period during which he performs night work, under Art. 8(1)(b) of Directive 2003/88/EC. Work involving special hazards or heavy physical or mental strain shall be defined by national legislation and/or practice or by collective agreements or agreements concluded between the social partners, taking account of the specific effects and hazards of night work, Art. 8(2) of Directive 2003/88/EC.

23 Art. 9(1)(a) of the Working Time Directive gives night workers the **right to a free health assessment** before taking up their work and thereafter at regular intervals. The free health assessment must comply with medical confidentiality pursuant to Art. 9(2) of Directive 2003/88/EC and by virtue of Art. 9(3) of Directive 2003/88/EC may be conducted within the national health system.

24 Night workers with health problems verifiably linked to their night work are entitled under Art. 9(1)(b) of Directive 2003/88/EC to be transferred to day work as far as a transfer is possible and the night worker is suited to the work.

25 Under Art. 10 of the Working Time Directive the work of certain categories of night workers can be made subject to certain guarantees, under conditions laid down by national legislation and/or practice, in the case of workers who incur risks to their safety or health linked to night-time working.

26 Under Art. 11 of Directive 2003/88/EC an employer who regularly uses night workers must bring this information to the attention of the competent authorities if they so request.

27 There is a special rule to protect shift workers embodied in Art. 13 of Directive 2003/88/EC which deals with the **pattern of work**. If an employer intends to organise work according to a certain pattern, he must take account of the general principle of adapting work to the worker. This is to be done especially with a view

to alleviate monotonous work and work at a predetermined work-rate, depending on the type of activity and of safety and health requirements, especially as regards breaks during work time.

VI. Derogations

By virtue of Arts. 17–19 of Directive 2003/88/EC it is possible to derogate from certain provisions of the directive. The provisions are meant to contribute to a more flexible application of the directive subject to compliance with the principles laid down therein (Report from the Commission of 1st December 2000 on the state of implementation of Council Directive 93/104/EC of 23rd November 1993 concerning certain aspects of the organisation of working time [Working Time Directive], p. 4). **28**

Essentially, there are **three types of derogation**. Art. 17(1) of Directive 2003/88/EC permits derogations from Arts. 3–6, 8 and 16 of the Working Time Directive where, on account of the specific characteristics of the activity concerned, the duration of working time is not measured and/or predetermined or can be determined by the workers themselves. Such derogations are permitted particularly for managing executives or other persons with autonomous decision-taking powers, family workers and workers officiating at religious ceremonies in churches and religious communities. Derogations can be laid down by the Member States with due regard for the general principles of the protection of health and safety. **29**

Art. 17(2) of Directive 2003/88/EC permits derogations from Arts. 3–6, 8 and 16 of the Working Time Directive subject to paragraphs 3–5. These derogations may be adopted by means of laws, regulations or administrative provisions, by means of collective agreements or agreements between the social partners. Derogations under Art. 17(2) of the Working Time Directive are subject to the fundamental requirement that the workers concerned are afforded equivalent periods of compensatory rest or that, in exceptional cases in which it is not possible for objective reasons to grant such equivalent compensatory rest periods, they are afforded appropriate protection. **30**

31

Case 428/09 – **Union syndicale Solidaires Isère**
[2010] ECR I-9961

In the case Union syndicale Solidaires Isère the *ECJ* considered the question whether casual or seasonal staff carrying out a maximum of 80 days of work per year in holiday and leisure activity centres are workers for the purposes of Directive 2003/88/EC and, if this is the case, whether derogations pursuant to Art. 17 of the Directive are allowed. The disputed national law did not provide that such workers are entitled to a daily rest period with a minimum duration of 11 consecutive hours as stipulated by Art. 3. The *ECJ* held that persons employed under such contracts fall within the scope of Directive 2003/88. Regarding its scope the Working Time Directive makes reference to the basic directive 89/391. From its purpose of encouraging improvements in the health and safety of workers at work and from the wording of Art. 2(1), it must be taken to be broad in scope. Whether a person can be classed as a worker must be based on objective criteria and on an overall assessment of all the circumstances of the case. Being employed for a fixed term or only for certain days in a year does not rule out being classed as a worker. A derogation was only possible within the limits of Art. 17(3)(b) in this case. The Court found that the conditions stated therein are satisfied because the workers in question must ensure constant supervision of the children accommodated in those centres – including night time – and must therefore "protect [...] persons". The derogation is however subject to the conditions in Art. 17(2). Accordingly, the national provision must ensure that the workers are afforded equivalent compensatory rest periods that follow on immediately from the working time which they are supposed to counteract or, in exceptional cases in which it is not possible, for objective reasons, to grant such equivalent periods of compensatory rest, the workers concerned are afforded appropriate protection. The national rule in question was not able to ensure this.

32 Finally, by virtue of Art. 18 subparagraph 1 it is possible to derogate from Arts. 3–5, 8 and 16 by means of collective agreements or agreements between the social partners. This power is primarily incumbent on the social partners or parties to collective agreements at national or regional level. They may however delegate their power to a lower level. Derogation is subject to – just as Art. 17(2) sets out – the workers concerned being afforded equivalent compensatory rest periods or, in exceptional cases in which it is not possible for objective reasons to grant such equivalent compensatory rest periods, being afforded appropriate protection.

VII. Proposal for amendment

33 Presently there is a proposal for amendment of Directive 2003/88/EC (see the amended proposal for a directive of the European Parliament and of the Council amending Directive 2003/88/EC concerning certain aspects of the organisation of working time [presented by the Commission] of 31 May 2005, COM [2005] 246 final) which however has not been successful so far. The Commission still considers it necessary to revise the working time provisions as it stated in a communication in March 2010: "It intends to undertake such a review, based on an impact assessment with a strong social dimension and a full-scale consultation of the two sides of industry" (COM [2010] 106 final).

34 A **review of the Working Time Directive** is sorely needed. The sluggish progression is incomprehensible given the numerous infringements of the Directive. According to an analysis conducted by the Commission's offices in 2010, the implementation of the Directive 2003/88/EC by the Member States has been highly dissimilar. 19 countries disregard the obligations concerning on-call time (Austria, Belgium, Cyprus, Czech Republic, Germany, Denmark, Estonia, Greece, Spain, Finland, France, Hungary, Ireland, Netherlands, Poland, Sweden, Slovenia, Slovakia, United Kingdom). 21 countries do not comply with the obligations concerning compensatory rest periods (Belgium, Cyprus, Czech Republic, Germany, Denmark, Estonia, Greece, Spain, Finland, France, Hungary, Ireland, Lithuania, Lapland, Malta, Netherlands, Portugal, Sweden, Slovenia, Slovakia, United Kingdom). 4 countries are in breach of the provisions concerning the individual opt-out (Spain, France, Hungary, especially though the United Kingdom in sec. 4 Working Time Regulations 1999). Only Luxemburg and Italy have implemented the Working Time Directive fully into national law – at least at this time (COM [2010] 801 final).

VIII. Comparative Law

35 The implementation of the Working Time Directive has proved to be quite different in the various Member States; the implementation report from the year 2008 is worth reading (COM[2010] 802 final; available at: http://eur-lex.europa.eu/LexUriServ/LexUriServ.do?uri=CELEX:52010DC0802:EN:HTML).

§ 8. Proof of employment terms

Literature: *Clark/Hall,* The Cinderella Directive? Employee Rights to Information about Conditions Applicable to their Contract or Employment Relationship, 21 Industrial Law Journal 1992, No. 2, 106–118; *Kenner,* Statement or Contract? – Some Reflections on the EC Employee Information (Contract or Employment Relationship) Directive after Kampelmann, 28 Industrial Law Journal 1999, No. 3, 205–231; *Nielsen,* The contract of employment in the member states of the European Communities and in community law, 33 German Yearbook of International Law 1990, 258–283.

With regard to proof of work conditions the **Directive 91/533/EEC** on an employer's obligation to inform employees of the conditions applicable to the contract or employment relationship (so-called Employee Information Directive) contains the requirements laid down by European law. The essential content of the Directive is that every worker must be provided with a written document from which he can ascertain the "essential aspects of the employment relationship" (Art. 2(1) in conjunction with Art. 3 of the Directive). 1

This obligation addressed at the employer to provide the employees with a written document about their basic working conditions is clearly a means to ensure greater transparency, particularly for those Union workers covered by atypical contracts (*Barnard*, EU Employment Law, 2012, p. 565). The EU legislator therefore acknowledges the challenge asssociated with the burden of proof regarding the concrete employment terms. However, the factual legal effects of the written document is in dispute (see on this below). 2

I. Development of Directive 91/533/EEC

The idea of regulating proof of work conditions was not invented by the European legislators. It has its origins in the form and proof requirements adopted by individual Member States as early as the 1970s. The background to this development was the fact that it was felt that the transparency of the employment market and of work conditions was being threatened by the development of a multitude of new forms of employment (tele and standby work, job sharing and job splitting) and one wanted to counteract this development by introducing new information obligations. 3

English and Irish law in particular served as pioneers and as the **model example for the ensuing European regulation** (*Bercusson*, European Labour Law, 1st ed., pp. 433 *et seq.*; *Kenner*, 28 Industrial Law Journal 1999, 205–231, 206). Sec. 1 of the British Employment Protection (Consolidation) Act 1978 obligated the employer to give the employee a written statement of the essential conditions of the employment contract. The Irish Minimum Notice and Terms of Employment Act 1973 contained a very similar provision in sec. 9. In France, too, there was an obligation to provide proof in that the pay slip (*bulletin de paie*) had to include certain information about the contract conditions such as the particulars of the parties. In **Germany** (and in other Member States such as **Portugal** and **Greece**, see *Nielsen*, 33 German Yearbook of International Law 1990, pp. 258 *et seqq.*), on the other hand, this development found no followers. There, general requirements of proof were unknown and proof was only prescribed by law in exceptional cases. 4

Owing to these differences in the laws of the Member States the Commission saw the need for a Europe-wide harmonization and submitted a proposal to the Council on 5 December 1990 on the basis of the then existing Art. 100 EC Treaty (the 5 successor provision Art. 114 TFEU is no longer applicable to worker rights; this competence can now be found in Art. 153(2)(b) TFEU) for an approximation directive. On 18 October 1991 this was adopted as the so-called **Employee Information Directive**. Just like the national laws, which were the catalyst for adopting the directive, its aim is to provide the employee with information about his rights. By handing over a written document from which he can see in "black and white" what the terms and conditions of his employment contract are, it wants to enable him/her to keep track of his/her rights and duties even in a flexible world of employment. Additionally, putting contract terms in writing increases legal certainty and prevents difficulties in proving an employment relationship. Moreover, the Employee Information Directive implements the employees' fundamental social rights laid down in No. 9 of the European Community Charter of Fundamental Social Rights (COM [1989] 248 final). As the Directive primarily has the protection of the employees in mind, the Member States may only derogate from the Directive in their favour (Art. 7 of the Employee Information Directive).

II. Scope of Application (Art. 1 of the Employee Information Directive)

6 Pursuant to Art. 1 of the Employee Information Directive this directive applies to every paid employee who has a contract or employment relationship defined by the law in force in a Member State and/or is governed by the law in force in a Member State. The application of the Directive is therefore subject to the condition that the contractual relationship the conditions of which one wishes to verify is an employment relationship. As to the **definition of employment contract or employment relationship** the Directive seems to refer to the law of the Member States (Art. 1(1): "employment relationship defined by the law in force in a Member State"); this is also the prevailing opinion: *Kenner*, 28 Industrial Law Journal 1999, 205–231, 216, 217 and for German literature see *Lörcher*, 41 AuR 1994, 450, 452 *et seq.*; *Wank*, 49 RdA 1996, 21, 22; EAS/*Friese* B 3050 para. 9; and also the Commission in their implementation report, p. 6, available under http://ec.europa.eu/social/main.jsp?catId=706&langId=en&intPageId=202. One may doubt this, because the Directive also applies to employment relationships that are not defined by the law of a Member State. Pursuant to the wording it suffices that an employment relationship is governed by the law in force in a Member State; it is not necessary for it to also be defined by the law of the Member State ("and/*or* is governed by the law in force in a Member State" [emphasis added]). Were one to actually apply the national definition of employment relationship, then the alternativity of the two alternatives of Art. 1(1) would lose all meaning. If an employment relationship within the meaning of the Directive is only ever an employment relationship as defined by national law, then the first alternative will always apply at any rate and no scope of application will remain for the second alternative. It follows that the Directive's definition of employment relationship cannot be congruent with that of national law. Rather, a determination must be made **autonomously on the basis of the Directive**. Only where the Directive makes no such determination must the Member States set out specifications, such as determining the length of time of "fixed-term employment contracts" within the meaning of Art. 8(2)(2) Employee Information Directive (Case 306/07 – Andersen [2008] ECR I-10279 paras. 27 *et seqq.*).

7 *Bercusson* makes a similar argument, although he bases the argument on the distinction between employment contract and employment relationship (European Labour law, 1st ed., pp. 429 *et seq.*, 2nd ed. pp. 651 *et seq.*). Under English law a person is only considered an employee if he has entered into or works under an employment contract. But as the directive sees an employment relationship as sufficient, the term in the directive is wider than in English law. Another argument for an autonomous interpretation of the term is the fact that the directive serves as an implementation of No. 9 Community Charter of Fundamental Social Rights, which uses the European definition of worker (COM [1989] 248 final). Therefore, it seems appropriate to apply it here also (cf. § 2 at paras. 12 *et seqq.*). It follows then that civil servants also fall within the scope of the directive.

8 It is my understanding that the scope of the Directive is determined by the sub-clause, based on the **European definition of worker**. In this respect, the second alternative is relatively straightforward. It is consistent with the Commission's first draft proposal ("This Directive applies to employment relationships that are subject to the law in force of the Member State" COM [1990] 563 final). It comprises all contractual relationships that are considered employment contracts under European law and are governed by the law of a Member State. In contrast, the meaning of the first alternative is less clear. It is obviously meant to separate the scope of the Directive from the proper law of the contract. In principle, the contracting parties to an employment contract are free to choose the proper law of the contract. With that, workers can take up employment in Europe without being governed by the law of a Member State and that of the European Union. Under the draft proposal they would also have not fallen within the scope of the Directive. The legislator obviously wished to prevent this by adding the alternative "defined by the law in force of a Member State". The Directive also applies to employment contracts that are subject to a non-European proper law of the contract, namely as an imperative worker protection provision (cf. Art. 9(1) of Rome I Regulation). However, the scope is in fact limited to such employment relationships that are considered employment relationships under the relevant national law. This is appropriate, as given that the Directive is applied concurrently with the national mandatory provisions on worker protection, the demarcation difficulties are kept to a minimum.

III. Contents

9 The Directive 91/533/EEC, Art. 2(1), obligates the employer to inform the employee of the essential aspects of the employment relationship. In which form the information must be given is set out in Art. 3.

1. Essential aspects of the employment relationship (Art. 2 of the Employee Information Directive)

10 **The essential aspects of the employment relationship** as set out in Art. 2(2) are:
- the **identities** of the parties (Art. 2(2)(a));
- the **place of work** or, where there is no fixed or main place of work, the principle that the employee is employed at various places and the registered place of business or, where appropriate, the domicile of the employer (Art. 2(2)(b));
- the **title**, grade, nature or category of the work for which the employee is employed (Art. 2(2)(c)); however it is not necessary for the employee to be able to ascertain from his grade of work whether he would be entitled to a higher salary category if he meets certain requirements (AG *Tesauro* in his opinions in Cases 253/96 et al. – Kampelmann and others [1997] ECR I-6907, para. 21);

- the **date of commencement of the contract or employment relationship** (Art. 2(2)(d));
- in the case of a **temporary contract or employment relationship, the expected duration** thereof (Art. 2(2)(e));
- the **amount of paid leave** to which the employee is entitled or, where this cannot be indicated when the information is given, the procedures for allocating and determining such leave (Art. 2(2)(f));
- the length of the **periods of notice** to be observed by the employer and the employee should their contract or employment relationship be terminated or, where this cannot be indicated when the information is given, the method for determining such periods of notice (Art. 2(2)(g));
- the initial **basic amount**, the other component elements and the frequency of payment of the remuneration to which the employee is entitled (Art. 2(2)(h));
- the **length** of the employee's normal **working day or week** (Art. 2(2)(i)); a possible obligation to work overtime, which by its wording does not constitute working time but is performed outside of normal working hours, is not included (Case 350/99 – Lange [2001] ECR I-1061, para. 16);
- where appropriate, the **collective agreements** governing the employee's conditions of work (Art. 2(2)(j)(ii)) or, in the case of collective agreements concluded outside the business by special joint bodies or institutions, the name of the competent body or joint institution within which the agreements were concluded (Art. 2(2)(j)(ii)).

11 Whether **more aspects of the employment relationship** aside from those enumerated in Art. 2(2) fall under the obligation to inform is disputed. Some legal scholars submit, with reference to the very specific enumeration in Art. 2(2), that the enumeration is exhaustive, for such an elaborate enumeration would not have been necessary if the catalogue were to be regarded as only exemplary (*Kenner*, 28 Industrial Law Journal 1999, 222; cf. also the submission of Advocate General *Tesauro* in Case 253/96 et. al. – Kampelmann and others [1997] ECR I-6907, para. 21 who is of the opinion that the directive only gives the employee a "minimum" of information and so excludes any obligations to provide more extensive information). The *ECJ*, in contrast, regards the list in Art. 2(2) as an illustrative, not an exhaustive enumeration (Case 350/99 – Lange [2001] ECR I-1061, para. 22). The Court relies on the word "at least" with which the enumeration is introduced. In the Lange case it regarded the employee's obligation to work overtime whenever requested by the employer as another essential element of the contract. In light of the unambiguous wording, the *ECJ*'s interpretation is convincing. The legislator of the Directive could not have formulated the exemplary nature of the catalogue any clearer. Moreover, the case at issue shows that there is a definite need for acknowledging elements not included in the list. It would run counter to the purpose of the directive, to wit, to protect employees from uncertainties regarding their obligations, to not acknowledge these additional elements. Further elements do not include the employee's obligation (in the case of a civil servant of the ECB) to perform his duties conscientiously and without regard to self-interest – this obligation constitutes a basic element of the good faith principle and is manifestly applicable, so consequently, there is no need for express stipulation (*CFI* Case T-333/99 – X/EZB [2001] ECR II-3021, para. 82).

For **expatriate employees** who are employed abroad longer than a month, Art. 4(1) in conjunction with (3) of the Employee Information Directive adds these essential aspects: 12
- the duration of the employment abroad (Art. 4(1)(a));
- the currency to be used for the payment of remuneration (Art. 4(1)(b));
- where appropriate, the benefits in cash or kind attendant on the employment abroad and the conditions governing the employee's repatriation (Art. 4(1)(c),(d)).

2. Means of information for the employer (Art. 3 Employee Information Directive)

In what form the information shall be given is set out in Art. 3 of the Employee Information Directive. From Art. 3(1) of the directive one can infer that it suffices when the employee is provided with a document from which he can see all relevant aspects mentioned in Art. 2(a), (b), (c), (d), (h) and (i). This can be a written employment contract as long as it contains all necessary information. If this is not the case, it must be supplemented by a second document (cf. Art. 3(2) subparagraph 2). This obligation must be fulfilled no later than two months after the commencement of employment (Art. 3(1)). Should he not satisfy the obligation in time, stricter conditions apply: If the employee is not given the document within the expiry period of two months, then the employer is obligated to give him a written declaration containing at least the information provided for in Art. 2(2). This is stricter than paragraph 1 where the obligation to inform is limited to Art. 2(2)(a), (b), (c), (d), (h) and (i). 13

Modifications of aspects of the employment relationship must be made available to the employee in the same fashion no later than one month after the date of entry into effect of the change in question (Art. 5(1)). This does not apply to changes of administrative or statutory provisions or collective agreements referred to (Art. 5(2)). 14

3. Legal effects of the written documents

Pursuant to the first indent of Art. 6, the Directive 91/533/EEC shall be without prejudice to national provisions concerning the form of the employment contract. As a result this attestation of employment merely has **declaratory meaning;** a contract is valid even without such proof of essential contract elements (Case 350/99 – Lange [2001] ECR I-1061 paras. 27, 29; cf. also the opinions of Advocate General *Tesauro* in the Case 253/96 et. al. – Kampelmann and others [1997] ECR I-6907 para. 10). This raises the question which legal consequence an employer's violation of the obligation to provide information has. This is set out in Art. 8(1) of the Employee Information Directive: pursuant to this the Member States must make sure that employees can pursue their claims by judicial process. The Member States must therefore create an enforceable claim for issuance of information. The *Landesarbeitsgericht* Hamm (State Labour Court in Hamm) referred the question to the *ECJ* for a preliminary ruling whether beyond that the directive modifies the burden of proof in the employee's favour, so as not to encounter difficulties of proof regarding the listed points of employment due to lack of a written document (*LAG Hamm* of 9 July 1996 – 4 Sa 828/95). The *ECJ* rejected this with reference to Art. 6 of the directive which stipulates that national procedural rules, and thus the rules 15 concerning burden of proof, shall be unaffected (ibid., para. 30). Although the objective would not be achieved if the employee were unable to use the information contained in the notification referred to in Art. 2(1) as evidence before the national courts. In light of the purpose of the Directive though, it suffices for the notification to enjoy such presumption as to its correctness as would attach, in domestic law, to any similar document drawn up by the employer and communicated to the employee (ibid., paras. 32, 33). By the same principles the directive does not require the employer's failure to comply with his legal obligations to provide information to be deemed obstruction of evidence. Whether such behaviour is considered obstruction of evidence, should be judged according to principles of national law (Case 350/99 – Lange [2001] ECR I-1061, para. 35). The general principle remains – concerning the obligations laid down by the directive – that the directives must be implemented effectively and **sanctions for infringements of the Directive** must be effective, proportionate and dissuasive (cf. § 1 at 38).

4. Other instructions for implementation

16 The Directive gives the Member States a broad discretion as to how to achieve the level of protection required. Under Art. 8(1), the Member States must create an enforceable right to information. This can be achieved, according to Art. 9(1) in conjunction with Recital 13, by legislation or by agreements between social partners, specifically collective agreements. The latter will suffice even for employment relationships of workers who are not members of a union as long as the worker can rely on the rights conferred by the collective agreement, i. e. the worker can enjoy the protection provided for in the Directive (Case 306/07 – Andersen [2008] ECR I-10279, paras. 27 *et seqq.*). Such an employment relationship is "covered" by a collective agreement in terms of Art. 8(2); thus, the worker may be required to give the employer prior notice as set out in Art. 8(2) before enforcing his rights before the courts. The reason for this interpretation is the fact that the worker, even when he is not a member of the union, enjoys the protection provided by the collective agreement. Unlike in the case of individual employment contracts there is no structural imbalance of bargaining power (ibid., paras. 31 *et seqq.* and 49). Under Art. 8(2) the formality of prior notification may not be required for workers with a temporary employment relationship. This provision is meant to include workers whose contract is of such short duration that the obligation to notify the employer before taking legal proceedings could compromise effective access to judicial means of redress (ibid., para. 51). It is for the Member States to determine the duration (ibid., paras. 52 *et seqq.*).

IV. Implementation into national law

17 The **German legislator** implemented the Employee Information Directive by means of the ***Nachweisgesetz*** (Law on notification of conditions governing an employment) of 28 May 1995 (BGBl. I p. 946). In **French and English Law** it was merely necessary to adapt the existing provisions. French law already provided that an employee must be presented with a copy of proof that he was hired (*déclaration préalable à l'embauche*, Art. L. 1221–9 Code du travail) and a pay slip (*bulletin de*

paie, Art. L. 3243-1 *et seq.*) which meets the requirements of the Directive in most cases (on this and on implementation shortcomings *Lardy-Pélissier/Pélissier/Roset/Tholy*, Code du travail, 30th ed., 2010, Art. L. 1221-3). In English law information obligations are set out in the Employment Rights Act 1996 c. 18 Arts. 1 *et seqq.* The **German *Nachweisgesetz*** applies to all employees. It is submitted that employees within the meaning of the directive include civil servants, therefore, in keeping in line with an interpretation in conformity with the Directive (§ 1 at 41 *et seq.*), in application of the principle of analogy they are also employees within the meaning of the *Nachweisgesetz*. Excluded from the scope of application are employees that are employed only temporarily for no more than one month.

Some legal systems did not make use of the exceptions (**Luxembourg, Belgium**), others however created exceptions which are by far more extensive (cf. Italy: no obligation to provide information between married couples and relatives, Austria: special rules for domestic workers [§ 1(3) AVRAG], the most extensive is probably Sweden: Domestic workers, family members, employees in managerial or comparable positions, sheltered employment and temporary work for a public institution are excluded from the scope; all examples are available in the Commission's implementation report under: http://ec.europa.eu/social/main.jsp?catId=706&langId=en&intPageId=202. 18

In German law § 2(1) *Nachweisgesetz* obligates the employer to provide the employee with proof of the essential information one month before the agreed commencement of the employment relationship, thereby implementing the obligation to provide information as set out in Art. 2(1) of Employee Information Directive. However, an express regulation of legal redress pursuant to Art. 8(1) Employee Information Directive is lacking. Under the general rules, an employee, as required by Art. 8(1) Employee Information Directive, has a cause of action for written proof of employment in a court of law by means of an action for performance. Furthermore, an employee can refuse performance until he is provided with the respective proof. In German law a damages claim under § 280 *Bürgerliches Gesetzbuch* is also conceivable should the employee have suffered losses or damages by not being issued the proof of contract information (cf. *BAG* of 29 May 2002 – 5 AZR 105/01). In other countries criminal measures and administrative fines and monitoring by public authorities serve as additional incentives for the employer to fulfil his obligations. For instance, in **French law** Art. R. 154-3 *Code du travail* in conjunction with Art. 131-13 Code pénal stipulates administrative fines of up to 450 EUR for violation of the obligation to provide information. In Germany there are **administration fine provisions** only for individual areas such as the temporary employment business, cf. § 16(1) No. 8 *Arbeitnehmerüberlassunggesetz* (Law on Temporary Employment). Unlike in France, German employees therefore must enforce their rights themselves. The implementation by the German legislator is therefore in line with Art. 8(1) Employee Information Directive which specifically stipulates that the employees themselves shall pursue their rights, whether this is considered realistic or not. In **English law** it was a criminal offence under the original Contracts of Employment Act 1963 for an employer to refuse to give particulars of the employment contract. This was repealed in 1965. Currently, employees have the right of recourse to Employment Tribunals to obtain a declaration rectifying the statutory particulars. However, the fact that Employment Tribunals there have no capacity to award compensation or impose a fine for non-compliance it is seen as disincentive to 19 employees to even make a claim (see *Kenner*, 28 Industrial Law Journal 1999, 222; also critical of this "weak enforcement mechanism" *Clark* and *Hall*, 21 Industrial Law Journal 1992, 117; *Davies* and *Friedland*, Labour Law – Text and Materials, p. 279 *et seqq.*).

§ 9. Posting of Workers

Literature: *Barnard*, The UK and Posted Workers: The Effect of Commission v Luxembourg on the Territorial Application of British Labour Law, 38 Industrial Law Journal 2009, No. 1, 122–132; *Bercusson*, Thompsons Labour and European Law Review 1997, Issue 7, 6–7; *Catala/Bonnet*, Droit Social Européen, 1991; *Dicey/Morris/Collins*, On the Conflict of Laws, 15th ed., 2012; *Görres*, Grenzüberschreitende Arbeitnehmerentsendung in der EU, 2003; *Nettekoven*, Die Erstreckung tariflicher Mindestlöhne in allgemeinverbindlichen Tarifverträgen auf entsandte Arbeitnehmer im Baugewerbe, 2000; *Shaw*, Social Law and Policy in an Evolving European Union, 2000; *Shaw/Hunt/Wallace*, The Economic and Social Law of the European Union, 2007.

I. Introduction

1. Description of the posting situation

Transnational worker mobility exists on the one hand, in the form of an employee leaving his home country and accepting a job in a different state, thereby becoming fully integrated into the employment system there. This situation represents the typical case of freedom of movement for workers (Art. 45 TFEU) which was discussed at length in § 2, paras. 1 *et seqq*. On the other hand, there are forms of transnational worker mobility where the connection to the home country remains and the integration into the employment system of the host country is, accordingly, of a lesser degree. A company bringing in its own employees for a project outside of the home country or a temporary work agency sending employees on assignment to a foreign company are examples of such cases. These cases are referred to as the **posting of workers**. 1

2. Guarantees by virtue of the fundamental freedoms, particularly Art. 56 TFEU

The possibility of posting workers is secured in primary law by the fundamental freedoms of the TFEU. The (active) freedom to provide services (Art. 56 TFEU) is particularly relevant. 2

Case 113/89 – **Rush Portuguesa** [1990] ECR I-1417

The Portuguese Republic acceded to the European Community in 1986. Pursuant to Art. 215 *et seqq.* of the Act of Accession, the freedom of movement of workers was restricted for Portuguese workers for a transitional period in order to prevent mass migration and its concomitant strain on the employment markets. Before the transitional period had expired, a Portuguese construction company entered into a subcontract for an assignment in France. In order to carry out the construction work, the construction company posted Portuguese workers to France without obtaining a work permit beforehand. In subsequent proceedings, the French court submitted to the *ECJ* the question, *inter alia*, whether the requirement of a work permit for posted Portuguese workers was in conflict with the freedom to provide services.

The *ECJ* held that the freedom to provide services included the right to move freely on another Member States' territory with all of one's staff without the obligation of obtaining a work permit for the workers. Imposing such conditions on the person providing services established in another Member State would otherwise discriminate against that person in relation to his competitors established in the host country who are able to use their own staff without restrictions, and moreover would affect his ability to provide the service (para. 12). The *ECJ* also held that the transitional provisions only related to the freedom of movement of workers (Art. 45 TFEU) and therefore applied only when workers sought access to the employment market. This is not the case where workers are sent to another Member State to work temporarily (para. 15).

In light of the concerns voiced by the French government in the proceedings, the *ECJ* expressed its opinion, *obiter,* on two other important questions: For one, although the making available of labour by an undertaking is a supplying of services within the meaning of Art. 56 TFEU (early on Case 279/80 – Webb [1981] ECR I-3305); as the activities are specifically intended to enable workers to gain access to the labour market of the host Member State, the derogation provisions of the Act of Accession apply in this case. For another, the Court repeated its opinion, which is expressed in the Seco case (Cases 62 and 63/81 [1982] ECR 223), that Community law does not preclude Member States from extending their legislation, or collective labour agreements entered into by both sides of industry, to any person who is employed, even temporarily, within their territory, no matter in which country the employer is established.

3 To the extent that the assignment of workers is necessary for the provision of services, Art. 56 TFEU therefore also guarantees the right of a person to post his own staff from the home state to a host state. The service provider is not forced to hire workers in the host state (local workers). The *ECJ* held in the **case Vander Elst** that this applies equally when the posted workers are not EU citizens but from third countries, (Case 43/93 – [1994] ECR I-3803). In the **Laval case** the *ECJ* stated that trade unions must be mindful of the freedom to provide services of a company posting workers. The case involved a union organisation that blocked a construction site in order to force a service provider situated in another Member State to negotiate the pay of its posted workers and to become party to their collective agreement (Case 341/05 – [2007] ECR I-11767). The posting of workers within the EU cannot therefore be prevented. This must be distinguished from the question, which the *ECJ* commented on previously in the cases Seco and Rush Portuguesa, as to which working conditions apply to posted workers (on this see below paras. 16, 30 *et seqq.*).

4 The **freedom of establishment** can also be relevant in posting situations, such as the assignment of staff from the headquarters of a parent company in the course of establishing an affiliate company in another European state. But the freedom of movement for workers, according to the prevailing opinion, is not considered to apply to the posting of workers in the context of contracts for work and services, as the posted worker specifically does not want to become integrated into the foreign employment market (Cases 49/98 and others – Finalarte [2001] ECR I-7831). The situation is different where employees are hired out to other states as temporary workers, as the temporary worker is under the control of the hirer and is therefore utilised in the same way as a worker employed in the host state (cf. also Case 113/89 – Rush Portuguesa [1990] ECR I-1417, 1444).

3. Consequences for immigration and social law

The posting of workers bears on immigration law. Fewer problems arise with workers that are citizens of a Member State, for – as EU citizens – they enjoy privileged freedoms of movement at any rate. This did not however apply to the ten Middle and East European Member States who acceded to the EU in 2004 (Malta, Cyprus, Estonia, Latvia, Lithuania, Poland, Czech Republic, Slovakia, Slovenia and Hungary). Transitional regulations restricted workers from these states from accessing the previous Member States' employment markets for up to seven years. These regulations expired on the 30 April 2011. Since the 1 May 2011 all citizens of the acceding Member States enjoy full freedom of movement for workers and therefore have unrestricted access to all employment markets within the EU. This does not apply to the citizens of the Member States Bulgaria and Rumania who acceded to the European Union on the 1 January 2007. The regulations set up for the transitional period will however expire by the 31 December 2013. For Croatia the period ends by the 30 June 2020. Within the transitional period a Member State is free to require a work permit for workers who are posted to its territory in order to provide services (Case 307, 308, 309/09 – Vicoplus [2011]). After the transitional period it would constitute an unlawful restriction of the freedom to provide services under Art. 56 TFEU for a Member State to require employers, established in another Member State and posting workers to the territory of the first Member State, to send a prior declaration of posting (Case 515/08 – Santos Palhota [2010]). 5

In contrast, workers from third countries outside the EU do not enjoy freedoms of movement in their own right. But if they are sent by a company from an EU Member State, the freedom to provide services enjoyed by the posting company results in an ancillary freedom of movement for the posted worker. For the ancillary freedom of movement to apply, the worker must be lawfully and permanently employed in the home state (cf. Case 43/93 – Vander Elst [1994] ECR I-3803; Communication from the Commission COM [2006] 159: Guidance on the posting of workers in the framework of the provision of services, p. 8). 6

Provisions relating to residence of posted workers from third countries have **not been harmonized as yet** at Community level. The first draft proposal of a Services Directive by the Commission provided some rules in its Art. 25. After the European Parliament rejected the proposal, the Commission submitted a modified proposal in which Art. 25 was stricken. National provisions must therefore be tested directly against Art. 56 TFEU and must in particular meet the requirements of the principle of proportionality. (see e. g. Case 244/04 – Commission ./. Germany [2006] ECR I-885, where the relevant German rules and practices relating to residency were objected to as being unnecessary). 7

The relevant social law issues that arise in connection with the posting of workers cannot be discussed here (hereunto see the posting rules relating to social law in Art. 14 of Regulation (EEC) No. 1408/71 or Art. 12 of Regulation (EC) No. 883/2004 which superseded Regulation (EEC) No. 1408/71, as well as the academic literature on European social law such as *Catala/Bonnet*, Droit Social Européen, 1991; *Steinmeyer*, in: Fuchs, Europäisches Sozialrecht, 5th ed., 2010; *Shaw*, Social Law and Policy in an Evolving European Union, 2000; *Shaw/Hunt/Wallace*, The Economic and Social Law of the European Union, 2007). 8

II. Country-of-origin principle and place-of-work principle

1. Explanation

9 In cases of posting workers, the question arises which legal system applies to the work conditions of the posted worker. One must distinguish between **two basic principles**: Under the country-of-origin principle the work conditions are laid down by the state from which the worker was sent. Under the place-of-work principle, the laws of the state to which the worker has been sent are applicable.

2. The law according to the general conflict of laws

10 The law that applies to situations connected to several countries – as is the case when posting workers – is generally determined by the conflict of law rules. This is determined by European law, specifically by Regulation (EC) No. 593/2008, the so-called Rome I Regulation (see in detail § 11). This applies to contracts entered into after the 17 December 2009 (Arts. 28 *et seq.* Rome I Regulation). If no choice of law is selected pursuant to Art. 3 Rome I Regulation, the applicable law is determined by objective connecting factors according to Art. 8(2) Rome I Regulation. It is stated therein that the applicable law of the employment relationship is the law of the state in which the employee habitually carries out his work, even if he is temporarily posted to another state, in the alternative, the law of the state of the hiring establishment (Art. 8(3) Rome I Regulation), in so far as there is no closer connection to another state (Art. 8(4) Rome I Regulation). All criteria point towards the country of origin being the relevant connecting factor in cases of posting workers. Laws of the state where the work is carried out are only applied to the extent that they are internationally mandatory rules within the meaning of Art. 9 Rome I Regulation. Whether a rule is internationally mandatory is a matter of interpretation. The decisive factor is whether the norm gives effect to important social policies and does not just protect individual interests (see in detail § 11, para. 20; *Dicey/Morris/Collins,* On the Conflict of Laws, 2006, paras. 33–090).

3. Advantages and disadvantages

11 The result of the country-of-origin principle is that service providers from countries with lower wage levels and lower social security contributions possess competitive advantages over companies from countries with higher standards, as they can offer their services at lower prices. This corresponds to the **competitive position in trade**: manufacturers from low-wage countries have an advantage when it comes to price. In terms of competition therefore, treating the posting of workers situation in the same way as the trade situation supports the country-of-origin principle. In addition, the country-of-origin principle prevents the added burden for transnationally active service providers of being forced to consider several legal systems.

12 However, the country-of-origin principle has some severe disadvantages. Where companies from countries of low wages and social standards enjoy competitive advantages, on the other side of the coin the companies in high-wage countries such as Sweden, France or Germany suffer significant competitive disadvantages. In the medium term and long term this will either lead to a decline of the wage levels and

social standards in those countries or those companies will be squeezed out resulting in increased unemployment. This problem particularly affects the building industry, where the labour costs represent regularly a high percentage of the overall costs. Critics speak of the danger of social dumping. The social dimension was emphasized some years after in the UK, where the Lindsey Oil Refinery dispute made the headlines. The protestors were outraged that at a time of recession and high unemployment a contractor did not hire local British workers to work on a large engineering project in the UK and voiced concerns about undercutting the price of local labour by hiring foreign workers (for a detailed analysis of this dispute see *Barnard*, 38 International Law Journal 2009, 245 *et seqq.*). In addition, there is a **danger of social friction as a result of a "split employment market"**, in which posted employees work in poorer conditions compared to their domestic colleagues. Finally, the regulatory power of the legislator and of the parties to collective agreements would be undermined in matters relating to social conditions if a large number of posted workers were to work outside the higher standards of high-wage countries. All of this distinguishes the importation of services significantly from the importation of goods and justifies accepting different social standards as a legitimate competitive advantage in the one case, but actively counteracting a competitive lowering of social standards in the other case.

III. Posted Workers Directive (PWD)

1. Short outline of its origins

In light of the disadvantages of the country-of-origin principle, the European legislator decided to pass special laws relating to the posting of workers and place more emphasis on the place-of-work principle. 13

By adopting the Directive 96/71/EC (Posted Workers Directive – PWD) based on Arts. 55, 47(2) EC (now Arts. 62, 53(2) TFEU), the European legislator created a set of rules that, ever since, has been the subject of political discussion time and time again. 14

The directive was politically highly controversial. The United Kingdom and Portugal in particular rejected it on grounds of principle (see the UK's opposition in Industrial Relations Legal Information Bulletin No. 444, March 1992, p. 9; see also *Bercusson*, Thompsons Labour and European Law Review 1997, Issue 7, pp. 6–7). 15

2. Approach: place-of-work principle regarding the "hard core" of work conditions

The approach of the PWD consists of introducing the place-of-work principle for the "hard core" (Recital 14 of PWD) of work conditions. Legally, this is achieved by declaring that certain work conditions are internationally mandatory rules. For purposes of the Rome I Regulation, the PWD can be seen as an act of the Community, which takes precedence over the rules of the Rome I Regulation, pursuant to Art. 23 Rome I Regulation, cf. *Blanpain*, European Labour Law, 2010, p. 433. 16

3. PWD's compatibility with primary law

There is disagreement as to the PWD's compatibility with European primary law. 17

18 **In favour** of the legality of the rules in principle: *Däubler*, 7 EuZW 1997, 613, 615 *et seq.*; *Hanau*, 49 NJW 1996, 1369, 1372; *Hickl*, 14 NZA 1997, 513, 515; *Schiek*, Europäisches Arbeitsrecht, 3rd ed., 2007, p. 286. Nevertheless the *ECJ* has since decided a number of cases in this area without questioning the legality of the directive. At least in practice, therefore, the PWD's legality must be assumed.

19 Which stance one takes on this point is probably based in part on whether one considers social dumping legitimate or even desirable. Based on the *ECJ*'s case-law, the approach taken in the directive must, in principle, be considered to be in line with primary law. Rules that force transnationally active companies that temporarily post their employees abroad to guarantee the local work conditions, may represent a restriction of the freedom to provide services, because they put an additional economic burden on the company. But this restriction can be justified. The *ECJ* has held in numerous decisions that Community law does not preclude the Member States from extending their national rules or collective agreements concluded by both sides of industry to any person who is employed, even temporarily, within their territory, and from enforcing those rules (see above para. 2: Case 113/89 – Rush Portuguesa [obiter] [1990] ECR I-1417; Cases 369 and 276/96 – Arblade [1999] ECR I-8453; Case 164/99 – Portugaia Construções [2002] ECR I-787; cf. also recital 12 of Directive 96/71/EC).

20 It was, however, considered a problem that **only overriding reasons in the public interest can act as justification for the restriction of a fundamental freedom**, whereas e. g. the **German** *Arbeitnehmerentsendegesetz* (Statute on Posted Workers) serves to protect the German building industry from alleged unfair competition by low wage companies from abroad and to reduce unemployment in the German employment market, as evidenced by the explanatory memorandum of the legislation (cf. the first question in the *ECJ* Case 164/99 – Portugaia Construções [2002] ECR I-787). But it is precisely these aims that would be considered unlawful. As the *ECJ* confirmed in the cases Finalarte and Portugaia Construções, measures that restrict the freedom to provide services cannot be justified by economic objectives such as the protection of domestic companies (Case 49/98 and others – Finalarte [2001] ECR I-7831; Case 164/99 – Portugaia Construções [2002] ECR I-787). The protection of workers does however represent an overriding public interest (Cases 369 and 276/96 – Arblade [1999] ECR I-8453; Case 49/98 and others – Finalarte [2001] ECR I-7831). According to the *ECJ*, it will suffice if the restriction serves to *objectively* achieve this goal. Whilst the intention and aims of the legislator may be an indication of the aim of the law, it is not conclusive (Case 49/98 and others – Finalarte [2001] ECR I-7831; Case 164/99 – Portugaia Construções [2002] ECR I-787). This approach was reaffirmed in the decision C-60/03 (Wolff & Müller [2004] ECR I-9553). And in Laval (Case 341/05 – [2007] ECR I-11767) the *ECJ* accepted that protection against social dumping may constitute an overriding reason of public interest. Considering the fact that Recital 5 of the PWD also reveals the objective of "fair competition" along with the protection of employees and that, objectively, the higher German minimum wage gives posted workers an advantage and does in fact prevent social dumping, the provisions of the *Arbeitnehmerentsendegesetz* are usually justifiable.

21 The European directive itself has, as yet, not been the subject of judicial review by the *ECJ*. However, there are decisions relating to the issue of posted workers where acts of Member States had to be assessed on the basis of the directive and the Court therefore had the opportunity to comment on the legitimacy of the directive (Case 60/03 – Wolff & Müller [2004] ECR I-9553; Case 341/02 – Commission ./. Germany [2005] ECR I-2733; Case 341/05 – Laval [2007] ECR I-11767). One can conclude from the Court's silence on this matter that it has no such concerns.

22 As a rule restricting fundamental freedoms, the extension of domestic provisions to posted workers to achieve the objective of worker protection, must be appropriate and necessary (Cases 49/98 and others – Finalarte [2001] ECR I-7831). Furthermore, companies from other Member States must not be discriminated against.

The extension is not necessary in cases where the rules of the home country afford essentially the same or a similar level of protection (Cases 49/98 and others – Finalarte [2001] ECR I-7831). Otherwise this would mean unnecessary **duplication**. Moreover, such cases often involve a discriminatory and therefore unlawful **additional burden** on the posting company. If the social security of the posted worker is already secured by contributions made in the home state, then the company is not required to pay for benefits in the host state that serve the same purpose (Cases 62/81 and others – Seco [1982] ECR 223; Case 272/94 – Guiot [1996] ECR I-1905; Cases 369 and 276/96 – Arblade [1999] ECR I-8453). 23

The fact that, in concluding a collective agreement specific to one undertaking, an employer established in one Member State can pay wages lower than the minimum wage laid down in a collective agreement declared to be generally applicable, whilst an employer established in another Member State cannot do so, represents unlawful unequal treatment (Case 164/99 – Portugaia Construções [2002] ECR I-787). 24

4. Posting workers and the Services Directive

On the 12 December 2006 the politically controversial Services Directive 2006/123/EC was adopted and was amended during the legislative process not least owing to the pressure exerted by European Parliament (**Directive 2006/123/EC** of the European Parliament and of the Council of the 12 December 2006 on services in the internal market). The Directive is without prejudice to the provisions of the PWD. Pursuant to Art. 1(6) the Directive does not apply to employment law in general. Moreover, Art. 3(1)(a) stipulates that the provisions of the PWD take precedence. Finally, Art. 17 No. 2 sets out that Art. 16 – as the central provision regarding the freedom to provide services – does not apply to matters covered by the PWD. 25

IV. Rules that apply to all forms of posting

1. The term "worker"

The rules only apply to employment relationships. According to Art. 2(2) PWD the term "worker" is that which applies in the law of the Member State, to whose territory the worker is posted. Thus, in contrast to the scope of application of Art. 45 TFEU there is no definition of "worker" in Community law. 27

Problems arise in particular in cases where individual persons offer their labour as a "one-man company". Technically, this is a self-employed subcontractor. But in these cases it is important to look at the actual work situation, although this can be difficult: If the work constitutes dependent employment, then it is an employment relationship. This is a case of so-called "**bogus self-employment**". Whether that person is irrevocably considered a self-employed person in his or her home country is irrelevant (e. g. persons who are certified as self-employed under English law with a so-called A 1 certificate). 28

2. Situations covered by the PWD

According to Art. 1(3) PWD the posting rules apply to the following transnational situations: posting of workers in the context of a contract to provide work or services (a), posting of workers to a company owned by the group of companies (b) and the hiring out by an agency for temporary work in another Member State (c). 29

3. Minimum work conditions by law, regulation or administrative provision

30 Art. 3(1) first indent PWD sets out which law, regulation and administrative provisions of the host state, irrespective of the law applicable to the employment relationship, must apply in the posting situation. It must be concluded, *argumentum e contrario*, from Art. 3(1) second indent PWD that "law, regulation and administrative provisions" mean only state rules and not collective agreements that have been declared universally applicable (cf. *Bercusson*, European Labour Law, 2009, p. 298). Thus, in accordance with the regulatory approach described above (para. 18), the PWD does not lay down Community-wide minimum work conditions but simply sets out which law is applicable in a conflict of laws situation.

31 The following matters are covered by the PWD in its Art. 3:

- Maximum work periods and minimum rest periods (a).
- Minimum paid annual holidays (b).
- The minimum rates of pay, including overtime rates not including supplementary occupational retirement pension schemes (c). Not all Member States have minimum wage laws. However, this is not an infringement of the PWD. The PWD does not demand a harmonization of minimum standards; it just lays down regulatory areas where the laws of the host state must be applied. The Union lacks the authority to regulate minimum wage substantively (Art. 153(5) TFEU).
- The conditions of hiring-out of workers, in particular the supply of workers by temporary employment undertakings (d).
- Health, safety and hygiene at work (e). Provisions in this area were already considered to be internationally mandatory even before adoption of the PWD.
- Protective measures with regard to the terms and conditions of employment of pregnant women or women who have recently given birth, of children and of young people (f).
- Equality of treatment between men and women and other provisions on non-discrimination (g).

32 Art. 3(7) PWD specifically sets out that the extension of national laws to posted workers shall not prevent more favourable work conditions from being applicable (cf. the principle of more favourability in Recital 17 PWD)

4. Minimum work conditions in collective agreements

33 The **provisions for the building industry and cleaning industry are exceptional** in that not only minimum work conditions laid down by state laws are declared internationally mandatory but, under certain circumstances, also rules in collective agreements. Art. 3(1) PWD provides that collective agreements can be extended to posted workers in the economic areas listed in the annex of the Directive. This is significant as the most important work condition economically – wage – is not always regulated by a state minimum wage. In Germany, Sweden, Denmark and Finnland, for instance, it is regulated by collective agreements. The principle of the most favourable provision in Art. 3(7) PWD also applies here. However, provisions in collective agreements must only be applied to posted workers if the collective agreements are universally applicable within the meaning of Art. 3(8) PWD. In those Member States where it is not possible to declare collective agreements universally applicable, the danger of undercutting local labour prices remains. In the UK there is no law giving extension to collective agreements, thus the company

posting workers to the UK must only adhere to minimum wage laws, thereby still being able to offer lower labour prices than local competition that may be bound by collective agreements. There is the possibility for Member States with no system to declare collective agreements universally applicable to base themselves on collective agreements or arbitration awards which are generally applicable to all similar undertakings in the geographical area and in the profession or industry concerned, and/or collective agreements which have been concluded by the most representative employers' and labour organizations at national level and which are applied throughout national territory. However, the Member State must opt into either of these possibilities (Case 341/05 – Laval [2007] ECR I-11767; *Barnard*, 38 Industrial Law Journal 2009, 245, 256). This option was not pursued by the Swedish government which lead to the problems arising in the Laval case, and this was not pursued in the UK.

5. Exceptions

The application of all work conditions listed in Art. 3(1) PWD – whether by law or collective agreement – can lead to disproportionate complications particularly in cases of only short-term posting. 34

If for instance a Polish construction company sends its workers to a construction site in Belgium for six months, it seems reasonable that the company must obtain information about possible minimum wage rules and pay those minimum wages applicable in Belgium to the workers for the duration of the posting. But if a Polish machine manufacturer sells a machine to Belgium and sends a few workers to Belgium for three days to assemble it, it may not be reasonable, or in accordance with the purpose of the PWD, for the Polish company to have to pay the posted workers the minimum wages applicable in Belgium for those three days. 35

These circumstances are taken into account by Art. 3(2) PWD which allows rules relating to minimum wage and minimum annual holidays to be excluded if the period of posting does not exceed eight days in cases of assembly and installation of goods. Some Member States included this exception using a copy-out technique in their implementation acts, such as **Belgium, Finland, France and Greece** amongst others. **Spain** stipulates the non-applicability of minimum leave and minimum rates of pay to any posted workers that are posted for no more than 8 days. The **United Kingdom** and **Ireland** have not made use of this exception (cf. Report from the Commission services on the implementation of Directive 96/71/EC of the European Parliament and of the Council of 16 December 1996 concerning the posting of workers in the framework of the provision of services, p. 12). 36

The PWD also gives Member States the option of not applying minimum wage provisions to posted workers (except in cases of hiring out for temporary work) if the length of the posting does not exceed one month (Art. 3(3) PWD) or leaves this decision to be made in a collective agreement that is universally applicable (Art. 3(4) PWD). Neither the Finnish legislator nor the German, Belgian, French or British legislator seized this opportunity: the provisions concerning posted workers apply from the first day of posting. If the amount of work to be done is not significant, the Member States may grant exemptions from minimum wage provisions and minimum annual holiday provisions, under Art. 3(5) PWD. Such an exception was initially laid down in German law but was repealed again in 2004. This potential exemption has not been incorporated in the Austrian transposition 37 act, in the Finnish, and French instruments, in the Greek Presidential Decree, the Irish Act, the Italian Decree, the Netherlands Act, in the United Kingdom, in the Swedish Act or in the Belgian Act either. However, in the Netherlands the parties to collective agreements may, if they wish so, decide to exclude workers posted to the Netherlands in the context of a non-significant posting from the scope of the extended collective agreements (cf. Report from the Commission services of January 2003 on the implementation of Directive 96/71/EC of the European Parliament and of the Council of 16 December 1996 concerning the posting of workers in the framework of the provision of services, p. 13).

6. Redress

38 Art. 6 PWD sets out that judicial proceedings may be instituted in the Member State in whose territory the worker is or was posted in order to enforce the right to the terms and conditions of employment. According to the general rules of international jurisdiction, a court in the country of origin would normally have jurisdiction in posting cases (Art. 19 Brussels I Regulation). Some countries have however made use of the authority set out in Art. 6 PWD, see Report from the Commission services on the implementation of Directive 96/71/EC of the European Parliament and of the Council of 16 December 1996 concerning the posting of workers in the framework of the provision of services, p. 20.

39 The **British government** made some changes to existing employment legislation in order to comply with the PWD. One example is sec. 196 of the Employment Relations Act 1996 which was repealed by sec. 32(3) of the Employment Relations Act 1999. Under the previous law, certain statutory employment protection claims could not be brought before an employment tribunal in the UK by a worker who ordinarily worked outside Great Britain. Without the geographical limitation, it was unclear under which circumstances the legislation applied, as read literally, it applied to anybody who worked under an employment contract anywhere in the world. This question was put to the House of Lords in *Serco Ltd v Lawson [2006] UKHL 3* where it was decided that there was an implied territorial limitation in that the employee must be in employment in Great Britain at the time of dismissal or, in the case of expatriate workers, the legislation would apply if the employee was posted abroad by a British employer for the purposes of a business carried on in Great Britain (see for more details *McMullen*, 27 Company Lawyer 2006, 342–343). Therefore, workers posted to the territory of the UK can bring claims before an employment tribunal in the UK. In **Italy** proceedings must be brought before the Italian courts during the performance of the contract or within one year of its expiry, Art. 4(3) of the Decreto Legislativo 25 febbraio 2000, no. 72.

§ 10. Employee Representation and Unions

Literature: *Dukes*, Case Note: The Right to Strike under UK Law: Something More Than a Slogan? NURMT v SERCO, ASLEF v London & Birmingham Railway Ltd., 40 Industrial Law Journal 2011, 302–311; *Hall*, Assessing the Information and Consultation of Employees Regulations, 34 Industrial Law Journal 2005, 103–126; *Jagodzinski*, EWCs after 15 years — success or failure?, 17 European Review of Labour and Research 2011, No. 2, 203–216; *O'Donoghue/Carr*, Dealing with Viking and Laval: From Theory to Practice, 11 Cambridge Yearbook of European Legal Studies 2008/9, pp. 123–163; *Stewart/Bell*, The Right to Strike: A Comparative Perspective - A Study of National Law in six EU States, The Institute of Employment Rights, 2008; *Wooldridge*, The Framework Directive on informing and consulting employees, 24 Company Lawyer 2003, 182–184.

I. Collective Labour Law in the EU

The regulations concerning collective labour law are few and far between 1 compared to those concerning individual labour law. The subject matter remains the individual Member States' domain. This will probably not change in any fundamental way in the near future. Essential aspects of collective labour law are outside the scope of the EU's legislative authority. Pursuant to **Art. 153(5) TFEU** no provisions may be laid down at European level concerning the law of association or the law of strike and lock-out. This is true despite the existence of Art. 28 CFREU which enshrines the right of workers, employers and their respective organisations to negotiate collective agreements and take collective action at primary law level. For Art. 51(2) CFREU states that the Charter does not establish any new power for the Union (see in detail below, para. 6). And quite rightly so: Such an explosive political subject matter should not be put in the hands of those pursuing European harmonization. A provision relating to this was already included in the Social Agreement; see Art. 2(6). This is different with regard to the law concerning collective agreements. At present no provisions exist but under Art. 153(3) third indent TFEU one certainly could adopt provisions on this matter. However, no European collective agreements exist at this time. Whether this will ever change, remains to be seen.

Many Member States recognize a right to strike: The **United Kingdom** have statutory provisions 2 regulating industrial action (see the Trade Union and Labour Relations (Consolidation) Act 1992; for details and a recent review see *Dukes*, 40 International Law Journal 2011, 302 *et seqq.*). The **German** legislator has not provided any regulations. But the right to strike is recognized by the courts and is derived directly from the right to associate enshrined in Art. 9(3) of the constitution (*Grundgesetz*). In **Belgian Law** the right to strike is not recognized as such in the Constitution, however it may be derived from Art. 23(3) of the Constitution, which provides for the right to collective bargaining. Due to the fact that Belgium is party to various international instruments, which regard the right to strike as fundamental, it is also considered fundamental in Belgian law. Still, it does not provide for a detailed regulation on how to exercise the right to strike, i. e. that it is up to the unions and employer associations to regulate the content of the right on the basis of the principle of subsidiarity (*Stewart/Bel*, The Right to Strike: A Comparative Perspective. - A Study of National Law in six EU States, The Institute of Employment Rights of 2009 based on papers prepared for a conference held at the University of Leicester, 15–18 April 2008). In **Spanish law**, however, the right to strike is recognized in Art. 28 of the Spanish Constitution as a fundamental right of workers to defend their interests, without prejudicing legally imposed measures to assure the maintenance of essential community services (La Constitución Española de 1978, Artículo

28(2)). The right to strike is regulated in detail in the Royal Decree 17/1977 on Work Relationships (Decreto-ley 17/1977, de 4 de marzo, sobre Relaciones de Trabajo) with some nuances introduced by the Spanish Constitutional Court in its decision of 8 April 1981.

3 This is unsatisfactory, particularly for companies that are organized in many different European countries. Agreeing on a uniform collective agreement in these cases is only possible under the domestic law of a Member State which could come into conflict with the international private law of another state. Mostly, a solution is found by agreeing to parallel collective agreements under e.g. French and German law.

4 The most important subject matter, on which European collective labour law provisions have been adopted, is codetermination. There is the European Works Council Directive 94/45/EC, last amended by Directive 2006/109, by reason of the accession of Bulgaria and Romania and the Directive regarding the involvement of employees in a European Company (Societas Europaea, SE; Directive 2001/86/EC) as well as the Directive concerning the information and consultation of employees 2002/14/EC.

5 Additionally, there are numerous directives containing provisions concerning duties to inform, consult and advise employee representatives under domestic law, such as in the Part Time Work Directive (97/81/EC), the Fixed Term Work Directive (99/70/EC) and, before that, in the Collective Redundancies Directive (98/59/EC). The Directive on Temporary Agency Work also contains provisions which give employee representatives consultation rights, see Directive 2008/104/EC).

II. European law governing collective agreements and labour disputes?

6 The statements above have indicated already: There is no genuine European law governing collective agreements or labour disputes. At first blush this seems strange, considering the fact that Art. 28 CFREU, which has now become part of European primary law pursuant to Art. 6(1) EU-Treaty, gives workers, employers and their respective organisations the guaranteed right "in accordance with Community law and national laws and practices, […] to negotiate and conclude collective agreements at the appropriate levels and, in cases of conflicts of interest, to take collective action to defend their interests, including strike action". This guarantee is broad in scope: it guarantees **collective autonomy** as well as the **freedom to take industrial action**. But as the CFREU does not extend the powers of the Union, Art. 28 CFREU acts primarily as an **interface** which makes sure that industrial action that is legal under national law is observed at European level.

7 This pivotal function is apparent in the well-known *ECJ* decisions "Viking Line" and Laval:

Case 341/05 – **Laval** [2007] ECR I-11767 and
Case 438/05 – **Viking Line** [2007] ECR I-10779

The Latvian company Laval posted around 35 workers to Sweden to work on building sites operated by a Swedish company for the purposes of the construction of school premises in Vaxholm. After unsuccessful negotiations regarding a collective agreement, the Swedish building and public works trade union carried out collective action in protest, consisting of, *inter alia*, preventing the delivery of goods onto the site, placing pickets and prohibiting Latvian workers and vehicles from entering the site. In January 2005, other trade unions announced sympathy actions, consisting of a boycott of all Laval's sites in Sweden, with the result that the undertaking was no longer able to carry out its activities in that Member State. Laval sought a declaration that both the blockading and the sympathy action affecting all its worksites were illegal and an order that such action should cease. It also sought an order that the trade unions pay compensation for the damage suffered.

The Swedish Arbetsdomstolen made a reference to the Court of Justice for a preliminary ruling with the question, *inter alia*, whether Arts. 12 EC and 49 EC and Directive 96/71/EC precluded trade unions from attempting, by means of collective action, to force a foreign undertaking which posts workers to Sweden to apply a Swedish collective agreement.

In its judgment, the *ECJ* pointed out that the right of trade unions of a Member State to take collective action by which undertakings established in other Member States may be forced to sign the collective agreement for the building sector – certain terms of which depart from the legislative provisions and establish more favourable terms and conditions of employment as regards the matters referred to in Art. 3(1), first subparagraph, (a) to (g) of Directive 96/71/EC and others relate to matters not referred to in that provision – is liable to make it less attractive, or more difficult, for such undertakings to carry out construction work in Sweden, and therefore constitutes a restriction on the freedom to provide services within the meaning of Art. 49 EC. The Court went on to say that, in principle, blockading action by a trade union of the host Member State which is aimed at ensuring that workers posted in the framework of a transnational provision of services have their terms and conditions of employment fixed at a certain level, falls within the objective of protecting workers but that the obstacle which that collective action forms cannot be justified with regard to such an objective. The collective action such as that at issue in the main proceedings cannot be justified in the light of the public interest objective, where the negotiations on pay, which that action seeks to force an undertaking established in another Member State to enter into, form part of a national context characterised by a lack of provisions, of any kind, which are sufficiently precise and accessible that they do not render it impossible or excessively difficult in practice for such an undertaking to determine the obligations with which it is required to comply as regards minimum pay. Consequently, the *ECJ* held that Art. 49 EC and Directive 96/71/EC are to be interpreted as precluding a trade union, in a Member State in which the terms and conditions of employment covering the matters referred to in Art. 3(1), first subparagraph, (a) to (g) of that Directive are contained in legislative provisions, save for minimum rates of pay, from attempting, by means of collective action in the form of a blockade of sites such as that at issue in the main proceedings, to force a provider of services established in another Member State to enter into negotiations with it on the rates of pay for posted workers and to sign a collective agreement the terms of which lay down, as regards some of those matters, more favourable conditions than those resulting from the relevant legislative provisions, while other terms relate to matters not referred to in Art. 3 of the Directive. It also stated that national rules, which fail to take into account collective agreements to which undertakings that post workers to Sweden are already bound in the Member State in which they are established, give rise to discrimina-

tion against such undertakings, in so far as under those national rules they are treated in the same way as national undertakings which have not concluded a collective agreement.
The *ECJ* ruled in the same vein in Viking Line. The case concerned the question whether the trade union International Transport Workers Federation (ITF) could prevent the Finnish shipping company Viking Line from registering one of its vessels under Estonian law in order to hire a cheaper Estonian crew. The ITF had sent a circular to all its 600 affiliated unions in 140 countries decreeing that only the Finnish Seamen's Union may negotiate with Viking Line about the re-flagging. Viking's plans having been thwarted, it brought an action against the ITF in the United Kingdom where ITF is situated.
The Court observed that such collective action as exercised by the ITF was a restriction of freedom of establishment, as it had the effect of making less attractive, or even pointless, the exercise by an undertaking of its right to freedom of establishment. In considering a possible justification of the restriction, the *ECJ* conceded that the right to take collective action for the protection of workers was a legitimate interest which, in principle, justified a restriction of one of the fundamental freedoms guaranteed by the Treaty and that the protection of workers was one of the overriding reasons of public interest recognized by the Court. Whether the restriction was justified was left up to the national court who should apply a test of proportionality. In principle, a restriction of freedom of establishment by collective action could therefore be justified. The Court however held that to the extent that the "flags of convenience" policy of the ITF prevents ship owners altogether from registering their vessels in a State other than that of which the beneficial owners of those vessels are nationals, the restrictions on freedom of establishment resulting from such action cannot be objectively justified.

8 Art. 28 CFREU is however not just an interface for national law. The provision contains minimum standards such as the express guarantee of the right to strike. To determine what this guarantee entails one must take a closer look at the Union's authorities for regulating the law of collective bargaining and labour disputes.

1. The Union's competences for regulating the law of collective bargaining and labour disputes

9 As mentioned above: At present the Union has only limited competence to regulate the law of collective bargaining and labour disputes. Under Art. 4(2)(b) TFEU there is a shared competence only "for the aspects defined in this Treaty". This refers to Arts. 151 *et seqq.* TFEU.

10 a) No rules governing the right to strike and impose lock-outs can be adopted at European level. This is stated expressly in Art. 153(5) TFEU. European law, especially the freedom of establishment, can nevertheless set boundaries for national laws governing industrial disputes, as the cases Viking Line and Laval show. This limitation of competence applies to the authority to create and define the law; it does not apply to possible restrictions – the latter would be pointless, as it would create "inestimable" rights.

b) An authority to **harmonize the national law governing collective agreements** 11
could only be derived from the general provisions of Arts. 153–155 or 352 TFEU. These provisions too must be reconciled with Art. 153(5) TFEU though, which expressly rejects competencies regarding the right to association and the right to strike and impose lock-outs. The general clause in Art. 352 TFEU must yield to this expressly adopted restriction of the authority of the EU. Whether the right to association mentioned in Art. 153(5) TFEU includes the right to collective bargaining is questionable. Restraint should be exercised here. When strike and lock-outs are mentioned specifically, it seems more likely to conclude that the law governing collective agreements, despite its functional connection to the law of industrial disputes, is not excluded from the competencies under Art. 153 TFEU, but rather that it is included in "the representation and collective defence of the interests of workers and employers" of paragraph 1(f). The TFEU therefore gives a foundation for the harmonization of the national law of collective agreements. However, it is unlikely to be made use of within the foreseeable future, not only because of the requirement of unanimity in Art. 153(2) TFEU – the principle of subsidiarity also strongly militates in favour of the autonomy of the national legal orders.

c) In contrast, it is questionable whether the Treaties contain an **authority to** 12
adopt an autonomous European collective agreement. This is made clear by Art. 153(2) TFEU which only authorizes the adoption of directives, i. e. can only give instructions on how to shape the national law but cannot create genuine European foundations. Art. 155 TFEU also gives no authority to create a supranational law governing collective agreements. Even though Art. 155(1) TFEU clearly confirms the possibility of supranational collective agreements (*Sciarra,* in: Liber Amicorum Lord Wedderburn, 1996, pp. 189, 199; *Treu,* in: Liber Amicorum Lord Wedderburn, 1996, pp. 169, 173) and although an "agreement" under Art. 155 TFEU – the subject matter of which could go beyond that of a European collective agreement – could be extended to matters of association and collective bargaining law, there would be no way of implementing such an agreement. Enforcement by virtue of the legislative powers of the EU does not go beyond the procedure based on Art. 153 TFEU. And the nature of a European law of association and collective bargaining rules out the other means of enforcement, that is, domestic implementation under the rules of the respective Member States.

d) Furthermore, the Union can lay down the staff regulations of its officials and 13
servants which would encompass an authority and – following Art. 28 CFREU – a duty to regulate collective bargaining and labour disputes. This is the only possible case under the Treaties where a genuine European, supranational law governing collective bargaining and labour disputes can be created. In other areas there is only the competence to create directives (Art. 153(2)(b) TFEU).

2. The guarantee in Art. 28 CFREU

Art. 28 CFREU will remain an interface until there is a uniform legal framework 14
for collective labour law. The significance of Art. 28 CFREU will therefore be limited in most collective labour law disputes. The law of collective bargaining and industrial action is national law and the Member States are only bound to the Charter when they are implementing Union law (Art. 51(1) CFREU). This refers to the executive or legislative implementation of Union law or the restriction of fundamental rights by

the Member States (the latter is disputed by some but the *ECJ* mentions this specifically in Laval and Viking Line). Consequently, collective agreements or industrial action measures will only fall within the scope of Art. 28 CFREU when there is a transnational connection, but not in a "normal", national labour dispute.

3. Political attempts

15 The limited scope of Art. 28 CFREU may seem unsatisfactory; attempts to create **legal bases for a European law of collective bargaining** or for European collective agreements have their roots in various stages of development of the EU. Unfortunately, they are (therefore) not tailored to work in harmony. The Commission of the European Communities submitted a proposal to the Council of Ministers in the 1970 s for a Regulation concerning a European Company (COM [1970] 600 final of 10 October 1970), which at that time contained special provisions in Arts. 146 *et seqq.* regarding the ability of European Companies to conclude collective agreements. These proposals were not pursued any further (on their content cf. *Hood*, The European Company Proposal, 22 The International and Comparative Law Quarterly 1973, No. 3, pp. 434–461; *Storm*, 26 Business Lawyer 1971, pp. 1443–1454; *Sanders*, The European Company, 6 Georgia Journal of International and Comparative Law, Issue 2, pp. 367–394). In the amended proposal for a regulation embodying a statute for a European Company of 25 August 1989 (Commission Draft Regulation on a Statute for a European Company, COM No. 268 final (August 25, 1989), published in 57 Common Market Law Review 1990, 120) the provisions concerning the employees' position had already been eliminated. They can be found in Directive 2001/86/EC supplementing the Statute for a European Company with regard to the involvement of employees (on this see paras. 27 *et seqq.*). Art. 4 thereof provides that an agreement – obviously not intended as a collective agreement – shall be negotiated between the managing or administrative bodies of the companies and the employees of these companies, wherein arrangements for the involvement of the employees shall be set out.

16 There were also attempts to create a European guarantee of collective autonomy and industrial action. Numbers 11 and 12 of the former Community Charter of Fundamental Social Rights of Workers of 9 December 1989 can be mentioned here:

Freedom of association and collective bargaining

11. Employers and workers of the European Community shall have the right of association in order to constitute professional organizations or trade unions of their choice for the defence of their economic and social interests. Every employer and every worker shall have the freedom to join or not to join such organizations without any personal or occupational damage being thereby suffered by him.

12. Employers or employers' organizations, on the one hand, and workers' organizations, on the other, shall have the right to negotiate and conclude collective agreements under the conditions laid down by national legislation and practice. The dialogue between the two sides of industry at European level which must be developed, may, if the parties deem it desirable, result in contractual relations in particular at inter-occupational and sectoral level.

This was complemented by Arts. 5 and 6 of the European Social Charter (ESC). 17
This also guarantees the workers' right to associate (Art. 5) and the right to bargain collectively.

"Article 6 – The right to bargain collectively

With a view to ensuring the effective exercise of the right to bargain collectively, the Parties undertake:

to promote joint consultation between workers and employers;

to promote, where necessary and appropriate, machinery for voluntary negotiations between employers or employers' organisations and workers' organisations, with a view to the regulation of terms and conditions of employment by means of collective agreements;

to promote the establishment and use of appropriate machinery for conciliation and voluntary arbitration for the settlement of labour disputes;

and recognise: the right of workers and employers to collective action in cases of conflicts of interest, including the right to strike, subject to obligations that might arise out of collective agreements previously entered into."

The Charter of Fundamental Rights as well as the ESC were cited by the *ECJ* in 18
Viking Line and Laval to argue for the right to industrial action. The significance is however marginal compared to Art. 28 CFREU. The ESC is a treaty of international law and is therefore outside of European law in its narrow sense, as the *ECJ* also explained.

III. European Works Councils

The first great milestone in regulating collective labour law was the adoption of 19
the Directive establishing a European Works Council (Directive 94/45/EC) on 28 October 1996. It was adopted on the basis of Art. 2(2) of the Social Agreement (equivalent to Art. 153(2) TFEU). The Directive 94/45/EC prescribed the information and consultation of employees in transnational cases. This was to be achieved by setting up a European Works Council as a special body either by **agreement** between the employee representatives and the company or on the basis of mandatory **statutory provisions** in absence of an agreement. Initially, it was disputed whether Art. 153(2) TFEU included the authority to create new employee representative structures or whether existing employee representative bodies would merely be given additional rights. The implementation of the Directive in all Member States has rendered this question obsolete.

The original Directive was revised in 2009. The new Directive 2009/38/EC 20
brought changes to the authorities of the employee representatives – it is made clear that the EWC only has authority in transnational cases (Art. 1(3)); the definitions in Art. 2 were amended. The negotiation procedure was also amended. Art. 4(4) obligates the central management to obtain certain information, pursuant to Art. 5 the special negotiating body shall be established in accordance with the same guidelines as the European Company. An exciting new feature can be found in Art. 6(2)(b) which expressly forbids the parties to a collective agreement to discriminate on grounds of gender. This constitutes the first express reference to anti-discrimination in European collective labour law. Of great significance in practice is the fact that the European legislator stipulates a renegotiation in cases of "structural changes" (Art. 6(2)(g)). For a recent review of the EWC, see *Jagodzinski*, EWCs after 15 years – success or failure?, 17 European Review of Labour and Research 2011, No. 2, 203–216.

1. Scope

21 The Directive covers Community-scale undertakings and Community-scale groups of undertakings of a certain size. "Community-scale undertaking" according to the legal definition of Art. 2(1)(a) means any undertaking with at least 1000 employees within the Member States and at least 150 employees in each of at least two Member States. Thus, the Directive covers only larger entities. The thresholds were heavily contested even at the time of the original directive's adoption; employer representatives pushed for higher numbers. The amended Directive did not change the thresholds. Subsidiarity was manifest in Art. 13 of Directive 94/45/EC, whereby existing voluntary agreements, as long as they have the inherent quality of ensuring employee rights, have precedence (for further information on Art. 13 see: European Works Councils: The Uncertain Future of 'pre-Directive' Agreements: an Analysis of Art. 13 of the European Works Council Directive, 24 Industrial Law Journal 1995, Issue 4, 382–387). It is not quite clear at what time these voluntary agreements have to have been in force: at adoption of the directive or the enactment of the implementing legislation. Art. 14 of Directive 2009/38/EC sets out a similar rule. This transitional problem naturally loses importance over time.

2. Content

22 The Directive gives two options, either the establishment of EWC (which is undoubtedly the alternative it primarily strives for), or the establishment of a decentralized employee information and consultation procedure. The choice between the two possibilities must be made by employers and employees, after negotiations. This legal responsibility lies with a special negotiating body, see Art. 2(1)(i) of Directive 2009/38/EC. This is a body that is established solely for negotiating an agreement with the central management and then comes to an end (ad-hoc body). Where the central management and the negotiating body are unable to conclude an agreement within three years, Art. 7 stipulates the establishment of an EWC in accordance with the subsidiary requirements set out in the annex. The fact that these only come into action in the alternative and the primary regulation is left to the parties' own authority is also a manifestation of subsidiarity.

3. Competencies of the EWC

23 The competencies of the EWC do not include codetermination (unlike – in part – in the SE), but merely information and consultation. This is why it has been dismissed by employers as a "tourist event for works councils" in the past. The substance of the information duties is described in no. 1(a), 2, 3 of the annex of the Directive.

4. Purview of the right to information

24 In the ***Bofrost*** **case** the *ECJ* had to deal with the issue of substance and purview of the right to information under Art. 11 of Directive 94/45/EC (Case 62/99 – Bofrost [2001] ECR I-2579; for details see *Thüsing/Leder*, SAE 2002, 171). It especially had to deal with the question whether the works councils have a right to information even where it has not yet been established that the management to which the workers'

request is addressed is the management of a controlling undertaking within a group of undertakings and the required information has been deemed confidential by the management. According to the *ECJ*, for the Directive to serve its purpose of improving the employees' right to information and consultation in Community-scale groups of undertakings, it is essential that the workers concerned be guaranteed access to information enabling them to determine whether they have the right to demand the opening of negotiations with central management and the workers' representatives. With that, the *ECJ* has given employee representatives a wide-ranging right to information based on the idea that the Directive must serve a useful purpose; this flanks the right to initiate negotiations in order to establish a cross-border works council enshrined in Art. 5(1) by granting employee representatives the right to be informed about whether the preconditions for this right are fulfilled. Being mindful of the fact that the employee representatives' right to information must be as functional as possible, the *ECJ* finally established the employer's duty to "communicate" documents. The wording of Directive 94/45EC supported this line of argument, given that Art. 11(2) spoke of information being "made available" which can be more than just a verbal communication. The *ECJ* did however draw a line: It had to be "essential information" for setting up transnational employee information and consultation, the communication of documents had to be "necessary" in order to achieve this goal and the management of the undertaking had to have access to the information or at least be able to gain access. Art. 4(4) of Directive 2009/38/EC took this decision into consideration and incorporated it.

In the matter of ***Kühne and Nagel*** the central issue was also the right to 25
information (Case 440/00 – Kühne & Nagel [2004] ECR I-787; confirmed in a very similar case referred by the *Labour Court Bielefeld* Case 349/01 – Anker [2004] ECR I-6803; see *Waas*, The Obligation to Disclose Information – A central management's duty where a European Works Council is established, 3 European Legal Forum 2004, 199–204). The *ECJ* clarified here that in cases where the central management of a Union-scale group of undertakings is not located in an EU country, the employee representatives shall still be provided with information. The obligation to provide information includes information on the average total number of employees and their distribution across the Member States, the establishments of the undertaking and the group undertakings, and information on the structure of the undertaking and of the undertakings in the group. Where the central management does not provide the information, the deemed central management (Art. 3(6)(2) of Directive 94/45/EC: in this case the business of the undertaking or the undertaking of a group of undertakings which employs the most employees in the EU) must request the information essential to the opening of negotiations for the establishment of such an EWC from the other undertakings belonging to the group which are located in the Member States. The deemed central management has a right to receive all necessary information. The management of each of the other undertakings belonging to the group which are located in the Member States is under an obligation to supply the deemed central management with the information concerned in order for it to be passed on to the employee representatives. This too is addressed by Art. 4(4) of Directive 2009/38/EC, obligating the deemed central management (cf. Art. 3(6)(2) of Directive 2009/38/EC).

5. Comparative Law

26 There is comprehensive documentation on the Commission's internet website regarding the implementation of the directive in other European states: http://ec.europa.eu/social/main.jsp?catId=707&langId=en&intPageId=211. It provides all the implementation laws as well as summary reports on the implementation process. Also there is material regarding the future development of the directive. A collection of EWC agreements is available at www.ewcdb.org/ and www.worker-participation.eu.

IV. Co-Determination in the Societas Europaea

27 The EWC model was developed further in the European Company (or Societas Europaea, abbrev. SE). The idea of codetermination in the SE has been around for over a generation. The need to create a uniform European Company arose early on in the harmonization process of European commercial law; Community-scale undertakings should not only be able to be established as a **German** *Aktiengesellschaft* or a **French** *Société Anonyme*, but as a genuine European Company. Germany was hesitant for a long time, concerned that the conversion, merger or other transformation of a German company that is codetermined into a European Company would lead to a decrease in worker protection, as long as the European Company had no regulations securing codetermination. The question of codetermination therefore quickly became a stumbling block. After more than 30 years of discussion the Directive concerning codetermination in the European Company (Directive 2001/86/EC) was adopted on 8 October 2001. Whereas the Statute of the European Company is regulated by Regulation (Regulation No. 2157/2001), the associated rules on codetermination were put into a Directive in order to give the domestic legislators greater constructive discretion.

28 In July 2013 there were almost 1865 European Companies in the EU and EEC (for current data see www.worker-participation.eu). More specific information is not available because there is no central registry for SEs, although the Commission is considering this issue presently. Since the SE has only been made available in most Member States since the expiry of the transposition period in 2004, these numbers are impressive. One must be mindful of the fact that the SE is mainly aimed at large incorporations due to its structure. In Germany e.g., companies such as Allianz, BASF or MAN have chosen the SE. The most SEs can be found in the Czech Republic however, but many of the companies are so-called shelf companies which do not engage in commercial activity.

1. The development prior to the finished directive

29 Almost exactly 50 years ago, demands to create a European trading company were voiced for the first time. The **impetus** for this came **from the French side**: *Thibièrge* demanded the creation of a uniform European company in a lecture given at a notary congress in 1959 (cf. *Thibièrge*, Le Statut des Sociétés Etrangères, in: Congrès des Notaires de France, 1959, p. 260 *et seqq.*). As early as 1952 though, proposals for a European company were submitted to the Council of Europe. These however pertained only to companies that managed public services and exercised public authority. These proposals were met with refusal, with the result that the Council of Europe did not pursue the project any further. The **French government**

took it up again in March 1959. It formulated a proposal to establish a European trading company on the basis of a uniform draft bill to be implemented into each partner state's legal system. The Commission followed this path set by the French government and went a step further: in a petition of April 1966 it developed the idea of establishing this European trading company not on the basis of individual national legal systems but on the basis of a genuine European law in form of a treaty to be adopted by the partner states. In December 1966 the commercial lawyer *Sanders* from Rotterdam in his capacity as a member of an expert panel appointed by the Commission, formulated a draft proposal of a statute for a European company (*Sanders*, European Stock Corporation: Text of the Draft Statute with Commentary, Commerce Clearing House, 1969), which was then submitted to the Council of Ministers as a Commission proposal in 1970 (COM [1970] 600 final, OJ C-124/1). Constant alterations to proposals for the statute of this company type ensued; each proposal was cause for fresh criticism and fresh agreement, and oftentimes its ultimate failure seemed just as within their grasp as its success. Again and again the issue of codetermination turned out to be the critical obstacle to a consensus. Unlike the problems that arose in the area of tax law and commercial law which were more about the harmonization of national provisions in a technical sense than about developing European solutions to questions of principle, the decision regarding codetermination in the intended company required the taking of a political stance and the answering of the question whether and to what extent the Member States wanted codetermination similar to the German or a comparable model or not (cf. e. g. *Blaurock,* Steps Towards a Uniform Corporate Law in the European Union, 31 Cornell International Law Journal 1998, 377, 384, 390). This lead to the issue of codetermination being dealt with separately in a directive proposal on the basis of Art. 44(2)(g) EC (now Art. 50(2)(g) TFEU) instead of being a subject matter of the Statute of the European Company.

The Directive concerning European Works Councils adopted in September 1994 **30**
gave the issue **"employee involvement"** a new importance. It was clear that it would not suffice to apply this Directive's provisions to the European Company without adapting them, and that the question of the involvement of employees would need to be revisited. To this end, the Commission assembled the **Davignon Group**, a panel of six experts comprised of representatives of academia, employer and employee representatives, named after its chairman *Davignon*, the former vice president of the European Commission and president of the *Société Générale de Belgique*. Their final report (Working Party of Experts "*European Systems of Worker Involvement*" [with regard to the European Company Statute and the other appending proposals], OJ C-227/01 of 26 July 1997; the employers' representative was my dear father *Rolf Thüsing*) was presented to the Council in May 1997; their solution to the question of codetermination was a proposal that represented a compromise between the positions of the employers and trade unions. There followed an unofficial textual proposal based closely on this report under the Luxembourg presidency which was superseded in the following year of British presidency to a proposition wherein the answer to the question of codetermination deviated considerably from the proposals of the expert panel, suffered small changes under Austrian presidency and was finally adopted as a directive. **Consequently, the SE is based on two legal acts**: The Regulation (EC) No. 2157/2001 of 8 October 2001 and the Directive 2001/86/EC of 8 October 2001 (*History of the European*

Company Statute, available at: www.worker-participation.eu/European-Company/History; *Sasso*, Societas Europaea: Between Harmonization and Regulatory Competition, 4 European Company Law 2007; *Lenoir*, The Societas Europaea or SE – The new European company, Report by the French Minister of Justice, HEC EUROPE INSTITUTE, 2007; *Blackburn*, The Societas Europea: the Evolving European Corporation Statute, 61 Fordham Law Review 1993, Issue 4).

2. The SE's basic structure of codetermination against the backdrop of divergent national laws of codetermination

31 In their attempt to find a solution to the question of codetermination for the European Company established by merger, creation of a holding company or joint subsidiary, the *Davignon* expert group, and now the Directive, followed the negotiation approach already favoured by the majority: the shareholders and employee representatives of the companies participating in the establishing of the European Company shall form a negotiation body which, within time limits which are consistent with the establishing of the new company, shall be balanced so as to allow discussion of the respective interests without one side or the other being able to stand in the way of the establishing of the European Company – such is ideally the pursued goal (cf. Report section 94). In the absence of an agreement, default rules shall apply to secure a balanced solution. Employee representatives shall account for a fifth of the members of the management board or the supervisory board, with a minimum of two members (cf. Report section 83). No difference was made with regard to the codetermination rules in force up to that time in the participating companies. Rather, the objective pursued was a uniform set of rules for all European Companies, varied only to the extent of what was agreed in the respective negotiation procedure. The fact that only seven Member States of the European Union had rules which make provision for participation of employee representatives in the various company bodies (management board, supervisory board) lead to the pursuit of uniform rules

32 I. e. **Germany** (Codetermination on the supervisory board: a third up to a half of the SB members); Austria (Codetermination on the supervisory board of companies and groups of companies: a third of SB members and a third of members on committees established by the SB); **Luxembourg** (Codetermination on the management board: a third of the MB members); **Denmark** (Codetermination on the management board in companies and groups of companies: a third of MB members and two members in groups of companies); **Sweden** (Codetermination on the management board: two or three MB members) and **Finland** (Codetermination on the management board or supervisory board in companies and groups of companies: a quarter of MB or SB members). In **France** only two or four members of the works council may participate in the meetings of the management board in an advisory role and with the possibility of raising an issue and demanding a well-reasoned answer.

33 For a company that wishes to merge transnationally with another company it cannot make any difference what codetermination rules previously existed in the contending companies of the merger in order to avoid any distortion of competition as a result of national codetermination laws. The default rules applicable in the absence of an agreement providing for an employee involvement of a fifth of the board members also have special significance: even where participating companies had rules in place providing for employee involvement of a third or even equal involvement on management boards, the employee representatives would have an

incentive to arrive at an agreement, because the default rules would fall short of the previous *status quo*. The appeal of solutions tailored to the needs of the individual companies could have been increased this way which is why this proposal was welcomed by the corporate side. However, it proceeded in a different direction and the directive adopted differs in many respects from the concepts of the *Davignon* report. They have the negotiation approach in common but have different approaches as regards the default rules applicable in the absence of an agreement. Now, codetermination is determined by the codetermination rules that previously existed in the companies participating in the establishment of the European Company. In the absence of a two-thirds majority of the negotiation group agreeing on an alternative solution, under section 3(a) of the annex to Art. 7 of the directive, the codetermination rules of the participating company that are most favourable will apply; i. e. the previous optimum of one of the companies will continue to apply to the new company after transformation (before-and-after-principle, cf. Recital 18 of Directive 2001/86/EC). **German** commentators name this policy as the **"scrambled egg theory"**: it only takes one bad egg to ruin the omelette, and only one participating company subject to codetermination rules to lead to codetermination in the new European Company as long as the number of employees exceeds a certain threshold. The disadvantages for companies with a high standard of codetermination are obvious: an entrepreneur from **France**, for instance, where employee representatives on supervisory boards of private companies only have consultation rights and no voting rights (cf. *Blanc-Jouvan*, La participation des travailleurs à la gestion des entreprises, in: Gamillscheg, Mitbestimmung der Arbeitnehmer, 1978, p. 54), will be reluctant to merge with a German company which is subject to codetermination rules of the coal and steel industry because he disapproves of this form of codetermination, and may merge with a company from another Member State. The operative reason for this solution is the fear of numerous companies "**escaping codetermination**". There is much to be said for this but it is uncertain as to what extent this fear is warranted – and there is unlikely to be any empirical evidence.

On these issues see the 2010 Report by the European Commission, available at http://ec.europa.eu/internal_market/company/se/index_en.htm.

3. Objectives of employee participation in the SE

An array of legislative intentions have been offered with regard to the objectives of 34
employee participation in the decisions of a company, the contours of which however have remained fuzzy. At times, scholars have gone back as far as the protection of human dignity (*Knudsen*, Employee Participation in Europe, 1995, SAGE; *Gold*, "Taken on board": An evaluation of the influence of employee board-level representatives on company decision-making across Europe, 17 European Journal of Industrial Relations 2011, No. 1, 41–56; *Sjåfjell*, Towards a sustainable European Company Law: A Normative Analysis oft he Objectives of EU Law, with the Takeover Directive as a Test Case, 2009, p. 67 *et seqq.*). Historically, it was most likely the **wish to democratise the employment environment** that triggered the ever-increasing legislation over the years. Aside from this there is the general aim of protecting employees which was achieved by involving the employee side in the normally one-sided decisions made by the employer; in recent times it was hoped that obligatory or

voluntary employee involvement would lead to increased employee motivation and also an improved productivity on account of the expertise of the representatives. Which of these aims were decisive for the European legislator in developing its rules on employee involvement has not been revealed. It presents a cluster of motives without giving more weight to one or the other. In the far-reaching Directive 2002/14/EC establishing a general framework for informing and consulting employees in the European Community the focus is put on the "need to strengthen dialogue and promote mutual trust within undertakings", on making work organisation more flexible "while maintaining security", on the possibility of making "employees aware of adaptation needs", but also on promoting "employee involvement in the operation and future of the undertaking and increase[ing] its competitiveness" (Preamble 7 of Directive 2002/14/EC).

35 Regarding employee involvement in the SE, the Directive 2001/86/EC is only slightly more concrete. There is a general reference to the **social objectives of the Community** (Preamble 3) and the wish to ensure information and consultation procedures at transnational level (Preamble 6). In this respect, the directive builds on the Preamble of the Directive on the establishment of a European Works Council 94/45/EC (now Directive 2009/38/EC), where similar vows and desires can be found ("Whereas appropriate provisions must be adopted to ensure that the employees of Community-scale undertakings are properly informed and consulted when decisions which affect them are taken in a Member State other than that in which they are employed"), which, however, do not reveal the aim and value of employee involvement itself either. Its reasonableness is postulated without giving reasons, one shows commitment to the cause without saying why. This commitment however only applies to a *part* of the wide spectrum of employee involvement. The issue is not codetermination as a whole. It is apparent that there are limits with regard to the object of involvement as well as to its instruments:

36 Information and consultation procedures shall be ensured at "transnational level" (Preamble 6, Art. 1(i) and (j), Directive 2001/86/EC). Therefore, the **transnational element** is a necessary requirement for the directive concerning the involvement of employees in the SE to apply. This is not a new idea and follows the same path traced by previous directives: A requirement of transnational relevance can be found in the EWC-Directive 94/45/EC (see Preamble; No. 1(a) of the subsidiary provisions under Art. 7) and is evidenced by the *travaux préparatoires* to Directive 2001/86/EC: the information and consultation of the representative body was always meant as a supplement or substitute of codetermination on the supervisory or management body of the company; the codetermination, though, is transnational *per se* because it is relevant for the whole transnationally organised company. Just as the decisions of the codetermined body concern the company and therefore have a potentially transnational significance, the information and consultation is also designed for a transnational context, as the legal definition of "information" in Art. 2(i) of Directive 2001/86/EC illustrates quite verbosely. A forerunner of this can be found in the report of the *Davignon* group which had a groundbreaking effect on the development of codetermination in the European Company and continued to have a defining effect on its further development (see for instance paras. 37, 40).

37 In addition to the aforementioned limited scope of employee involvement there is a **restriction of the means**: Aside from the codetermination on the supervisory or

management boards of the company, there is only the information and consultation of the employees and their representatives. Whereas the default rules of codetermination are largely subject to the *status quo* of the participating companies, a uniform default rule shall apply in the case of information and consultation, which would also serve as a minimum standard for all companies irrespective of national origin. Information and consultation, therefore, are not on equal footing with codetermination; rather, the European legislator's perspective presupposes codetermination and creates employee rights of a lesser intensity, which, however, do not apply to the individual undertakings but to the company as a whole. This **vertical relationship of the codetermination rights**, in turn, is evidenced by the genesis of the directive. The previous draft proposal of the Directive concerning employee involvement in the SE of 25 August 1989 (OJ 1989 C-263 69, see *Hockelin*, European Company Statute: Company Strucutre and Employee Involvement Across EC Borders, North Carolina Journal of International Law and Commercial Regulation 1991, Issue 3, 587–630, pp. 614 *et seqq.*; *Linmondin*, The European Company (Societas Europaea) – A Successful Harmonisation of Corporate Governance in the European Union?, 15 Bond Law Review 2003, Issue 1, 145–180, pp. 155 *et seqq.*; *Keller*, The European Company Statute: Employee Involvement – and Beyond, 33 Industrial Relations Journal, Issue 5, 424–445, pp. 426 *et seqq.)* gave the shareholders and employees a right to choose between four models of employee involvement: at its head was a dual system of employee representation on the supervisory or management bodies modelled on the German example. The lowest form of employee involvement was a model based on French law, which provided for a body consisting of employee and shareholder representatives equipped with consultation and information rights (for more information on these models: *Rehfeldt*, Employee involvement in companies under the European Company Statute (ECS) – Case Study: SCOR SE, available at: www.eurofound.europa.eu/pubdocs/2010/787/en/2/EF10787EN.pdf). These codetermination rules were quite rightly seen as having the same objective, but of being of a varying intensity. The *Davignon*-report and the following Luxemburg proposal of 1997 pursued this idea, but modified it to the effect that it provided for a uniform minimum rule concerning information and consultation as well as codetermination on the supervisory and consulting bodies. Here too one did not have employee codetermination in its true sense in mind (for details on the *Davignon* report, see *Lower*, Employee Participation in Governance: A Legal and Ethical Analysis, 2010, pp. 180 *et seqq.*).

The **aims and instruments of operational codetermination** by works councils must be distinguished from those of company codetermination. Codetermination regarding policy-making is a form of labour codetermination. It relates to the employer-employee relationships. The employer and the works council as the employee representative stand on opposite sides just as in the employment relationship. The works council (central works council, central works council of affiliated companies) is involved in certain employer decisions (dual system). Company codetermination is not a form of labour codetermination but of employee involvement in the selection and control of the company management (single model). The regulated issues are different: The works council cannot prevent the sale of significant company assets or off-shoring, just as the employee representatives on the supervisory board cannot object to a dismissal. **38**

V. The instrument of the "negotiation solution"

39 The negotiation solution fits into these parameters of employee involvement in the SE as a way of achieving a set of rules that suit the individual company as best as possible.

1. Origin and forerunner

40 It is to the ***Davignon* group's merit** that the negotiation solution was implemented into the directive concerning employee involvement in the SE. With a solution in mind that is tailored to suit each individual company (see para. 41), it is largely based on the model of the European Works Council Directive 94/45/EC, the negotiation model of which is parallel in its function, and the wording of which is partly identical to the provisions of Directive 2001/86/EC (of course, significant differences remain, see *Davis*, Workers on the Board of the European Company?, 32 International Law Journal 2003, 75, 83; these were reduced somewhat by Directive 2009/38/EC regarding e.g. the composition of the special negotiating body). The Directive 94/45/EC itself is based on the experiences of the Member States which were already acquainted with "negotiated" codetermination under domestic law – both with respect to codetermination on the supervisory board as well as at operational level on the basis of collective agreements (such as in Italy; see hereunto *Biagi*, 15 Comp. Lab. L. 1994, 155, 160; also in Sweden *Flodgren*, in: Bruun et.al., The Nordic Labour Relations Modell, 1992, pp. 46 *et seqq.*).

41 The main reason for this new step was the possibility of achieving a European set of rules despite the very different national rules. The choice of a negotiation solution in the Directive 94/45/EC (now Directive 2009/38/EC) may be a result of the fact that the directive itself was a result of negotiations. In compliance with the procedure set out in the Maastricht Treaty and the Social Agreement of 7 February 1992, which was amended by the Amsterdam Treaty, the European social partners' agreement made it possible to adopt a directive which had been attempted for a long time – though to no avail – in the past (see the repeated **failure of the *Vredeling*-Directive**).

2. Scope

42 European law is quite monosyllabic with regard to the spectrum of possible agreements. It is expressly set out that the negotiating partners may agree on the default rules, see Art. 7(1)(a) of Directive 2001/86/EC. In order to concede the possibility of more restrictive or more extensive rules, it will require additional arguments beyond referring to the inadequate wording of the law.

a) Waiver of notification and consultation rights

43 The negotiating partners cannot agree to waive their transnational notification and consultation rights altogether. Importance must be attached to the objective presented in the 6th recital that in *all* cases of creation of an SE, information and consultation procedures at transnational level should be ensured. Assuming that it is possible to agree on rules that are more restrictive compared to the default rules – which can be very extensive depending on the national law – with regard to codetermination on management and supervisory boards, then, especially with respect to waiving all rights to appoint any employee representatives to the supervisory and management bodies of a company, the objectives of the Directive can

surely only be met if, pursuant to the draft proposal of the Directive of 1991, notification and consultation represents the minimum level that can be agreed upon within the powers of the negotiating partners. The power is conferred on the negotiating partners in order to implement the objectives of the directive in a suitable manner; a waiver of all notification and consultation rights would frustrate these objectives and would be in conflict with the motive that led to the negotiation solution. This is not covered by the negotiating partners' assigned mandate.

There is, admittedly, little **practical significance to this debate.** Due to the existence of default rules, it is unlikely that the result of a negotiation – assuming its legal admissibility – will ever be the waiver of all notification and consultation rights: The special negotiation body has no incentive to waive rights that are guaranteed in the absence of an agreement. Therefore, it is the extension of notification and consultation rights that has greater practical importance, as these rights may be conceded by the management in return for a reduction of involvement on the supervisory and management bodies of the company. 44

It is important to distinguish waiving notification and consultation rights from **restricting** these rights to certain parts of the company or company groups. It can be assumed that there is a wide scope to set up such restrictions. If the prevailing opinion in academic literature favours including states outside the European Union (see below), then it must also be possible the other way around. The scope of the agreement is not stipulated by law. A limitation could be seen in the prohibition of arbitrary acts or, generally, the equal treatment principle as an unwritten element of European primary law (hereunto the Case 144/04 – Mangold [2005] ECR I-9981, s. § 4 at paras. 20 *et seqq.*). However, without objective reasons, a functional negotiation would not result in an agreement excluding certain worker groups anyway. 45

b) Extension of participation rights

It is less certain as to what extent an agreement can be made to extend participation rights beyond notification and consultation under Art. 6 of Directive 2001/86/EC. This is viewed by some scholars as permissible with no restrictions whatsoever in light of the "**precedence of private autonomy**" as set out in the directive, the autonomous negotiation power and the general direction of European law which has achieved an ever more extensive employee involvement by virtue of the Directives 2009/38/EC, 2001/86/EC and 2002/14/EC. A line is drawn only where the agreement would infringe upon representation rights already in place under national law. In this case, the national law itself would have to allow the exercise of participation rights via the SE Works Council. 46

This is in fact in strong contrast to the majority opinion among scholars regarding the European Works Council. Here, it is assumed that the directive and its implementation only give the parties the authority to lay down rules regarding transnational notification and consultation of employees, i. e. that the agreement cannot validly provide, beyond the notification and consultation of employee representatives, that business action can only be taken with the employee representatives' prior consent The basis of this is a teleological argument in light of the objectives of Art. 6 of Directive 2009/38/EC. Indeed: The latter argument does emphatically support the majority opinion. Pursuant to Art. 6(1) of Directive 94/45/EC the agreement can only contain the "detailed arrangements for implementing the information and consultation of employees provided for in Art. 1(1)" – this is 47 also true for Art. 5 of Directive 2002/14/EC. Rules regarding rights of prior approval go beyond notification and consultation. It is merely a matter of concretizing (*"Modalitäten der Durchführung"*; *"modalités de mise en œuvre"*) the information and the notification; not extending it.

48 It is doubtful whether this strict assessment can be applied to the agreement concerning the SE Works Council. The use of the EWC-Directive as a guideline for the SE-Directive – with regard to its central concept as well as in many individual points – certainly supports this contention. However, a similarly clear provision showing a lack of authority to extend the scope cannot be found in the SE-Directive 2001/86/EC. In light of the concept of the negotiation mandate, this silence probably says more than words. If it is uncontested that the codetermination rights can be more restrictive than the default rules, then in return, it must be possible to extend the notification and consultation rights. The European legislator made it clear by stipulating the appointment to the supervisory board that the agreement need not be neutral with regard to the level of involvement, but instead that a reasonable provision can be found somewhere within the parameters of the default rules. For the same reasons it has allowed a restriction, it allows an extension of participation rights. A suitable compromise may require both: a restriction of involvement on the supervisory body is possible because the notification and consultation rights were increased; within the basic parameters of the two participation rights a middle ground can be agreed upon.

3. Legal nature of the agreement

49 The Directive 2001/86/EC gives no details about the legal nature of the agreement. In fact, Art. 6 states that "Except where otherwise provided in this Directive, the legislation applicable to the negotiation procedure provided for in Arts. 3 to 5 shall be the legislation of the Member State in which the registered office of the SE is to be situated." As the legislation applicable to the negotiation procedure is governed by the law of the state in which the SE is registered and the directive contains no provision regarding the legal nature of the agreement, this question can only be answered by the law of that Member State: the agreement is part of the negotiation procedure, in that it constitutes its conclusion.

50 Therefore, the national law determines the legal nature of a participation agreement, with the result that the legal nature of the agreement can differ from Member State to Member State.

VI. Information and Consultation Directive 2002/14/EC

1. Generally

51 By virtue of the **Directive 2002/14/EC establishing a general framework for informing and consulting employees in the European Community,** Community-wide general standards were put in place for the first time regarding the involvement of employees at national level. Consequently, it has been referred to on numerous occasions as the "breakthrough towards a European works constitution" (*Reichold,* 20 NZA 2003, 289). The information and consultation rights under Art. 4(2) constitute the heart of the directive. According to Art. 4(2)(a) the information (but not the consultation) shall cover the recent and probable development of the undertaking's or the establishment's activities and economic situation. Both the information and the consultation shall cover, for one, the situation, structure and probable development of employment within the undertaking or establishment and any anticipatory measures envisaged, in particular where there

is a threat to employment (Art. 4(2)(b)), and for another, decisions likely to lead to substantial changes in work organisation or in contractual relations, including collective redundancies and transfers of undertakings (Art. 4(2)(c)). In the case of Art. 4(2)(c) the consultation must take place with a view to reaching an "agreement" (Art. 4(4)(e)). This is all very similar to the information rights in the context of the European Works Council and the SE Works Council, see paras. 22 *et seqq.* The European Commission began reviewing the Directive in 2010.

The directive led to considerable changes especially in the **United Kingdom and Ireland**, the labour law of which did not thus far have a general system for the information and consultation of employees (on implementation in the United Kingdom: *Bercusson*, 31 ILJ 2002, 209 *et seqq.*; *Hall*, 34 ILJ 2005, 103 *et seqq.*; *Lorber*, 19 IJCLLIR 2003, 297; *Lorber*, 22 IJCLLIR 2006, 231; an overview of implementation instruments is available at: http://eur-lex.europa.eu/LexUriServ/LexUriServ.do?uri=CELEX:72002L0014:EN:NOT). German law suffered much less effects. The level of employee involvement (using this as an umbrella term for information, consultation and codetermination, cf. Art. 2(h) of Directive 2001/86/EC) went far beyond that of other industrialized countries; **Germany** is the **"World champion in codetermination matters"** (*Junker*, 31 ZfA 2001, 225, 242). German law also exceeds the minimum standard stipulated by Directive 2002/14/EC by far in many respects, especially with respect to the degree of involvement rights. 52

2. Genesis

The genesis of the directive has a lot to do with the closure of the Renault factory in the Belgian town of Villvoorde. On the 27 of February 1997 the manager of Renault Industrie Belgique informed the local works council and also the business press, that the *Président Directeur Général* of the French parent company had decided to shut down the factory in Villvoorde for economic reasons per the 31 of July 1997. Neither the local employee representatives nor the European Works Council which had been created within Renault were informed or consulted about this decision ahead of time. This course of action taken by the Renault company provoked considerable outrage among the public, as well as in the Commission, and triggered a demand for stricter rules regarding the information and consultation of employees. This was the context in which the Commission submitted the directive proposal on the 17 of November 1998 (COM [1999] 612 OJ C 2/3). This is why the Directive 2002/14/EC is sometimes referred to as the "**Renault-Directive**". After that first proposal, more than three years went by before the Directive 2002/14/EC was adopted on the 11 of March 2002, which just shows how contentious the issue of employee involvement is at European level. During the legislative procedure the Commission had to mediate between the involvement-friendly positions of the European Parliament and the sceptical stance taken within the Council. 53

3. Aims of the Directive

In the Preamble of Directive 2002/14/EC various reasons are given. First of all, the first recital states that, pursuant to Art. 136 of the Treaty (now Art. 151 TFEU), a particular objective of the Community is to promote social dialogue between management and labour. Recital 2 refers to the not legally binding Community Charter of Fundamental Social Rights of Workers of 9 of December 1989. Point 17 thereof provides that the information, consultation and participation for workers is a fundamental social right. This reasoning does not take up as 54 much space as the line of argument aimed at increasing competitiveness and employability of the employees, which can be found primarily in recitals 7–14. It was felt that there was "a need to strengthen dialogue and promote mutual trust within undertakings in order to improve risk anticipation, make work organisation more flexible and facilitate employee access to training within the undertaking while maintaining security, make employees aware of adaptation needs, increase employees' availability to undertake measures and activities to increase their employability, promote employee involvement in the operation and future of the undertaking and increase its competitiveness" (Recital 7). Timely information and consultation is said to be a prerequisite for the success of the restructuring and adaptation of undertakings to the new conditions created by globalisation of the economy (Recital 9). **The Directive is seen as part of the European employment strategy**, the key elements of which are the concepts "anticipation", "prevention" and "employability" (Recital 10). Accordingly, the recitals emphasize the anticipatory approach. Previous legal frameworks at national and Community level have not always prevented serious decisions from being taken without adequate procedures having been implemented in advance to inform and consult them (Recital 6). The existing legal framework for employee information and consultation is said to adopt an excessively *a posteriori* approach to the process of change and neither contributes to genuine "anticipation of employment developments" nor to risk "prevention" (Recital 13).

4. Framework Directive with minimum requirements

55 The Directive 2002/14/EC is a **framework Directive**. It is for the Member States to provide for provisions within the established framework and adapt them to their own national situation (Recital 23). Accordingly, the Directive expressly refers to the national law and practice of the Member States several times, such as with respect to the practical arrangements of the information and consultation (Art. 4(1)), and also for the terms establishment (Art. 2(b)), employer (Art. 2(c)), employee (Art. 2(d)) and employees' representative (Art. 2(e)). This way, the Member States can draw on existing structures, but must make sure that the principle of effectiveness is not undermined (Art. 1(2)). The directive is – as always – **without prejudice** to **national provisions that are more favourable to the employees** (Art. 4(1) and Art. 9(3)). Considering the approach of Directive 2002/14/EC to increase the competitiveness of undertakings, it would have made sense to lay down an absolute limit of burden that can be put on the undertakings but this would not have been covered by the legal basis (Art. 137 EC as amended in the Amsterdam Treaty). Pursuant to Art. 137(5) EC as amended in the Amsterdam Treaty (= Art. 153(4) 2nd indent TFEU) the directives based on this provision shall not prevent any Member State from maintaining or introducing more stringent protective measures.

5. Scope of application

56 The directive applies, according to the choice made by Member States, to undertakings employing at least 50 employees in any one Member State, or establishments employing at least 20 employees in any one Member State, pursuant to Art. 3(2).

a) The terms "undertaking" and "establishment"

57 The possibility of the rules applying to "establishment" instead of only "undertaking" was not included in the original Commission proposal (COM [1998] 612 final). By inserting this option by means of the second Commission proposal, the fact is taken into account that in several Member States it is not the undertaking but rather the establishment that is used as a reference point for the participation rights of employees (cf. the annex to the original Commission proposal, COM [1998] 612 final). Thus, the provision helps avoid friction when implementing the directive. The term "undertaking" is defined in Art. 2(a) as "a public or private undertaking carrying out an economic activity, whether or not operating for gain, which is located within the territory of the Member States". This phrasing follows strongly that of Art. 1(c) of Directive 2001/23/EC which in turn, is an attempt to codify the case-law of the *ECJ* on the previous Directive 77/187/EEC (cf. Recital 8 of Directive 2001/23/EC). Public undertakings are not only entities formed under private law and owned by a public authority, but also bodies governed by public law. The directive does not however apply to public administrations (cf. Recital 20). The decisive factor that distinguishes public undertakings covered by the directive from public administrations not covered by the directive is the carrying out of economic activity. Under Union law, this functional criterion is to be interpreted widely and includes the entire area of public services. Precluded from the scope is only the part of the civil service that is acting in its exercise of public powers. In the European Trade Union Institute Report on "Better defending and promoting trade union rights in the public sector" (available at: http://library.fes.de/pdf-files/gurn/00366.pdf, pp. 39 *et seqq.)* it is suggested to apply the competition law notion of undertaking to Directive 2002/14, which would mean that pursuant to the case-law in this field of European Law the Directive would not apply to undertakings which exercise typical public authority tasks.

58 **Establishment** is, pursuant to Art. 2(b), a "unit of business defined in accordance with national law and practice, and located within the territory of a Member State, where an economic activity is carried out on an ongoing basis with human and material resources". This reference to the national law of the Member States is a particularity in European Labour Law. For the purposes of Directives 2001/23/EC and 98/59/EC which are closely related to this subject matter, the *ECJ* specifically rejected the use of the national definitions (Case 449/93 – Rockfon [1995] ECR I-4291, para. 25; Case 270/05 – Athinaïki Chartopoïïa AE, [2007] ECR I-1499, para. 23).

b) The term "employee" and threshold calculations

59 The application of the Directive is subject to the number of employees in each establishment/undertaking, pursuant to Art. 3(1)(1). Employee in terms of the directive means "any person who, in the Member State concerned, is protected as an employee under national employment law and in accordance with national practice" (Art. 2(d)). Thus, reference is made to **national employment law**, see also § 5, paras. 42 *et seqq.* The method of calculating the threshold is determined by the Member States (Art. 3(1)(2)). However, the Member States cannot preclude certain persons from the calculations of the thresholds if they are protected as employees by the individual national employment laws, nor can they exclude them from the scope of the implementation provisions entirely. This was decided by the *ECJ* in the case *CGT et. al.* of 13 January 2007.

> Case 385/05 – **CGT and others** [2007] ECR I-611
>
> The matter concerned a provision in Art. L 610-10 of the **French** *Code du travail*, under which employees under the age of 26 were not included in the calculation of staff numbers which was essential to appoint the employees' representatives. The *ECJ* held that this provision was not in conformity with the Directive 2002/14/EC. According to the opinion of the Court, it is the directive that exclusively determines which persons are employees in terms of the directive and must therefore be included in the calculation of the threshold, namely all persons protected by the national employment law. Although it is for the Member States to determine the method of calculating the threshold, Art. 3(1)(2), however, does not permit a definition of the term employee. The directive does not prescribe in what way the employees within the scope must be taken into account in the calculations of the threshold, but it certainly prescribes that they must be taken into account.

60 It follows from this judgment that, for the purposes of the Directive 2002/14/EC, the general definition of employee according to the law of the relevant Member State is significant. The Member States may not use an employee definition in the implementation acts that is narrower than the definition otherwise applicable in national employment law. This result is persuasive. If one were to allow the Member States to codify a special employee definition, then they would effectively be determining the scope of the Directive themselves. The *ECJ* has held with respect to other directives concerning employment law that the reference to national employee definitions does not allow certain persons, that are otherwise considered to be employees under employment law, to be excluded from the scope of the relevant implementation acts (Case 22/87 – Commission/Italy [1989] ECR 143, paras. 17 *et seq.*; Case 334/92 – Wagner Miret [1993] ECR I-6911, paras. 12 *et seqq.*; cf. also Case 313/02 – Wippel [2004] ECR I-9542, para. 40 about Directive 97/81/EC).

6. The participants in information and consultation

61 It is the employer and the employees' representatives who participate in the information and consultation procedure, but not the individual employee or the workforce as such. Despite its title, which refers to the information and consultation of "employees", Directive 2002/14/EC does not at any point provide direct participation. Employees' representatives means, pursuant to Art. 2(e), "the employees' representatives provided for by national laws and/or practices". The reference to the national laws takes the fact into account that there are highly different systems of employee representation in place in the Member States (cf. the overview annexed to the Commission proposal; COM [1998] 612 final). One must distinguish, in particular, between the **dual channel** models, where, aside from the trade unions, other elected employee representatives exist in the individual undertakings or establishments, and the **single channel** models, where the employees' interests are represented exclusively by the trade unions (cf. for instance *Barnard,* EC Employment Law, pp. 451, 512 *et seqq.*; *Kenner,* EU Employment Law, pp. 66 *et seq.*). A significant indication for the interpretation of the term employees' representatives

can be found in the "Joint Declaration of the European Parliament, the Council and the Commission on employee representation" (OJ 2002 L-80/34) annexed to the Directive 2002/14/EC in which reference is made to the judgments of the *ECJ* of 8 June 1994 in cases 382/92 (Commission ./. United Kingdom [1994] ECR I-2345) and 383/92 (Commission ./. United Kingdom [1994] ECR I-2479). In both judgments the *ECJ* held with regard to the respective wordings in the Transfer of Undertakings Directive and the Collective Redundancy Directive that the Member States could choose how the employee representatives are designated but could not leave the question of their existence to the discretion of the employer (Case 382/92 – Commission ./. United Kingdom [1994] ECR I-2435 para. 18; Case 383/92 – Commission ./. United Kingdom [1994] ECR I-2479 para. 19). Consequently, the *ECJ* declared a British provision as contrary to the directive, which only regarded trade unions recognized by the employer as employee representatives. In **Germany**, the law guarantees the right to create works councils even against the will of the employer, yet there are still a great number of undertakings without a works council. Therefore, it is quite likely that, even in undertakings that do fall within the scope of the directive, no information or consultation will take place. This would not, however, constitute a violation of the directive's requirements. The Directive allows the existence of unrepresented undertakings/establishments if the employees are responsible for the lack of employee representation. Pursuant to recital 16, the Directive is without prejudice to those systems which provide for the direct involvement of employees, as long as they are always free to exercise the right to be informed and consulted through their representatives. The election of a works council can be seen as such a free exercise of rights.

Therefore, the directive accepts the existence of undertakings without a works council. There is 62
also no need to involve "**ad-hoc representatives**" or the employees themselves in lieu thereof in these undertakings.

7. Participation rights

As to its content, the Directive 2002/14/EC is confined to granting information 63
and consultation rights. An establishment of enforceable rights of codetermination would be contrary to the legal basis (Art. 137(1) third indent in conjunction with Art. 137(2) EC as amended by the Amsterdam Treaty = Art. 153(1)(e) in conjunction with Art. 153(2) TFEU). A provision on codetermination should have been based on ex-Art. 137(3) 3rd indent EC (= Art. 153(1)(f) in conjunction with Art. 153(2) TFEU).

It must be noted, however, that **consultation in terms of Union law** requires the 64
"exchange of views and establishment of dialogue" (Art. 2(g)). The employee representatives do not just have the right to submit an opinion (Art. 4(4)(c)), but must also be given the opportunity "to meet the employer and obtain a response, and the reasons for that response, to any opinion they might formulate" (Art. 4(4)(d)).

8. Negotiation solutions

Pursuant to Art. 5 the Member States may entrust the social partners at the 65
appropriate level – including at undertaking or establishment level – with defining the practical arrangements for informing and consulting employees. The arrangements agreed upon may be different to, and less favourable than, the provisions set

out in Art. 4. Art. 5 merely gives the Member States an option. There is no duty to enable negotiation solutions. On the negotiation solution model signifying its subsidiarity, see paras. 40 *et seqq.*

9. Enforceability and sanctions

66 Under Art. 7 of Directive 2002/14/EC the Member States shall ensure that employee representatives, when carrying out their functions, enjoy adequate protection and guarantees to enable them to perform properly the duties which have been assigned to them. In the Holst case (Case 405/08 [2010] ECR I-0095) the *ECJ* held that the Member States were not obligated to provide protection for employee representatives against dismissal beyond the usual standard. The Directive does not however preclude such higher standards of dismissal protection.

67 Under Art. 8(1) the Member States must provide for appropriate **judicial remedies** to enforce compliance with obligations arising from the directive. This requires enforceable claims to performance. A claim to performance with regard to the consultation duties will have no effect if the employees are presented with a *fait accompli* before the conclusion of proceedings. The Directive emphasizes the anticipatory approach. Its aim is to prevent serious decisions affecting the employees being taken before implementing appropriate information and consultation procedures (cf. Recital 6). Information and consultation must therefore take place before a final decision has been taken, or worse still, its implementation has begun. The *ECJ* stated in the *Junk* case concerning Directive 98/59/EC that it is significantly more difficult for the employee representatives to achieve the withdrawal of a decision already taken than to secure the abandonment of a decision that is being contemplated (Case 188/03 – Junk [2005] ECR I-885, para. 44). This can easily be applied to Directive 2002/14/EC. If the obligations to be enforced with the aid of measures under Art. 8 include the duty to consult *before* a decision is made, then it makes sense that any judicial remedy is only sufficiently effective if it can prevent decisions being taken or implemented before the conclusion of the participation procedure. Otherwise the right to participation could be frustrated prior to the decision. As a result, especially effective expedited judicial relief is required, which raises the question of injunctive relief in favour of the employee representatives.

68 Aside from appropriate legal measures, the directive also requires effective, proportionate and dissuasive **sanctions** (Art. 8(2)). The consequence that the employer's decision would have no legal effect in the case of a serious breach, which was contained in the original Commission proposal (COM [1999] 612 C 2/3 [7]), was struck out on account of the Council's objections (see the Common Position adopted by the Council of 23 July 2001, OJ 2001, C-307/16 [25]). Under Art. 7(7) of the **Spanish Law** of Infractions and Sanctions in the Social Order (Real Decreto Legislativo 5/2000, de 4 de agosto) a violation of information and consultation rights constitutes a grave infraction, for which a maximum fine of 6 250 EUR is set out in Art. 40(1)(b). In the **German** *Betriebsverfassungsgesetz* (§ 121(2)) a fine up to 10 000 EUR can be imposed. Whether these sanctions, especially the ceilings, are sufficiently effective and dissuasive, is doubtful. The maximum penalty of £ (GBP) 75 000 payable by employers for non-compliance in the UK, Art. 23(2) of the Information and Consultation of Employees Regulations 2004, could however be more dissuasive.

10. Protection of certain special interest undertakings

Art. 3(2) allows Member States to lay down particular provisions applicable to certain ideological undertakings or establishments, i. e. those which directly and essentially pursue political, professional organisational, religious, charitable, educational, scientific or artistic aims. This provision is in the tradition of a few other clauses of ideological protection (see Art. 4(2) of Directive 2000/78/EC; Art. 8(3) of Directive 94/45/EC, now Directive 2009/38/EC). A condition of Art. 3(2) is that provisions of that nature already exist in national legislation at the date of entry into force of the directive. Thus, established rights are to be protected. **Germany, Sweden and Austria** can therefore make use of the option in Art. 3(2). Even in special interest undertakings there must be **"conformity with the principles and objectives of the directive"**. 69

The substantive extent of the ideological protection is still uncertain. There is no elaboration in the documents on the question of when the "principles and objectives" of the directive are complied with. The interpretation of this typical compromise rule is difficult. Part of academic literature suggests that it will suffice to guarantee the existence of a trusting social dialogue without concrete and exact instructions. In any case it can be said that applying the principle of effectiveness as found in Art. 1(2) – under the title "object and principles" – must not lead to undermining the clearly intended preferential arrangement in Art. 3(2). 70

VII. Excursus: Codetermination policies in the various European states

Prior to the adoption of the *Davignon* report and again in the Commission proposal for Directive 2002/14/EC, the existing regulations on operational and company codetermination in the Member States were compiled. The results show a wide variety. To summarize, no Member State has no form of codetermination at all, some, however, only have company codetermination or just operational codetermination. So far as operational codetermination has been implemented, it is usually confined to hearings and consultations. Any regulations beyond this are subject to the employer's voluntary decision; the threshold for obligatory regulations vary considerably (see for details *Baums/Ulmer*, Employees Co-Determination in the Member States of the European Union, Recht und Wirtschaft, 2004). 71

Nevertheless, **a comparison of codetermination models** is a difficult task. For instance, in some countries codetermination is governed by the trade union; in others the works council and trade union are separate. In numerous countries employee participation is not codified but is the result of (collectively) agreed regulations by the social partners. So a simple glance at the statutes is not very helpful. One example is **Sweden**: This country has the lowest degree of codetermination regulation in statutory employment law and at the same time has an exceptional level of participation possibilities. Staff participation in Austria is also above-average, albeit achieved in a different way compared to the Swedes: Employees and undertakings are mandatory members of their respective associations. The employers' unions usually adopt the collective agreements that the employer associations and trade unions concluded – with the effect that almost all workers are covered by collective agreements. 72

The opposite model can be found in the **Mediterranean countries**: there, there are hardly any laws on codetermination rights. On the other hand, in Italy and France there exists an extensive right to strike that is guaranteed in the constitution: 73

pre-strike ballots prior to an industrial dispute are not necessary, there is no duty to maintain industrial peace and in Italy even politically motivated strikes are expressly permitted. The relationship between employers and workers is characterized more by conflict in the workplace than by consensus in society – with the result that considerably more working days are lost due to strike than in consensus-oriented systems such as in Germany or Austria.

74 The **transition countries** hold a special position – i. e. the countries of **Eastern and Central Europe** where the market economy is still young. There, though the workers have fewer rights than in "old" Europe – they still have to be involved. An example of this is Hungary: An undertaking of more than 50 employees must create a works council that – depending on the size of the company – has 3 to 13 members.

75 Only the works councils in **Germany and Austria** are entitled to be – in some cases – entirely released from their work duties. However, in **France** this entitlement to time off can be accumulated by the works council, the general works council and trade union; in Italy it is even transferable to other persons. In the UK too, employee representatives have the right to paid time off to perform their functions.

§ 11. International Labour Law

Literature: *Anton,* Private International Law, 3rd ed., 2011; *Chitty,* Chitty on Contracts, 3rd ed., 2008; *Dicey/Morris/Collins,* On the Conflict of Laws, 14th ed., 2010; *Editorial,* The consequences of employing a mobile workforce – a patchwork of protections, I.C.C.L.R. 2000, 11[12], 399–406; *Kaye,* The New Private International Law of Contract of the European Community, 1993; *Kloss,* The Enforceability of Foreign Collective Agreements, 46 Modern Law Review, 1983, 774–776; *Krebber,* Conflicts of Laws in Employment in Europe, 21 Comparative Labor Law & Policy Journal, 2000, 501–541; *Morse,* Consumer Contracts, Employment Contracts and The Rome Convention, 41 International and Comparative Law Quarterly 1992, 1–21; *Schiek,* Autonomous Collective Agreements as a Regulatory Device in European Labour Law: How to Read Art. 139 EC, 34 Industrial Law Journal 2005, 23–56; *Smith/Cromack,* International Employment Contracts – The Applicable Law, 22 Industrial Law Journal 1993, 1–13.

I. Internationalisation of the labour market

The posting of workers abroad has extremely old roots. Saint Paul sent Timothy 1 to Thessaloniki (1 Thessalonians 3:1), Pope Gregory II sent Boniface to Germany, Frederick II, Landgrave of Hesse-Cassel placed his soldiers at the King of England's disposal for the American War of Independence – and the Polish nobility sent a young duchess to the court of Augustus the Strong in Saxony, in order to become a favourite for his more special services. Thus, **this subject is not brand new.** Admittedly, the posting of workers today takes on a different form. Cases with a foreign element are increasing in labour law; the internationalisation of the markets includes the labour market. Legal advisors and the courts must deal more and more with arrangements in employment contracts regarding postings and transfers abroad. Based on existing decisions, the following chapter will illustrate the settled law and also discuss some new problems.

II. Applicable law in cross-border employment relationships

Cross-border employment relationships can be looked at from **two angles**: there 2 is the posting of workers abroad on the one hand, and the hiring of foreign workers on the other. The conflict of law rules apply equally in both cases.

1. Basic types of employment contracts

If an employee is sent to work abroad for a while, **several arrangements** are 3 possible. Short-term posting for only a few days or weeks poses no problems and can be done on the basis of the existing local contract without any need for modification. The usual rules apply. Cases where the employment relationship with the previous employer is terminated and a new employment relationship with the foreign employer is entered into – for instance with a subsidiary company within the corporation – are just as straightforward. But in practice it is the types somewhere in between that are much more common: those which do not quite release the employee from the rules of one legal system and do not quite admit him into the other legal system. On the one hand, there is the situation where an employee is posted abroad under the existing contract which is supplemented by additional arrangements relating to the posting. The employee remains loyal to his employer but his rights and duties under the employment contract are adapted to the changed circumstances. On the other hand, there is the case – particularly in groups of companies – of an employee being transferred to a foreign employer. The previous employment relationship is suspended and a new, fixed-term employment relationship is established with the foreign employer. Thus, the employee temporarily swaps employers and his new employment relationship may be subject to different laws.

4 In addition to these, there is a third possibility – to which academic literature has paid little attention but has been hinted at in court decisions – namely the situation of a foreign employer entering the existing employment relationship as an additional party, with the result that the employee has a joint employment relationship with two employers from then on. The question of the applicable law is particularly difficult to answer in this case (see paras. 14 *et seqq.*).

2. Determining the applicable law

5 Since the reform of the conflict of laws in 2009, the question of which legal system is applicable in these different scenarios is determined exclusively by European law. The Regulation (EC) No. 593/2008 of 17 June 2008, the so-called **Rome I Regulation**, has now replaced the previously applicable Convention on the law applicable to contractual obligations, in order to unify the national conflict of laws systems. Whereas the Convention was a treaty which needed to be transposed into the national laws of the individual Member States, the Rome I Regulation, due to its legal nature, has a direct effect. Pursuant to its Art. 1(1), the Regulation applies to contractual obligations in civil and commercial matters in situations involving a conflict of laws, whereby the term "contractual" serves to distinguish it from the Rome II Regulation which applies to non-contractual obligations.

a) The basic pattern

6 When searching for the applicable law it is necessary to proceed in several steps. The first question to ask is whether the contracting parties have agreed on a specific applicable law. In a second step the applicable law must be determined using objective criteria. This objective applicable law is essential if no choice of law has been agreed on, and even if there has, it is applied if the contractual choice of law would deprive the employee of the mandatory protection that would otherwise be afforded to him. Consequently, **hybrid forms** could arise. The thus ascertained applicable law to the employment contract is then supplemented by rules that are internationally mandatory, irrespective of the applicable law, and by rules concerning the performance of the employment contract, of which the law of the place of performance is invariably the applicable law. The following paragraph will elucidate this basic pattern in more detail.

b) Choice of law under Art. 3 Rome I Regulation

7 In principle, as with any contract, there is a freedom of choice of law pursuant to Art. 3 Rome I Regulation. So the contracting parties can agree upon which legal system shall govern the contract. This is also in line with the traditional approach of the common law: The leading authority remains the decision of the Privy Council in *Vita Food Products Inc. v Units Shipping Co. Ltd* [1939] 1 All ER 513 in which it

was established that the law chosen by the parties would be respected provided that choice was bona fide, legal and not contrary to public policy. Consequently, it is possible to select any law, even one that has nothing to do with the employment relationship whatsoever – this is different in, for example, Switzerland; there, Art. 121(3) IPRG provides that the parties can only agree on the law of the usual place of work or the residence of the employer. This choice of law, which makes sense for the parties for reasons of legal certainty, can be express or implied into the contract. In the past, the courts have been quite liberal in accepting an **implied choice of law**. A reference to a German collective agreement in an employment contract has frequently been considered a choice of German law (*BAG* of 26 July 1995 – 5 AZR 216/94). The *Cour de Cassation* has ruled similarly regarding French collective agreements and French law (*Cour de Cassation*, Chambre sociale of 16 November 1993 [90-16030], Bulletin 1993 V, p. 183 in a shipping case). And a jurisdiction clause is also a powerful implication that the parties have selected the law of the country of jurisdiction because it can be assumed that a judge will rule in accordance with his own law (see **for English law** *Evans Marshall & Co Ltd v Bertola SA* [1973] 1 W.L.R. 349; *The Komninos S* [1991] 1 Lloyd's Rep. 370).

It poses a problem though when the **German** ***Bundesarbeitsgericht*** (*BAG* of 27 July 1997 – 8 AZR 328/95) deduces that there is an implied choice of law from the fact that the nationality of the contracting parties, the place of conclusion of the employment contract and also the principal place of performance are all of one particular country, i. e. it is a case with a predominantly domestic or foreign element. In these cases it cannot be assumed that the parties consciously decided on an applicable law and made an – albeit implied – agreement to that effect, but rather that employer and employee assumed that a particular law applied without needing a contractual agreement. Choice of law requires a conscious agreement and that cannot be derived from the fact that the applicability of a certain law would make sense and be practical; these are criteria that are considered in the context of ascertaining the objective connection (nevertheless, similar to the German court, the *Cour de cassation* Cass.soc, 10 juillet 1992, JCP'93, 22063, obs. Rodière (Arrêt AIR AFRIQUE); see also *Anton*, Private International Law, 1990, p. 325). 8

A choice of law clause can refer to a legal system as a whole or it can be a partial choice of law. A partial choice of law is to distinguish from a *dépeçage*. A partial choice of law means that only certain provisions of a legal system shall be applied. There is some dispute about the admissibility of *dépeçage*, i. e. the possibility for the parties to an employment contract to choose different applicable laws for different issues of their employment relationship. The wording of the Convention, which is identical to the wording of the Regulation, generally allowing *dépeçage* for contracts, makes no exception for employment relationships, which is the reason for some to allow it (see *McLachlan*, B.Y.I.L. 1990, 311 *et seqq.* for more details). It is also a recognised notion in the common law (*Re United Railways of the Havana and Regla Warehouses* [1960] Ch. 52; *Libyan Arab Foreign Bank v Bankers Trust Co* [1989] Q.B. 728). 9

A partial choice of law as well as a subsequent choice of law will remain possible in the future (Art. 3(2) Rome I Regulation). A **partial choice of law**, as with any contract, must refer to parts of a legal system that are severable and independent of each other. As a result, it is possible, for example, to subject the employment relationship of an employee posted to the USA to the employment conditions there, but at the same time ensure the employee is afforded the dismissal protection under German law. 10

c) Objective connecting factor under Art. 8(2) Rome I Regulation

11 In the absence of a choice of law, the applicable law is determined by looking for the law with the closest connection on objective grounds. Under **Art. 8(2) Rome I Regulation** the relevant factor is the country in which the employee habitually carries out his work, even if he is temporarily employed in another country; in the alternative, under paragraph 3, if he does not habitually carry out his work in one and the same country, the applicable law will be that of the country where the place of business through which the employee is engaged is situated. Both connections are subject to a closer connection with another country that may appear from the circumstances as a whole; in that case, the law of the other country is the applicable law. There is no exhaustive list of possible factors to be taken into account, nor does the wording give a preference for certain factors that would be more determinative than others. The "circumstances as a whole" indicate that the majority of factors must point to a country other than the one of the habitual place of work or the engaging place of business. The factors to be taken into account are similar to those that can be the basis of an implied choice of law; they obviously do not have to be as strong. Possible factors are: the common nationality of the parties, the language of the employment contract, the currency in which the salary is paid, the indication that the contract was drafted against the background of a particular domestic employment law, the domicile of the employee, the need to treat a number of employees equally, social security benefits for the employee in a particular state, and a strong link to an earlier contract to which the law of that country was applicable (see *Krebber*, 21 Comp. Lab. L. & Pol'y J. 2000, 501, 526, 527; *Court of Appeal*, decision of 21 December 1988, *Attock Cement Co Ltd v Romanian Bank for Foreign Trade* [1989] 1 W.L.R. 1147; *BAG* of 24 August 1989 – 2 AZR 3/89; *Cour d'appel de Paris*, decision of 7 June 1996, Rev. Crit. d.i.p. 55 [1997]).

12 Consequently, for the **standard case** there are quite clear connecting factors for determining the applicable law. An employee who is hired for a fixed term to perform his work exclusively in a certain foreign state, will be governed by the law of that state. Admittedly, this can lead to unreasonable results, in view of the fact that the standard connecting factors were selected in order to afford the employee the protection of the law of his home state in the standard case. The Swiss Federal Court, in light of the similar provision of § 121 IPRG, in a case concerning an employee who was hired in Switzerland for fixed-term work in Guinea, assumed without further consideration that Swiss law applied – in all probability because Guinea perhaps does not have much of an employment law to speak of (Swiss *Bundesgericht* of 28 June 1982, BGE 108 II 115; similarly also *Bundesgericht* of 18 December 1951, SJIR X 1953 [346]: doorman in Ethiopia).

13 **English and German courts** display **more awareness** of the problems in these cases: **English courts** have attached weight to circumstances such as the place where the contract was made, the place of performance or whether the contract is closely linked with another contract containing a choice of law clause (*Cantieri Navali Riuniti SpA v NV Omne Justitia* [1985] 2 Lloyd's Rep. 428; *James Miller and Partners Ltd v Whitworth Street Estates (Manchester) Ltd.* [1970] A.C. 50; *Forsikringsaktieselskapet Vesta v Butcher* [1988] 1 Lloyd's Rep. 191). Criteria that justify the applicability of **German law** outside of the standard connecting factors, are the nationality of the contracting parties and the place of business of the employer, the use of a particular language, the place where the contract was made and also the employee's place of residence, though none of these criteria are of major importance on their own (see *BAG* of 24 August 1989 – 2 AZR 3/89). Based on

these factors, the *Bundesarbeitsgericht* found a closer connection than the standard connection of the place of work in a case concerning a British national whose residence was in Great Britain who worked as a cashier on a ferry which sailed under German flag; the applicable law was English law (*BAG* of 24 August 1989 – 2 AZR 3/89). However, the suggestion that the closest connection should invariably be determined by reference to the displacement rule in Art. 8(4) in lieu of the standard connecting factors in Art. 8(2) or (3) in the case where employer and employee are of the same nationality and have the same place of business/residence in another country, is not convincing. This does not reflect the practice of the courts, who are much more careful in examining the criteria (decidedly following the standard connecting factors *Cour de Cassation*, Ch. soc. of 7 May 2002 [99–46083], Bulletin 2002 V, p. 147: In the case of a French citizen who worked for a French company for nine years on the basis of an employment contract signed in California, the applicable law with regard to the termination of his contract was that of California. A different result may be concluded by virtue of an (implied) choice of law of the parties: *Cour de Cassation*, Ch. soc., of 28th October 1997 [94–42340], Bulletin 1997 V, p. 242: Hiring of a mechanic to work in Karachi): The employee's place of residence may be changed when work is taken up abroad, which would then militate in favour of referring to the standard connecting factors. It is submitted that the fact that the employee's nationality is not that of the country of performance can only be decisive when the employer specifically insists upon it being so.

The rule that **temporary employment** in another country does not displace the standard connecting factor of Art. 8(2) Rome I Regulation deserves some elucidation. As to when an employment is only temporary, the prevailing opinion is that every posting that is not permanent is immaterial and even a longer spell abroad does not make the overseas place of work the closer connection. 14

The standard connecting factor under Art. 8(2) Rome I Regulation is also decisive, when as in the **example given above** (para. 4) a foreign and a domestic employer are joined by a single employment contract. If the employee returns to his home country, then the law of the home country remains the applicable law even during his stay abroad and the employment relationship with the foreign employer is governed by the same law. The suggestion expressed by some scholars that the termination of such an employment contract is subject to both the rules of home law and the foreign law combined is therefore incorrect, because foreign law is not applicable in this case. 15

Conversely, **in cases of a double, not joint employment relationship** it is not correct to assume that the home law governs the second employment relationship which relates exclusively to the work abroad. In this case the habitual place of work during the whole fixed term of the employment relationship is the foreign state, therefore it is the standard connection under Art. 8(2) Rome I Regulation that leads to the right result. This is not only confirmed by the wording of the provision but also by practical considerations: For the time working abroad for a foreign employer it must be possible to be on equal legal footing with the other employees there, even when an employment relationship in the home state is still in existence. Otherwise, the foreign employer would be forced to treat the employee transferred to him differently than his other employees. This does not seem very helpful and it is submitted that it is right to obey the wording of the provision. 16

d) Art. 8(1)1 Rome I Regulation – Comparing favourability

The aforementioned broad outline of the objective applicable law is not only significant in the absence of a choice of law. For even if employer and employee have agreed on a particular applicable law, the objective applicable law must be determined. Under Art. 8(1) Rome I Regulation the choice of law must not have the effect of depriving the employee of the protection afforded to him by provisions that cannot be derogated from by agreement under the law that, in the absence of choice, would have been applicable. The reasons for this are clear. If the employer dislikes French employment law, he could ask or pressure the employee into agreeing to apply the employment law of Cambodia. There, employees are entitled to annual leave of only eighteen days, receive no continued payments in the case of illness, there is no dismissal protection to speak of and no works councils (see Introduction to 17

Cambodian Law, pp. 285 *et seqq.*; available at: http://www.kas.de/kambodscha/de/publications/31083/). Tempting conditions – with the result that all cries for a more flexible employment law would be rendered superfluous. Overriding mandatory rules for the protection of employees shall not be evaded by such a choice of law or even, for instance, by selecting US-American law (no paid minimum annual leave, no continued payments in case of illness, no paid maternity leave, no general dismissal protection, no works councils). Therefore, it is necessary at this stage to compare the favourability of the chosen law and the objective applicable law.

e) Change of applicable law

18 Once the applicable law has been determined by means of the above illustrated rules, the question is raised whether it may have been changed in the course of the employment relationship. Is an employment contract governed by one applicable law **from the cradle to the grave** or can it change? A subsequent choice of law is certainly possible, i. e. if employer and employee agree to replace the applicable law. It is not quite so clear whether the applicable law can change even without an agreement between the parties if the objective connecting factors change. Art. 3(2) and (5) of Rome I Regulation has a clear rule concerning the general law of contract: it is down to the time the contract is concluded and no change in circumstances can change the applicable law. The same restriction cannot be deduced from Art. 8(2) Rome I Regulation. So it is inferred that the objective applicable law determined according to Art. 8(2) Rome I Regulation is variable.

19 This corresponds to the **decisions of the *Cour de Cassation***. If an employee is posted abroad permanently, the law governing the employment contract will change automatically under Art. 8(2) Rome I Regulation, even if his employer does not change (*Cour de Cassation*, Ch. soc. of 17 December 1997 [94–45524], Bulletin 1997 V, p. 321: A Moroccan citizen was hired for work in Morocco but was then posted to France until the contract ended 12 years later). The decisive factor is that both employer and employee assume at the time of posting that the employee will not be returning to the home country to take up work. The same is true for the case where the **place of business relocates abroad** and the employee follows. The above-stated applies even if the relocation involves a transfer of undertaking, i. e. if the Transfer of Undertakings Directive comes into play. In fact it is not the change of employer that leads to a change of the applicable law, and so it is submitted that the value judgments contained in the Rome I Regulation are not in conflict with this result.

f) Art. 9 Rome I Regulation – Overriding mandatory provisions

20 The applicable law selected by the parties or determined by objective connection is complemented by Art. 9 Rome I Regulation. Following this, Arts. 3 *et seqq.* Rome I Regulation apply without prejudice to provisions of the national law that are mandatory, irrespective of the law otherwise applicable under the Regulation. This means that although an employment contract is subject to a foreign law, some provisions of the home law will prevail over the foreign law.

21 Art. 9 Rome I Regulation, like Art. 8(1) Rome I Regulation, refers to mandatory provisions but goes beyond that, as not every mandatory rule protecting their employees is internationally mandatory. The international mandatory character of a statute is easy to assess if the statute explicitly addresses the issue of its territorial application, such as U.S., English and Irish statutes often do. Modern statutes often indicate their mandatory character by stating that the statutory rules apply irrespective of the law which governs the contract of employment (e. g. Equal Pay Act 1970 s.1(1) as amended by Sex Discrimination Act 1975 ss.1(11) – the Equality Act

2010 does not have this definition anymore – and Employment Rights Act 1996 Pt VIII ss. 203, 204(1)). But even without such a reference, provisions in employment law are considered internationally mandatory if they not only regulate the balance between the interests of the individual parties but also require to be **applied unconditionally because they give effect to important social policies**. This specific aim of a provision is often difficult to determine, for whether a statutory right to annual leave serves the employee's interests in terms of rest or serves the public health as a matter of social policy, is a value judgment and one which can be debated about endlessly. But it is only when it can be said with sufficient certainty that the principal aim of a provision is the protection of a public interest that the special rule in Art. 9 is appropriate (see *Duarte v Black & Decker Corp* [2007] EWHC 2720). There have been only a small number of judgments on this subject. In the **English context**, it has been held that the rules under English law with respect to restrictive covenants in employment contracts are not mandatory rules (see *Duarte v Black & Decker Corp* [2007] EWHC 2720).

As in the case of all overriding mandatory provisions within the meaning of Art. 9 Rome I Regulation, it must be ascertained whether the situation has a **sufficient connection to one country**. This requirement is not contained in the wording specifically, but can be concluded from the nature of overriding mandatory provisions: no law shall be forced upon the parties where there is no significant connection. If all relevant connecting factors point to a foreign law, then Art. 9 Rome I Regulation is not applicable (see *Morse*, Chitty on Contracts, 2008, Vol. 1, para. 30–062). 22

The approach in English law goes too far. Section 204(1) ERA 1996, headed 'Law governing employment', provides 'For the purposes of this Act it is immaterial whether the law which (apart from this Act) governs any person's employment is the law of the United Kingdom, or of a part of the United Kingdom'. The leading text in the field (*Dicey/Morris/Collins*, On the Conflict of Laws, 2006, para. 33–090) says that the ERA 1996 applies '*prima facie* to all contracts of employment, whatever their governing law, and will be treated as a mandatory provision for the purposes of Art. 6 and Art. 7(2) of the Convention'. They also suggest (paras. 33–096 – 33–103) that the Equal Pay Act 1970, the Sex Discrimination Act (and by implication the other discrimination statutes), TULR(C)A 1992, the National Minimum Wage Act 1998 and the Public Interest Disclosure Act 1998 will also be regarded as mandatory. Under Art. 3(1) Posted Workers Directive, the host state must apply a 'nucleus of mandatory rules' (Recital 13 PWD) to posted workers working in its territory, whatever the law applicable to the employment relationship. Following *Laval* and *Rüffert*, the list of areas covered by Art. 3(1) (restrictions on working time, minimum rates of pay, conditions of hiring out of workers, health and safety, protection of pregnant workers and those who have recently given birth and equality legislation) is exhaustive and construed narrowly (confirmed in Case 354/05 – Commission v Luxembourg [2006] ECR I-67, para. 26). The general classification of its national labour legislation as an overriding internationally mandatory provision is not compatible with this (see also *Barnard*, 38 Industrial Law Journal 2009, 122–132). 23

g) Art. 12(2) Rome I Regulation – Having regard to the law of the country in which performance takes place

The **last step in the search for the applicable law** leads us to Art. 12(2) Rome I Regulation. Pursuant to this Art., in relation to the manner of performance, 24 "regard shall be had" to the law of the country in which performance take place. This also applies to the manner of performance in employment relationships. One can mention here, by way of example, the rules governing bank holidays. Bank holidays in the foreign workplace should apply in the same way to the workers that fall under the labour law of a different country, even if the host country has different or more or less holidays than the home country. Other examples include maximum working hours and accident prevention regulations. There is still scope for more than this. Since the work performed always amounts to performance of the contract, any law governing this can fall under the category "manner of performance".

25 This can include regulations concerning **performance by the *employer***, such as the payment of the salary. Germany forbids the truck system, i. e. paying employees in commodities, in § 107(2) *Gewerbeordnung*. Other countries have similar provisions and additional rules: Art. 115 of the Labour Code of Cambodia forbids the payment of wages in the form of alcohol and drugs, the Philipino Labour Code prohibits in Art. 104 the place of payment other than near the place of undertaking. So an employee whose contract is governed by German law could rely on these provisions, too – if he wishes to.

III. Forum

26 In principle, the question of international jurisdiction of a national labour court is determined by the general rules. Following this, in German law, e. g., if a labour court has geographical jurisdiction then it will usually have international jurisdiction (see *Bundesarbeitsgericht (BAG)* of 9 October 2002 – 5 AZR 307/01; *BAG* of 17 July 1997 – 8 AZR 328/95). Therefore, if a court has geographical jurisdiction under the general rules, then the fact that there is a foreign element will have no significance. For the territory of the European Union these general rules were superseded by the Convention on Jurisdiction and the Enforcement of Judgments in Civil and Commercial Matters of 27 September 1968 ("the Brussels Convention") with respect to claims relating to employment contracts (but not collective agreements and works agreements). The Convention was then replaced on 1 March 2002 for the European Union, save for Denmark, by the Council Regulation 44/2001 on Jurisdiction and the Recognition and Enforcement of Judgments in Civil and Commercial Matters (OJ 2001 L-12/1, 16 January 2001, "the Brussels I Regulation"; the Brussels I Regulation has since been extended to Denmark). The Brussels I Regulation contains special jurisdiction rules, just as the Brussels Convention did, for individual employment contracts in its Arts. 18–21. The rules are broadly similar to those of the Brussels Convention (*Droz/Gaudemet-Tallon*, Rec. crit. d. i. p. 90 [2001], 601). An employer domiciled in a Member State may be sued in the courts of the Member State where he is domiciled, Art. 19 No. 1 Brussels I Regulation. In addition, under Art. 19 No. 2 Brussels I Regulation, he can be sued – parallel to the structure of Art. 8(2) Rome I Regulation – in another Member State in the courts for the place where the employee habitually carries out his work or in the courts for the last place where he did so, or if the employee does not or did not habitually carry out his work in any one country, in the courts for the place where the business which engaged the employee is or was situated. Whereas this **basic pattern has remained unchanged** compared to the previous

law (see Arts. 3, 5 No. 1 Brussels Convention), there are three exceptions which I wish to explain briefly.

- As regards employers from foreign states, i. e. those whose domicile is not in the European Union, the application of the Brussels Convention was unclear and contentious (see *Junker*, ZZP Int 3 [1998], 179, 191 commenting on *ECJ* of 15 February 1989 – Case 32/88, ECR 1989, 341). The Brussels I Regulation sets out a clear rule in that it will suffice for a branch, agency or other establishment to be in a Member State in order for that Member State to have jurisdiction over employment matters. The employer is deemed to be domiciled in that Member State, Art. 18(2) Brussels I Regulation. 27
- In addition to the *usual* place of work being a determining factor of jurisdiction, the *last* place of work is now also of importance. Thus the complete course of the employment relationship is not examined, merely the last stage, the last location of posting. This is arguably more than a slight modification of the previous regime. Where an employee has worked in France for a year, then the Netherlands for a year and finally in Belgium for a year, in the event of dismissal it will be difficult to say in which country he "usually" carried out his work. Now it is clear that he can sue in Belgium (see the assenting approach under the previous law of the *ECJ* Case 37/00 – Weber [2002] ECR I-2013; *contra* at the time Advocate General *Jacobs* in his opinion of 18 October 2001). The relevant court must then – in so far as the applicable law was determined objectively – apply the relevant foreign law for the previous stages. 28
- The special rule of Art. 19 Brussels I Regulation, which applies instead of the general rules in Arts. 4 and 5 Brussels I Regulation, does not apply to claims brought by the employer. The rule in Art. 20 Brussels I Regulation remains applicable, according to which an *employer's* claim may only be brought in the courts of the Member State in which the employee is domiciled. This restriction was not contained in the Brussels Convention; under that, the employer could sue where the employee could sue. 29

IV. Unions and collective agreements

Up to this point we have discussed the law applicable to an employment contract. Due to the fact that Art. 8(2) Rome I Regulation does not cover collective labour law, the rules concerning this area had to be developed independently by the courts and academic literature. The law concerning collective agreements raise quite diverse problems. 30

In order to determine which law applies to a collective agreement, which employment relationships fall within its scope and how they are affected by the collective agreement, one cannot look to Art. 8 Rome I Regulation as this deals only with individual employment contracts. The Art. applies, by its heading, to *individual* employment contracts and, although the adjective "individual" does not appear in the text of Art. 6, this limitation was already emphasized in the Giuliano and Lagarde Report of 1986 (*Giuliano and Lagarde*, op. cit. supra no. 3, at p. 25.). The courts and legal scholars had to develop their own approaches on this matter. 31

An example of the possible problems in practice is the case of *Monterosso Shipping Co. Udv. International Transport Workers' Federation* [1982] I.C.R. 675. Art. 3(3) Rome I Regulation would presumably prevent avoidance of the non- 32 binding effect of collective agreements according to **British law** by a choice of law clause selecting a foreign law in a collective agreement which regarded the agreement as legally binding in cases where all the other elements relevant to the situation apart from the choice of foreign law were connected with England only. However, it seems likely that the question of whether terms of a relevant collective agreement are incorporated into a particular employment contract will be a matter to be determined by the law applicable pursuant to Art. 8 Rome I Regulation (see also *Kloss*, 46 MLR 1983, 774–776). This path is blocked for collective agreements following the German example of "normative agreements" (*Normenverträge*) – i. e. collective agreements that are the source of rights and obligations for employees without having to be transformed into an employment contract.

33 The nature and structure of obligations in a collective agreement is different compared to the typical contractual agreement. Therefore, collective agreements do not fit in with the concept that Art. 3 Rome I Regulation has in mind. Consequently, there is a consensus amongst legal scholars that the general rules for determining the applicable law are not directly applicable. However, there is some dispute concerning the applicability of those rules by way of analogy in order to determine the applicable law of a collective agreement. This applies – as already shown above – to Art. 3 Rome I Regulation and the choice of law option. Supporters argue that there is a significant practical need for a choice of law, especially in cases where supranational associations are involved in the collective bargaining process (the **European collective agreement** can be mentioned in this context – see *Schiek*, 34 Industrial Law Journal 2005, 23–56; see also § 10 at paras. 8 *et seqq.*). Others highlight the lack of comparability between a collective agreement and a contract (see also *Lyon-Caen*, La Convention Collective de Travail en Droit International Privé, J. du Droit Int'l 247, 260 (1964)).

34 Consequently, **objective connecting factors** must be examined **in order to determine the applicable law of a collective agreement**. The relevant factor in this assessment, according to prevailing opinion, is the focus of the provisions in the collective agreement, i. e. usually the primary area of operations for the employment relationships under the collective agreement. Some modify this suggestion to the effect that the applicable law shall be the law that applies to most of the contracts under the collective agreement, but it is submitted that the result will usually be the same. The same is true if you refer to the administrative seat of the parties to the collective agreement as an additional factor in determining the applicable law.

35 Beyond the existing case-law, a few **fundamental remarks** can be made to aid legal professionals **in practice**: Whether an employee who carries out his work abroad is subject to a collective agreement must be determined by interpreting the collective agreement. If he does not fall within the territorial scope of the collective agreement, it must be contractually agreed that it shall apply; this agreement, in turn, will be subject to the applicable law of the employment contract. Posting an employee abroad temporarily will not be enough to exclude him from the scope, just as in purely domestic matters an employee's temporary assignment to areas of responsibility outside the scope of a collective agreement will make no difference to its applicability. Even if an employee is hired exclusively for an activity abroad, he could still be subject to a collective agreement if the agreement is concluded precisely for such employment relationships. This is true for activities involving a constant change of work place such as airline personnel. The scope of these collective agreements is

not usually restricted to a particular area, so in these cases it will suffice for there to be a connection to the applicable law of collective agreements.

A question that will become more and more relevant in the future is how **cross-border collective agreements subject to one uniform law** can be achieved. What will be the result if a company concludes a collective agreement for French and German employees which is meant to be subject to a uniform law? Assuming that a choice of law is not possible, the applicable law must be determined by objective connection. If there is a balance between the two countries, there will not be a strong enough connection either way. There are suggestions that the law of a country shall apply according to the particular legal question in issue. But this is still quite vague, hardly reducing the problems occurring in practice. For the time being it will be best to conclude several collective agreements subject to the relevant laws, thereby avoiding problems of the proper law. This corresponds to current practice and is not likely to change until a uniform European applicable law of collective agreements is created on Brussels' initiative. This would certainly be desirable. But looking back to how long it took to achieve the European Company, it will probably be a long time before such ideas become law. The Commission proposal for a European Company at the beginning of the 1970 s contained special rules concerning the ability to conclude collective agreements and a uniform collective labour law (OJ 1970 C-124/10, October 1970, p. 1). This was dropped at a later date. See also § 10, para. 6. 36

§ 12. How to Find the Law

To finish, here are some purely practical tips: sometimes finding the relevant European provisions and decisions is already helpful on its own. Also, just reading the text of a foreign statute can be useful occasionally. For this, the internet is often the ideal place to start. For more in-depth knowledge, it is necessary to study the relevant text books and journals. 1

I. European law

The website of the European Community (www.europa.eu) is a useful tool not only for European law but also for labour law. These are particularly helpful: 2

- the website of the *ECJ*: All the *ECJ* decisions and Advocate General opinions since 17 June 1997 can be found under www.curia.eu. The search form under http://curia.europa.eu/jurisp/cgi-bin/form.pl?lang=en is particularly helpful. It allows you to search by date, key word or field. For those who want an in-depth instruction on the subject can use the extensive and therefore very useful digest of the case-law (http://curia.europa.eu/jcms/jcms/Jo2_11765/?hlText=digest). This contains the summaries of the judgments and orders of the *ECJ*, the *Court of First Instance of the European Communities* and the *Civil Service Tribunal of the European Union* delivered since their inception, structured systematically. Unfortunately, this is only available in French. The section listing annotations of judgments is also only available in French. This section contains references to annotations by legal scholars relating to the judgments delivered by the *ECJ*, the *Court of First Instance of the European Communities* and the *European Union Civil Service Tribunal* from 1954–2010 (http://curia.europa.eu/jcms/jcms/Jo2_7134/?hlText=annotations). 3
- the EUR-LEX site (http://eur-lex.europa.eu/en/index.htm): This site offers direct and free access to the laws of the European Union. Here you can consult the Official Journal of the European Union, as well as the Treaties, the legislation, case-law and preparatory acts. The search service offers various functions. 4
- the website of the European Commission's Directorate-General who is in charge of labour law and social law (http://ec.europa.eu/social/home.jsp?langId=en and – specifically for labour law – http://ec.europa.eu/social/main.jsp?catId=157&langId=en): The publications and implementation reports are particular interesting. For those who wish to dabble in comparative law or who just want to obtain a general idea of their neighbour's legal system, but also for those who are faced with the task of needing to present their own law in good English will find ample help here. 5
- the website of the European Commission on the subject of tackling discrimination in the European Union. This website contains information on all aspects of the measures taken by the EU – those of a legal as well as political nature – to combat discrimination. If you are particularly interested in anti-discrimination law (in European law as well as comparative law), you will find plenty of information under http://ec.europa.eu/social/main.jsp?catId=423&langId=en. The European Anti-Discrimination Law Review can be downloaded for free. 6

7 If you want to read the literature on this subject, have a look through the usual labour law journals as well as the *Common Market Law Review* and also the *International Journal for Comparative Labour Law and Industrial Relations*. The German law journal *Zeitschrift für Europäisches Arbeits- und Sozialrecht (ZESAR)* has dedicated itself to European labour law. The journal *Europarecht* on the other hand only rarely contains labour law related comments.

II. Comparative law

8 The internet is an ideal place to start researching comparative labour law, too. It will not take you very far but it will be more than adequate for a general overview. For more in-depth study, one should consult the national labour law journals. A good place to begin is the website of the European Foundation for the Improvement of Living and Working Conditions www.eurofound.europa.eu/emire/emire.html. For information beyond the borders of the EU see the databases of the International Labour Organization (www.ilo.org/public/english/support/lib/dblist.htm). There are currently no books relating specifically to comparative labour law. The best book in the German language is a compendium for legal professionals by *Henssler/Braun*, Arbeitsrecht in Europa, 3rd ed., 2011 including contributions regarding all the important countries of Europe. The more extensive *Encyclopaedia for Labour Law and Industrial Relations* can be found in university libraries and offers an – unfortunately not always up-to-date – overview of labour law in not only European states. An excellent library of comparative law literature can be found in Trier in the Institute for Labour Law and Labour Relations in the European Community (www.iaaeg.de).

1. British law

9 All British decisions can be found under www.bailii.org, the website of the British and Irish Legal Information Institute. There are also references to the law of other common law countries. It is possible to search either by subject matter or case name. The list of leading cases offers a good and well-informed outline (www.bailii.org/openlaw/employment.html). Reliable information relating to labour law can be found on the Department of Trade and Industry website (www.gov.uk/government/topics/employment). It comprises a number of documents along with an overview of employment rights (www.gov.uk/government/policies/making-the-labour-market-more-flexible-efficient-and-fair). Probably not quite as reliable but always up-to-date is the self-proclaimed "web's No.1 resource for British Employment Law", www.emplaw.co.uk. The latest decisions of the Employment Appeals Tribunal can be found on their website under www.employmentappeals.gov.uk/.

10 The leading law journal for labour law is the *Industrial Law Journal*; for a general idea of labour law *Tolley's Employment Law & Practice* can be recommended. *Employment Law* by *Tom Harrison* is worth a read – although it is of less practical use.

2. French law

11 The first stop to make when searching for French labour law should be www.legifrance.gouv.fr, where you can find a comprehensive outline of French law

– some parts are even in English, but unfortunately not the Code du travail. There are also references to legislation documents. The *Journal officiel de la République française* shares this official reference. The search service (www.legifrance.gouv.fr/initRechJuriJudi.do) takes you to the decisions of the *Cour de cassation*. The website www.juritravail.com is always up to date, which is helpful, but is not aimed at lawyers, and so their reports often lack precision. The site www.infotravail.com is similar. The official website of the Ministry of Employment (www.travail-emploi.gouv.fr), on the other hand, does not have an extensive labour law database. But one or two things can be found here sometimes, just as on the *Cour de cassation*'s website (www.courdecassation.fr).

The top ranking French legal journals are surely the *Droit social*, *Droit ouvrier* 12
and the *Revue de Jurisprudence Sociale*. All three can be equally recommended, perhaps with a little more emphasis on *Droit social*. Amongst the books *Droit du travail*, 27 e ed., 2012, by *Auzero/Dockès/Pélissier* from the series *Précis Dalloz* reigns supreme.

3. Dutch law

Online study of Dutch law is very worthwhile because Dutch law itself is very 13
comparative; it readily makes use of the experiences made by other countries to create new legislation. A first look can be taken at www.wetten.nl, where the most important Dutch laws are. The website under www.arbeidsrecht.nl, or (not quite as good) www.arbeidsrechter.nl is a more labour law specific site. The ministry of labour law's homepage is a little confusing but worthwhile (www.government.nl/ministries/szw). A very helpful list of literature sources relating to almost all labour law fields can be found – organized by subject – under http://www.ser.nl/nl/educatie/scriptieservice/themas.aspx (Literatuurlijsten van Sociaal-Economische Thema's). Those interested in anti-discrimination law will be pleased to see the homepage of the equal treatment commission (www.mensenrechten.nl), who present their latest decisions – some in English.

Of the Dutch labour law journals, *Sociaal Recht und Sociaal Maandblad Arbeid* 14
(SMA) should be highlighted in particular. For an in-depth insight into Dutch labour law, the books *Bakels/Bouwens/Asscher-Vonk*, Schets van het Nederlandse Arbeidsrecht, 21. ed. 2011, and *Heerma van Voss*, Inleiding Nederlands Sociaal Recht are highly recommended. A good general overview in English can be found in *Jacobs, Labour Law in the Netherlands* (2004).

4. Spanish law

The website of the Spanish ministry for labour and immigration (*Ministerio de* 15
Trabajo y Inmigracion) offers an informative introduction to Spanish labour and social law under www.empleo.gob.es/en/guial/index.htm.

The major publishing houses "La Ley" (laleylaboral.laley.es) and "Aranzadi" 16
(www.aranzadi.es/index.php/informacion-juridica) give helpful information on Spanish labour law, including a collection of the most important labour laws (such as "*Estatuto de los Trabajadores*" – all others are available at a fee) as well as current legislation and recent labour law court decisions.

The labour law journals "*Actualidad Laboral*" and "*Relaciones Laborales*" pub- 17
lished by "La Ley" fortnightly and the quarterly "*Revista Española de Derecho de*

Trabajo" published by "Aranzadi" can be recommended. For a more in-depth analysis of Spanish labour law the "classic" books are Derecho del Trabajo by *Manuel Alonso Olea et al.*, or Derecho del Trabajo by *Antonio Martín Valverde et al.*

5. Italian Law

18 Italian labour law is quite accessible online. The first stop should be made at www.dirittodellavoro.it. A list of numerous other helpful links can be found here, such as the Italian Labour Law E-Journal. The ministry of employment's homepage under http://www.lavoro.gov.it offers a catalogue of Italian labour legislation. The most helpful commentaries to get started with are *Grandi/Pera, commenario breve alle leggi sul lavoro.* Of the legal journals Diritto del lavoro, Lavoro et Diritto, Rivista Italiana di Diritto del Lavoro, Rivista Critica di Diritto del Lavoro should be mentioned. Another helpful journal is Massimario di Giurisprudenca del Lavoro.

Index

(bold = paragraph, light = marginal number)